CUTTING EDGE

THIRD EDITION

ELEMENTARY   **TEACHER'S RESOURCE BOOK**

WITH RESOURCE DISC

STEPHEN GREENE

SARAH CUNNINGHAM PETER MOOR

CONTENTS

TEACHER'S RESOURCE BOOK

Introduction

Teacher's notes

TEACHER'S RESOURCE DISC

Extra Resources

- Class audio scripts
- Video scripts
- Photocopiable worksheets with instructions
- Photocopiable worksheets index

Tests

- Progress tests
- Mid-course test
- End of course test
- Test audio
- Test audio script
- Downloadable test audio
- Test answer key

STUDENTS' BOOK CONTENTS

4

Pronunciation	Task	Language live/ World culture	Study, Practice & Remember
Word stress Short forms – *am, are, is* Stress in questions and short answers	Find information from documents **Preparation:** Reading **Task:** Speaking	**World culture** **Video and research:** Life in the Arctic	Study and Practice 1, page 138 Study and Practice 2, page 138 Study and Practice 3, page 138 Study and Practice 4, page 138 Study and Practice 5, page 139 Remember these words, page 139
Word stress *this, that, these, those* Short forms – *has/have got* Vocabulary – family	Talk about your five favourite people **Preparation:** Listening **Task:** Speaking	**Language live** **Writing:** Completing a form **Speaking:** Answering questions	Study and Practice 1, page 140 Study and Practice 2, page 140 Remember these words, page 141
Stress and weak forms – questions Stress and weak forms – telling the time	Describe life in your favourite town **Preparation:** Reading and listening **Task:** Speaking	**World culture** **Video and research:** Indian railway	Study and Practice 1, page 142 Study and Practice 2, page 142 Study and Practice 3, page 143 Remember these words, page 143
Verb forms – *he/she/it* Strong and weak forms – *does*	Choose a holiday activity **Preparation:** Reading and listening **Task:** Speaking	**Language live** **Speaking:** Meeting people **Writing:** Introducing a friend	Study and Practice 1, page 144 Study and Practice 2, page 144 Study and Practice 3, page 145 Remember these words, page 145
Weak forms – prepositions and articles Strong and weak forms – *can/can't*	Do a transport survey **Preparation:** Reading and listening **Task:** Speaking	**World culture** **Video and research:** Race across London	Study & Practice 1, page 146 Study & Practice 2, page 146 Remember these words, page 147
Linking in sentences Stress on word pairs	Describe a favourite place to eat **Preparation:** Listening **Task:** Speaking	**Language live** **Writing:** Describe a place to eat **Speaking:** Ordering food and drink	Study and Practice 1, page 148 Study and Practice 2, page 149 Remember these words, page 149
Strong and weak forms – *was/were* Regular past simple forms – *-ed* endings	Tell a life story **Preparation:** Listening **Task:** Speaking	**World culture** **Video and research:** The Information Age	Study and Practice 1, page 150 Study and Practice 2, page 150 Study and Practice 3, page 151 Remember these words, page 151

STUDENTS' BOOK CONTENTS

Pronunciation	Task	Language live/ World culture	Study, Practice & Remember
Linking – *did you*	Talk about an evening in or out **Preparation:** Listening **Task:** Speaking	**Language live** **Speaking:** Arranging an evening out **Writing:** Arranging an evening out	Study and Practice 1, page 152 Study and Practice 2, page 152 Remember these words, page 153
Stress – comparative adjectives	Choose souvenirs from your country **Preparation:** Listening **Task:** Speaking	**World culture** **Video and research:** Famous markets	Study and Practice 1, page 154 Study and Practice 2, page 154 Remember these words, page 155
Vocabulary – clothes	Analyse your personality **Preparation:** Reading and listening **Task:** Speaking	**Language live** **Speaking:** Asking for goods and services **Writing:** Describing people	Study and Practice 1, page 156 Study and Practice 2, page 156 Remember these words, page 157
Vocabulary – numbers	Devise a general knowledge quiz **Preparation:** Reading and listening **Task:** Speaking	**World culture** **Video and research:** Animals in danger	Study and Practice 1, page 158 Study and Practice 2, page 158 Remember these words, page 159
Weak forms – *going to*	Plan a festival **Preparation:** Reading **Task:** Speaking	**Language live** **Writing:** Information to promote a festival **Speaking:** Suggestions and offers	Study and Practice 1, page 160 Study and Practice 2, page 160 Remember these words, page 161
Weak forms and linking – *have to/don't have to*	Complete a careers questionnaire **Preparation:** Reading **Task:** Speaking	**World culture** **Video and research:** A dream come true	Study and Practice 1, page 162 Study and Practice 2, page 162 Remember these words, page 163
Strong and weak forms – *have* (Present perfect)	Take part in a game **Preparation:** Reading and listening **Task:** Speaking	**Language live** **Speaking:** Telephoning **Writing:** A text message	Study and Practice 1, page 164 Study and Practice 2, page 164 Remember these words, page 165

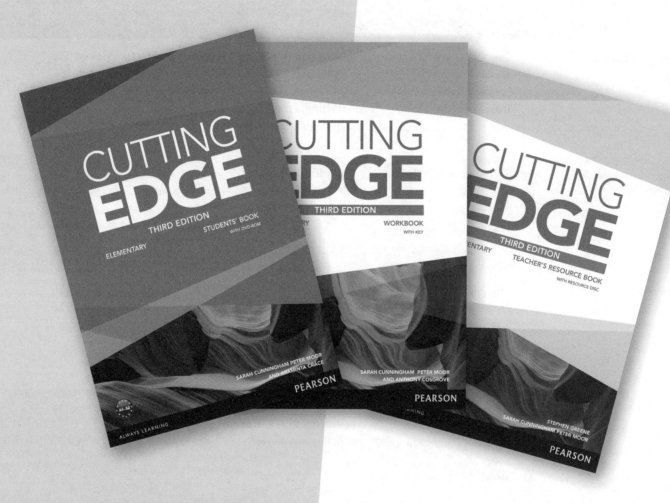

MESSAGE FROM THE AUTHORS

"Do you remember the first time you sent a text message? Or when you started checking information online? These things may seem like centuries ago or only yesterday, but one thing is for sure, in the last twenty years or so we have lived through a period of unprecedented technological change. Change which has affected all of our personal and working lives. Change that will not go away but will continue in ways that we haven't yet imagined.

Cutting Edge Third Edition, while retaining its most popular features, has changed to reflect and embrace the digital age. We have done this through new texts, enhanced features and design along with a whole suite of new digital components. We've added richer and more varied video content in the *Language live and World culture* lessons. These also deepen learners' knowledge and understanding of global issues, direct them to purposeful, focused research on the internet and guide them to summarise their findings through guided writing tasks.

The new *Share your task* feature encourages learners to film and compare their work with other *Cutting Edge* users. The fully revised *MyEnglishLab* for *Cutting Edge Third Edition* has a wide variety of interactive exercises to motivate and engage learners along with the gradebook so you can keep track of your learners' progress in an instant.

Grammar rules, vocabulary lists and test scores all play their part in language learning, but that's not the whole story; in the end, language learning is about connecting people. *Cutting Edge Third Edition* provides a window on the world with dramatic video clips, information-rich texts and engaging tasks. These provide a springboard for learners to engage in meaningful speaking and writing activities that reflect the reality of the 21st century.

We hope that you and your learners will enjoy using *Cutting Edge Third Edition* and we would like to thank you for the invaluable input you have given us over the years. We look forward to continuing and widening our ongoing dialogue with *Cutting Edge* users all over the world."

Sarah Cunningham and Peter Moor

OVERVIEW OF COMPONENTS

STUDENTS' BOOK

- Fourteen units with 90 to 120 hours of teaching material
- A comprehensive Study, Practice & Remember section
- Audio scripts of the class audio

DVD-ROM

- Audio material for use in class
- DVD content (World culture and Language live)
- Audio and video scripts
- Digital Mini Dictionary

WORKBOOK

- Additional grammar, vocabulary and pronunciation exercises to complement the Students' Book
- Additional functional language practice exercises
- Extra listening and reading material
- Extra writing practice

WORKBOOK AUDIO

- Audio material to practice listening, pronunciation and functional language
- Visit www.english.com/students/cuttingedge3e to download the audio

MYENGLISHLAB

Learning Management System that provides:
- Interactive workbook with instant feedback
- Extra practice in grammar, vocabulary and the four skills
- Progress, Mid-course and End of course tests
- Extra videos with interactive exercises

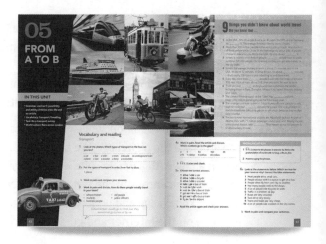

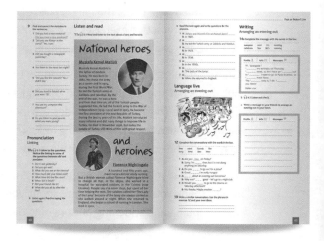

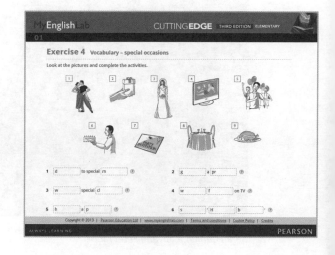

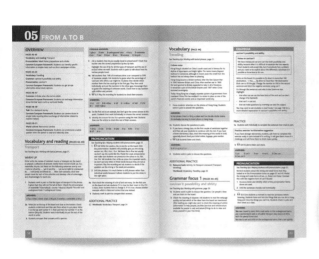

TEACHER'S RESOURCE BOOK

- Teacher's notes for every unit with alternative suggestions, culture notes and answer keys
- Generic teaching tips on useful areas such as: grammar, lexis, pronunciation, using video etc.

TEACHER'S RESOURCE DISC

- Class audio scripts and video scripts
- Photocopiable worksheets to provide additional practice of key language
- Editable and printable tests
- Test audio, audio scripts and answer keys

ACTIVE TEACH

Software for classroom use to help teachers get the most out of the course featuring:

- Answer reveal feature
- Integrated audio and video content
- Test master containing all course tests
- Large extra resources section
- Grammar and vocabulary review games
- A host of useful tools

WEBSITE

- Information about the course
- Sample materials
- Placement test
- A range of free downloadable worksheets
www.pearsonELT.com/cuttingedge3e

THE STUDENTS' BOOK

1 Key language highlighted at the start of each unit.

2 Personalised speaking activities recycle vocabulary and encourage learners to draw on their own knowledge and experience.

3 A variety of pre and post-reading activities are provided to get the most out of reading texts.

4 Information-rich texts reflect learners' interests and experience.

5 Topic-related vocabulary and focus on high-frequency, useful words and phrases.

6 Plenty of form-based and communicative practice of key language.

7 Special Pronunciation boxes focus on stress, weak forms and intonation.

8 Cross-referencing to Study, Practice & Remember sections for additional explanations, exercises and Study tips.

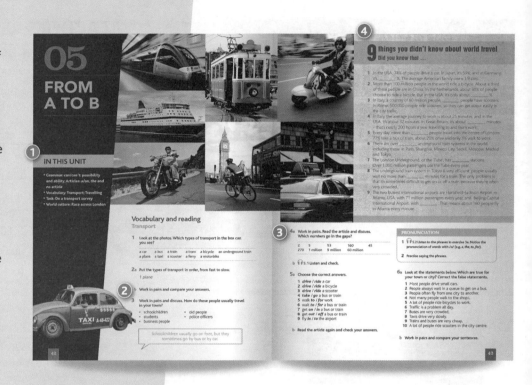

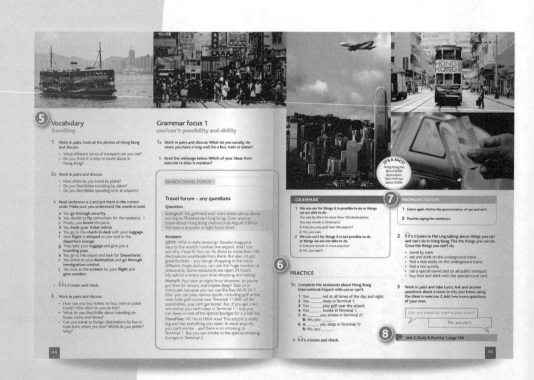

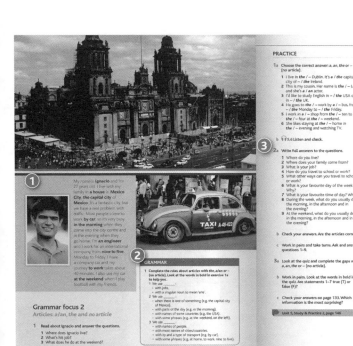

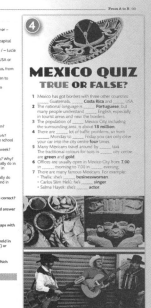

① Grammar presented in context through listening and/or reading texts.

② Learners are encouraged to notice grammar in context.

③ Speaking and writing activities are integrated throughout to extend and consolidate language covered in the unit.

④ Learners are encouraged to learn more about the world and other cultures.

⑤ A model or stimulus is provided to show learners what they are expected to do.

⑥ Structured speaking tasks help learners to achieve a particular goal or outcome.

⑦ Learners are encouraged to think and prepare before they do the task.

⑧ Useful language boxes help learners find the right expressions.

⑨ Share your task activities encourage learners to reflect and perfect their performance.

THE STUDENTS' BOOK

1 *Language live* spreads focus on functional language and writing.

2 Key functional language is presented through light-hearted DVD clips.

3 Pronunciation is integrated throughout.

4 Writing sections focus on particular genres of writing e.g. blogs, emails etc. as well as practising particular sub-skills e.g. drafting.

5 *Can do* box at the end of the unit highlights what learners have achieved in the unit.

6 *World culture* spreads explore contemporary issues of global interest.

7 Topics are introduced through authentic, documentary-style clips from TV programmes and other sources.

8 *World view* sections encourage learners to share ideas and experiences.

9 *Find out first/Find out more* sections develop online research skills.

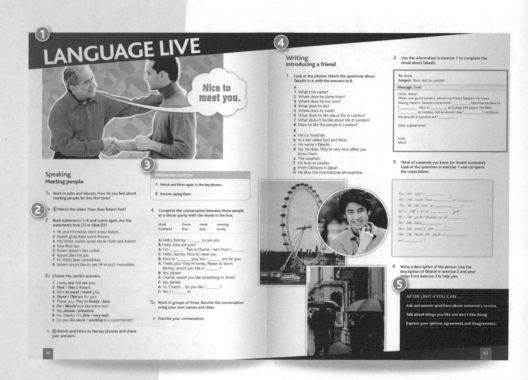

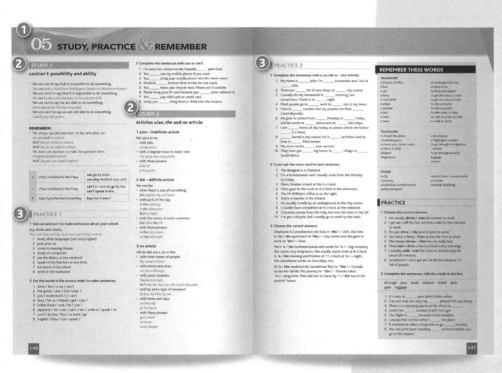

1 *Study, Practice & Remember* sections at the back of the Students' Book ensure systematic consolidation of new language.

2 *Study* sections provide a comprehensive overview of language covered in the unit.

3 Practice exercises can be used in class or set for homework.

4 *Remember!* boxes alert learners to key rules.

5 *Remember these words* sections provide a list of the most important words and phrases covered in the unit.

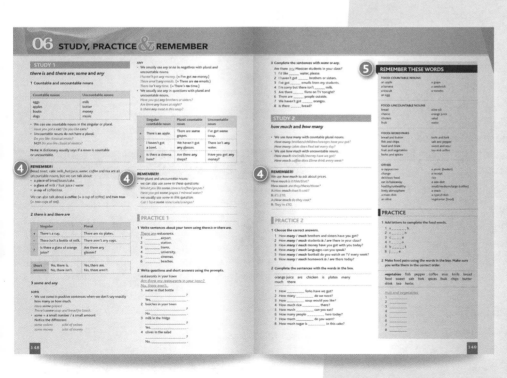

THE SUPPORT COMPONENTS

WORKBOOK

The Workbook contains a wide variety of grammar, vocabulary and functional language exercises that review all the areas studied in the Students' Book. It also features additional listening, reading and writing practice.

1 *Listen and read* sections encourage learners to develop listening skills using the accompanying audio files.

2 A variety of functional language practice activities consolidate areas covered in the Students' Book.

3 Writing exercises offer further practice of the genres covered in the Students' Book.

4 The workbook contains regular listening practice using the accompanying audio files.

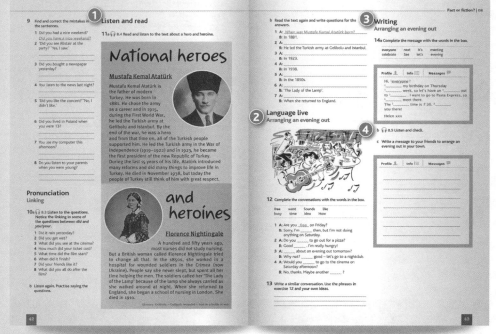

MYENGLISHLAB

MyEnglishLab provides a blended and personalised learning environment with materials that can be assigned at the touch of a button.

- Interactive workbook exercises with instant feedback and automatic grade book.
- Common error report that highlights mistakes that learners are making.
- Tips and feedback that direct learners to reference materials and encourage them to work out answers themselves.
- Mid-course and end of course tests.
- Extra video with interactive exercises for every unit.

ACTIVETEACH

Cutting Edge Third Edition ActiveTeach contains everything you need to make the course come alive. It includes integrated whiteboard software that allows you to add notes, embed files, save your work and reduce preparation time.

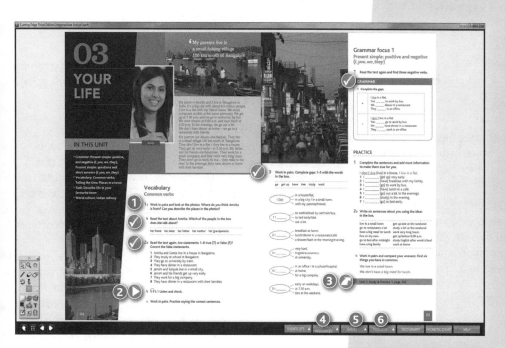

1 Answers to exercises are revealed at the touch of a button.

2 Audio and video content fully integrated with time-coded scripting.

3 Shortcuts to the relevant pages of the *Study, Practice & Remember* sections.

4 Extra resources section with photocopiables, teacher's notes, editable audio and video scripts, editable tests and more.

5 Grammar and vocabulary games for warm up and review activities.

6 Useful tools include a regular/phonetic keyboard, a stopwatch and a scorecard.

WEBSITE

The *Cutting Edge Third Edition* website provides a wealth of information and additional material to support the course.

• Information about the course, its components and the authors.

• Introductory author videos.

• Sample materials and free downloadable worksheets.

• A placement test.

www.pearsonELT.com/cuttingedge3e

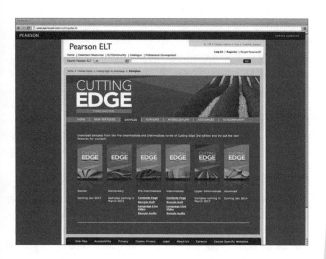

COURSE RATIONALE

The thinking behind Cutting Edge Elementary Third Edition

Overview

Cutting Edge Elementary Third Edition has a multilayered, topic-based syllabus which includes thorough and comprehensive work on grammar, vocabulary, pronunciation and the skills of listening, reading, speaking and writing. Structured speaking tasks form a central part of each unit. *Cutting Edge Elementary Third Edition* gives special emphasis to:

• communication

• the use of phrases and collocations

• active learning and research skills

• recycling and revision.

Topics and content

We aim to motivate learners with units based around up-to-date, globally relevant topics which help them gather information about the world and other cultures through the medium of English.

Cutting Edge Elementary Third Edition provides learners with many opportunities to share their opinions about the topics in focus and personalisation is strongly emphasized throughout. The differing needs of monocultural and multicultural classes has also been kept in mind throughout.

Approach to grammar

Learners are encouraged to take an active, systematic approach to developing their knowledge of grammar, and to use new language in a natural, communicative way.

Typically, there are two *Grammar focus* sections in each unit, in which grammar is presented using reading or listening texts. Each *Grammar focus* has a *Grammar* box which focuses on the main language points, and encourages learners to work out rules for themselves.

The *Grammar focus* sections are followed up thoroughly through:

• a wide range of communicative and written practice exercises in the *Students'* Book

• the opportunity to use new grammar naturally in the speaking tasks (see below)

• the *Study, Practice & Remember* sections which consolidate learning and clarify any remaining problems

• further written practice in the Workbook and interactive exercises in the fully revised *MyEnglishLab*.

(*See Teaching tips: Working with grammar* on page 20, and *Using the Study, Practice & Remember* sections on page 25.)

Approach to vocabulary

A wide vocabulary is vital to communicative success, so new lexis is introduced and practised at every stage in the course. Particular attention has been paid to the selection of high-frequency, internationally useful words and phrases, using information from the British National Corpus.

Vocabulary input is closely related to the topics and tasks in the units, allowing for plenty of natural recycling. Further practice is provided in the *Study, Practice & Remember* sections at the end of each unit and in the Workbook.

Fluent speakers make extensive use of 'prefabricated chunks' of language. Cutting Edge Elementary Third Edition gives particular emphasis to collocations and fixed phrases which are integrated throughout in:

• topic-based vocabulary lessons

• the Useful language boxes in the speaking tasks

• Language live lessons, which focus on phrases used in common everyday situations such as telephoning or making arrangements.

(See *Teaching tips: Working with lexis* on page 21.)

The speaking tasks

Cutting Edge Elementary Third Edition integrates elements of a task-based approach into its methodology. Each unit has a structured speaking task including surveys, mini-talks, problem-solving and narrative tasks. The primary focus is on achieving a particular outcome or product, rather than on practising specific language. The tasks provide the opportunity for realistic and extended communication, and because learners are striving to express what they want to say, they are more likely to absorb the language that they are learning. The tasks are graded carefully in terms of difficulty and, in order for them to work effectively, a model or stimulus is provided, useful language is given to help learners express themselves and thinking/planning time is included. Learners are also encouraged to record themselves or each other performing the tasks, and to share their recording with other learners through the new Share your task feature, thus providing extra motivation for rehearsal and accurate production.

(See *Teaching tips: Making tasks work* on page 23, and *Teaching Elementary learners* on page 26.)

In addition to the extended speaking tasks, *Cutting Edge Elementary Third Edition* offers many other opportunities for speaking, for example, through the discussion of reading and listening texts, communicative practice exercises, and the wide range of photocopiable activities in the *Teacher's Resource Disc*.

World culture

The World Culture pages are a new feature of Cutting Edge Elementary Third Edition and are designed to deepen learners' knowledge and understanding of global issues. This is done through the use of authentic video clips which act as a stimulus for internet-based research around the issues raised in the video. Learners are guided through the necessary steps to make their research focused and productive, and are given guidance on how to summarise their research through a guided written follow-up. The emphasis throughout is on creating a link between the classroom and the outside world, and the development of research skills which will prove of lasting value.

Language Live

Language Live pages are another new feature of *Cutting Edge Elementary Third Edition*. The main purpose of these pages is to help learners with the functional language they need to deal with everyday situations such as telephoning, shopping and making social arrangements. Learners are presented with key language through the medium of light-hearted DVD clips which provide an immediate and motivating context. They are then given the opportunity to practise the language further through roleplay activities, and to develop their writing skills through a related writing task.

Other features of *Cutting Edge Elementary Third Edition*

Listening

Cutting Edge Elementary Third edition places strong emphasis on listening. Listening material consists of:

- short extracts and mini-dialogues to introduce and practise new language
- words and sentences for close listening and to model pronunciation
- longer texts (interviews, stories and conversations), many of which are authentic, often in the Preparation section as a model or stimulus for the Task
- regular Listen and read sections in the Workbook to further develop learners' confidence in this area.

Speaking

There is also a strong emphasis on speaking, as follows:

- The tasks provide a regular opportunity for extended and prepared speaking based around realistic topics and situations.
- Much of the practice of grammar and lexis is through oral exercises and activities.
- The topics and reading texts in each unit provide opportunities for follow-up discussion.
- There is regular integrated work on pronunciation.
- Most of the photocopiable activities in the *Teacher's Resource Disc* involve extensive speaking practice.

Reading

There is a wide range of reading material in the *Students' Book*, including newspaper and website articles, factual/scientific texts, stories, quizzes, forms, notes, letters, blogs and emails. These texts are integrated in a number of different ways:

- extended texts specifically to develop reading skills
- texts which lead into grammar work and language analysis
- texts which provide a model or stimulus for tasks and models for writing activities.

Writing

Regular and systematic work on writing skills are developed in *Cutting Edge Elementary Third Edition* through:

- *Language live* pages in the *Students' Book*, which focus on writing e-mails and letters, writing narratives and reviews, drafting and redrafting, use of linkers, etc.
- *Writing sections* in the *Workbook*, which expand on the areas covered in the Students' Book
- written follow-up sections to many of the speaking tasks.

Pronunciation

Pronunciation work in *Cutting Edge Elementary Third Edition* is integrated with grammar and lexis and there are special pronunciation boxes in every unit. The focus is mainly on stress, weak forms and intonation. A range of activity types are used in the *Students' Book*, including discrimination exercises and dictation, and an equal emphasis is placed on understanding and reproducing.

Learning skills

Cutting Edge Elementary Third Edition develops learning skills in a number of ways:

- The discovery approach to grammar encourages learners to experiment with language and to work out rules for themselves.
- The task-based approach encourages learners to take a proactive role in their learning.

Revision and recycling

Recycling is a key feature of *Cutting Edge Elementary Third Edition*. New language is explicitly recycled through:

- speaking tasks which offer constant opportunities for learners to use what they have studied in a natural way, and for teachers to assess their progress and remind them of important points.
- extra practice exercises in the *Study, Practice & Remember* sections. These are designed to cover all the main grammar and vocabulary areas in the unit. After trying the exercises, learners are encouraged to return to any parts of the unit that they still feel unsure about to assess what they have (and have not) remembered.

(See *Teaching tips: Making tasks work on page 23 and Using the Study, Practice & Remember sections* on page 25.)

TEACHING TIPS

How to get the most out of Cutting Edge Elementary Third Edition

Working with grammar

In *Cutting Edge Elementary Third Edition*, learners are encouraged to take an active, systematic approach to developing their knowledge of grammar, and the opportunity to use new language is provided in a natural, communicative way. Learners are encouraged to notice language in context where possible, but with the necessary support to help them achieve understanding and do meaningful practice.

1 Get to know the material available

Every unit of *Cutting Edge Elementary Third Edition* has two *Grammar focus* sections, which include:

• introductory material in the form of a reading or listening exercise, to help contextualise the language (though the focus here is on overall comprehension rather than grammatical rules).

• a *Grammar* box which focuses learners on the main language points, and which uses questions to help learners notice the meaning and use.

• a *Study* section (part of the *Study, Practice & Remember* section) at the back of the *Students' Book* providing more detailed information about what is covered in the *Grammar* boxes.

• oral and/or written communicative practice exercises.

These language areas are recycled through the *Study, Practice & Remember* sections at the back of the *Students' Book*.

The *Workbook* includes additional practice material.

There are also a number of games and other activities designed to further consolidate the grammar areas covered in the *Teacher's Resource Disc*.

2 Be prepared to modify your approach

It is unlikely that you will discover that all learners are using the target language perfectly and need no further work on it. However, you may realise they only need brief revision, that you can omit certain sections of the *Grammar* box or go through some or all of it very quickly. Alternatively, you may decide to omit some of the practice activities, or set them for homework.

On the other hand, you may discover that many learners know less than you would normally expect at this level. In this case, spend more time on the basic points, providing extra examples as necessary, and leave more complex issues for another day.

3 Check what learners know but be prepared to clarify

The questions in the *Grammar* box are designed to check what learners already know and guide them towards understanding. It is important to check how far learners have understood the language and allow them to demonstrate what they know already. However, if you find that learners are stuck or can't answer, then don't be afraid to clarify and firmly establish what the correct answer is.

4 Be clear about what you are teaching

When planning a grammar lesson, an important first step is to make sure you fully understand the grammar point yourself. Read the *Study* section at the back of the book and make sure you are fully prepared for any questions learners ask. At the same time, it is important to be aware of what learners can realistically be expected to learn at this level, so don't 'overload' them with too many rules.

5 Help learners look for similarities and differences in their first language

Sometimes it can be useful for learners to think about and compare how similar meanings to the grammar being studied can be expressed in their own language. This is especially important if this is the first time learners have come across a grammar point. Even in multilingual classes, you can ask learners if they have a similar grammar point in their own language, without having to go into too much detail about what it is exactly.

6 Use Grammar boxes in different ways

Questions in the *Grammar* boxes can be tackled in different ways, depending on the ability/confidence of your learners and the relative difficulty of the language point in question. Here are some possible approaches:

• **Answer the questions individually / in pairs, then check them together as a class:**
This is a good way of encouraging a more independent attitude in your learners. Make sure that they understand what they have to do for each question, and monitor carefully to see how they are coping – if they are obviously all stuck or confused, stop them and sort out the problem. As you check answers, write up examples to highlight any important problems of form, meaning, etc. The *Study* section at the back of the *Students' Book* can be read at the end, either individually or as a class.

• **Answer the questions together as a class:**
With weaker classes, or for areas that you know your learners will find difficult, it may be best to read out questions to the whole class and work through them together, with examples on the board. Alternatively, set more straightforward questions for learners to answer in pairs, and do more complicated ones together as a class. As learners gain more confidence, you can set more and more questions for them to do on their own.

• **Learners work through the questions individually / in pairs, then check the answers themselves in the *Study* section:**
Stronger, self-sufficient learners may be able to take most of the responsibility for themselves. Most classes should be able to do this with the simpler *Grammar* boxes. It is still important that you monitor carefully to make sure that there are no major problems, and check answers together at the end to clear up any remaining doubts.

Working with lexis

1 Become more aware of phrases and collocations

Thousands of phrases and collocations make up the lexis in English, along with the traditional one-word items. If necessary, look at the list of phrase types below, and start noticing how common these 'prefabricated chunks' are in all types of English. They go far beyond areas traditionally dealt with in English-language courses – phrasal verbs, functional exponents and the occasional idiom, although of course they incorporate all of these.

- **collocations** (common word combinations), including:
  verbs + nouns (*leave school, have a drink*)
  adjectives + nouns (*best friend, bad news*)
  verbs + adverbs (*work hard*)
  verbs + prepositions/particles, including phrasal verbs (*listen to, wait for*)
  adjectives + prepositions (*interested in*)
- **fixed phrases,** such as: *Excuse me. / Here you are.*
- **whole sentences which act as phrases,** such as: *I don't know. / I agree with you.*

Such phrases blur the boundaries between 'vocabulary' and 'grammar' and in teaching these phrases, you will find that you are helping learners with many problematic areas that are traditionally considered to be grammar, such as articles and prepositions. Many common examples of these structures are in fact fixed or semi-fixed phrases. We are not suggesting that work on chunks should entirely replace the traditional grammatical approach to such verb forms, but recommend that it should be a useful supplement.

2 Keep an eye on usefulness and be aware of overloading learners

It is easy to 'go overboard' with collocations and phrases as there are so many of them, especially at this level, so keep it simple. In order to avoid overloading learners, limit your input to high-frequency, useful phrases. As you teach lexis, ask yourself questions such as: *How often would I use this phrase myself? How often do I hear other people using it? Do my learners need it? Is it too idiomatic, culturally specific or complex to bother with?*

3 Feed in phrases on a 'little but often' basis

To avoid overloading learners and ensure that your lexical input is useful, teach a few phrases relating to particular activities as you go along. For example, in a grammar practice activity, instead of simple answers such as *Yes, I do* or *No, I haven't*, feed in phrases such as *It depends, I don't really know.* The same is true of discussions about reading/listening texts and writing activities.

4 Point out patterns in phrases

Pointing out patterns will help learners to remember phrases. Many do not fit into patterns, but you can often show similar phrases with the same construction, like this:

5 Answer learners' questions briefly

One possible problem with a more lexical approach is that learners may ask a lot of questions beginning *Can I say ...?, What does ... mean?,* etc. Although learners should be encouraged to ask questions, there is obviously a danger of overload – and it may also be the same learner who is asking all the questions! Unless you feel that it is really important, answer briefly yes or no, and move on quickly. If you are not sure, the best answer is probably *I never hear anyone say it myself.* If the learner is still not satisfied, say that you will give them an answer the following lesson.

6 Make the most of emerging language

One simple way to make your learners more aware of collocation is to get into the habit of writing word combinations on the board wherever appropriate, rather than just individual words. The more learners see these words together, the more likely they are to remember them as a unit. Rather than just writing up *homework* or *party*, write up *do your homework* or *have a party*. Remind learners to write down the collocations too, even if they 'know' the constituent words.

7 Reinforce and recycle phrases

This is particularly important with phrases which, for the reasons given above, can be hard to remember. Most revision games and activities teachers do with single items of vocabulary can be adapted and used with phrases. You may find the following useful in addition:

- **Make a phrase bank:**
  Copy new words and phrases from the lesson onto slips of card or paper (large enough for learners to read if you hold them up at the front of the room) and keep them in a box or bag. This is a good record for you, as well as learners, of the phrases that the class has studied – do this frequently at the start and end of lessons to recycle the phrases often. Hold them up and ask learners to give you (choose as appropriate):

  - an explanation of the phrase
  - a translation of the phrase
  - synonyms
  - opposites
  - the pronunciation
  - situations where they might say this
  - a sentence including the phrase
  - the missing word that you are holding your hand over (for example, *on* in the phrase *get on well with*)
  - the phrase itself, based on a definition or translation that you have given them.

- **Have learners create their own review materials:**
  Take several small strips of paper into class, enough for a few for each learner. Ask them to look back over their notes (or look at the *Remember these words* sections at the back of the book) and choose 3-4 phrases they have learnt recently and write each one on a strip of paper. Circulate and check learners have formed the phrases correctly. Learners then tear each strip into separate words, shuffle them all together and give them to a partner, to put in order.

TEACHING TIPS

How to get the most out of Cutting Edge Elementary Third Edition

Helping learners with pronunciation

1 Aim for intelligibility

It is worth remembering that in today's world there are more speakers of English as a foreign or second language than there are native speakers, and so no-one can really say they 'own' the language or speak the most 'correct' form. It is therefore best to make sure learners can be understood rather than aiming for 'perfect' pronunciation, whatever that might be. Consonants (particularly at the beginning and end of words) are probably more important than vowels here. Use any tips you know for helping learners to reproduce them. You might focus them on a similar sound in their own language and then help them to adapt it, or use a trick like starting with /u.../ to get learners to produce the /w/ sound. Anything that works is valid here! Sometimes it is useful to contrast the problem sound with the one that learners are mistakenly producing, via a 'minimal pair' such as *show* and *so*. Say the pair of words several times, then ask learners to say which they can hear, before asking them to produce the words themselves.

2 Little and often is the key ... and be realistic

Don't wait for a *Pronunciation* box to come along in the *Students' Book*. Integrate pronunciation work whenever learners have a problem. 'Little and often' is a particularly good principle with pronunciation.

On the other hand, think about what you want to achieve: clarity and confidence are what most learners need, rather than perfection in every detail. Individuals vary widely in what they can achieve, so don't push too much when a particular learner is getting frustrated or embarrassed. Leave it and come back to it again another day. A humorous, light-hearted approach also helps to alleviate stress!

3 Drill in different ways, depending on the language

Choral and/or individual repetition is the simplest pronunciation activity to set up and possibly the most effective. It can help to build confidence by giving learners valuable practice in a 'safe' environment, as long as you don't overdo it (see above). There are different ways to drill language, and it's important to vary the way we do it. Some common drilling techniques include:

- **When drilling longer phrases:**
  Establish a rhythm and start by drilling only the stressed syllables. For example, for the phrase *What do you usually do at the weekend?* Start with *What – us – do – week*. Keeping the same rhythm, 'cram' in the other syllables, pronouncing them naturally. This helps learners feel how we use weak forms and sentence stress in English.

- **Drill the phrase backward to keep it sounding natural:**
  With longer words and phrases, start from the end and drill backwards. For example, with the word *comfortable*, work backwards *–ble – table – comfortable*. This allows you to isolate difficult parts of the word or phrase, but keep a natural-sounding pronunciation.

- **Vary your voice:**
  This can be a simple way to add variety to drills, by e.g. shouting or whispering. It also give learners different ways to practise saying the language.

4 Focus consistently on stress

This is an easy area in which to correct learners effectively. Get into the habit of focusing on word and sentence stress whenever you teach a new word/phrase with potential problems. If learners have problems, try one of the following ideas when you drill:

- Exaggerate the stress.
- Clap or click your fingers on the stressed syllable.
- Mumble the stress pattern, before saying the word: *mm-MM-mm attention*.
- Isolate the stressed syllable first, and then add the other syllables.

Don't forget to mark stressed syllables when you write new words on the board, by underlining or writing a blob over them, and encourage learners to do the same when they write in their notebooks.

5 Make learners aware of weak forms and word linking

As learners become more advanced, these features will also contribute to comprehensibility and fluency, and at any level they are important for the purposes of listening. As you teach new phrases and structures, draw learners' attention to weak forms and word linking as appropriate, and give them the opportunity to practise them, such as by using rhythm when drilling (see above). However, do not worry too much if they do not produce the weak forms and word linking spontaneously – this is more likely to come naturally when learners are more fluent.

6 Make learners aware of intonation

Intonation is a source of worry to many teachers and, consequently, learners. Teachers worry that their learners (or they themselves) cannot hear it, and that whatever they do their learners don't seem to 'learn' it. In reality, there are few situations in which wrong intonation leads to serious misunderstanding. Where problems do occasionally occur is in the area of politeness, and sounding sufficiently enthusiastic (although, even here, in real life many other factors – such as facial expression – can counteract 'wrong' intonation!).

In *Cutting Edge Elementary Third Edition*, we focus on these limited areas for intonation work. You shouldn't expect your learners to produce perfect intonation, but instead aim to raise awareness of it when appropriate. If learners have problems hearing and reproducing the intonation patterns that you choose to focus on, try some of the following ideas.

- Exaggerate the intonation pattern, before returning to a more normal model.
- Hum the intonation pattern before repeating the words (incidentally, this is very useful for hearing intonation patterns yourself, if you have difficulty).
- Use gestures to show the intonation pattern (rather like a conductor).
- Mark the intonation on the board using arrows.

Remember, though, that if learners are getting frustrated, or cannot 'get' the correct intonation, it is probably best to leave it and come back to it another time.

Making tasks work

1 Treat tasks primarily as an opportunity for communication

Some of the tasks in this course may be familiar; the difference is in how they are treated. The main objective is for learners to use the language that they know (and, if necessary, learn new language) in order to achieve a particular communicative goal, not to 'practise' specific language. Although it is virtually impossible to perform some of the tasks without using the language introduced in the unit, in others learners may choose to use this language only once or twice, or not at all. Do not try to 'force-feed' it. Of course, if learners are seeking this language but have forgotten it, this is the ideal moment to remind them!

2 Make the task suit your class

Learners using this course will vary in age, background, interests and ability. All these learners need to find the tasks motivating and 'doable', yet challenging at the same time. In *Cutting Edge Elementary Third Edition*, the tasks include more stages than in previous editions, in order to provide learners with the support necessary to make the most of the tasks. However, do not be afraid to adapt the tasks to suit your class if this helps. The teacher's notes contain suggestions on how to adapt certain tasks for monolingual and multilingual groups, learners of different ages and interests, large classes, and weaker or stronger groups. There are also ideas for shortening tasks, or dividing them over two shorter lessons. We hope these suggestions will give you other ideas of your own on how to adapt the tasks.

3 Make the most of the *Useful language* boxes

As learners are preparing, it is important that they are able to ask you about language queries, so that when they perform the task they can say what they personally want to say. Although the task should not be seen as an opportunity to 'practise' discrete items, there may be specific language that would be useful in order to perform the task successfully. Each task is accompanied by a *Useful language* box containing phrases which can be adapted by individual learners to express different ideas and opinions, as well as an opportunity to listen to the phrases used by speakers doing a similar task. The idea behind this is twofold: firstly, learners can hear how the phrases are used in context, and secondly this also helps draw their attention to the phrases in case they want to use them during the task. Some ideas for varying the way you do this include:

- Give learners a minute or two to say the phrases quietly to themselves so they know what to listen for before they listen.
- Have different learners listen for phrases under different sections of the *Useful language* box, then share their answers afterwards.
- After doing the exercise, have learners think of possible endings for the phrases, then read out their endings for their partner to guess the phrase.

4 Give learners time to think and plan

Planning time is very important if learners are to produce the best language that they are capable of. It is particularly useful for building up the confidence of learners who are normally reluctant to speak in class. Once learners have planned, discourage them from reading from notes. Give them time to look at their notes, and then ask them to close their notebooks. With certain learners this may have to be a gradual process.

5 Make notes for further input

Before or during the performance of the task, you may notice errors and gaps in learners' knowledge that you want to look at. It is usually best not to interrupt the flow of the task, but to make a note of points to cover later on.

6 Use the *Share your task* box

All the tasks in *Cutting Edge Elementary Third Edition* have a Share your task box which can either be done completely in class or as a combination of homework and classwork. These offer learners the opportunity to repeat or carry out a similar task and film or record it, enabling them to consolidate what they have learnt, and put into practice any suggestions and corrections that you have discussed. This is also an opportunity for learners to practise 'perfecting' what they say when reporting on the task, in order to record a version of themselves using English to a high standard, which should be motivating. Some ideas for filming/recording include:

- learners create a video/audio montage of themselves doing the task.
- learners create a TV/radio programme with a 'presenter' who introduces different people doing the task.
- depending on the task, learners could act out part of a narrative as a short film.
- encourage learners to add music or other background noise/ visuals, and to film in different locations to make their recordings more realistic.
- if learners are comfortable doing so, encourage them to post their recording on a blog or social networking site, then collect comments to share with the class.
- learners watch/listen to other learners' recordings, or show them to another class, and choose the best one.
- after learners have filmed/recorded themselves, collect in the recordings and plan a 'find someone who' task. Give learners a list of things which appear in their classmates' tasks and ask them to discuss whose task each thing appears in. They then watch/listen and check their answers.
- learners watch/listen to their classmates' tasks and then write a summary report.

See the Teacher's notes for further suggestions on how to use each *Share your task* box.

TEACHING TIPS

How to get the most out of Cutting Edge Elementary Third Edition

Using video material in class

The video lessons are a new feature of *Cutting Edge Elementary Third Edition*, and are intended to be modern, engaging ways of consolidating and extending some of the topics covered in the units. The video lessons occur at the end of every unit, and half the units have a *World culture* lesson, while the other half have a *Language live* lesson.

World culture lessons:

The *World culture* lessons contain one clip per unit: part of a TV programme. These lessons are intended to encourage learners to explore contemporary topics and develop the important 21st century skill of online research.

Language live lessons:

The *Language live* lessons contain two clips per unit: part of a story, used to introduce functional language and a *Key phrases* clip, where the functional language from the lesson is repeated in isolation. They are intended to introduce functional language in a light-hearted way and develop learners' writing skills through structured support.

1 Using video in class

Video can be an excellent way to study language as it is not only motivating but also illustrates the importance of non-verbal aspects of communication. In many respects, it is the 'next best thing' to observing real life. In order to get the best out of it though, observe the following guidelines:

- **Watch the clip yourself beforehand:**
  It is important to know what to expect so you can help learners understand the humour in the *Language live* clips (see below).

- **Do something visual first:**
  The exercises in *Cutting Edge Elementary Third Edition* are designed to go from easier to more challenging, but sometimes, with stronger classes, you might find that they'll benefit from first just watching the clip to get a general idea of what it's about, before watching again and doing the exercises in the *Student's Book*.

- **Don't replay the clip too many times:**
  Learners may become demotivated if they really can't understand something in the clip. Instead, make the most of the subtitles or time-coded scripts (see above). Always give learners a chance to comprehend by viewing only first, but if they run into difficulties with a particular part of the clip, use the subtitles/scripts to pinpoint the difficult language and explain as necessary.

- **Vary how you use it:**
  There are many different ways of using video in class, with different purposes. For example, learners can sit in pairs, one facing the screen and the other with their back to it. Play the clip with the sound off, and the learner facing the screen describes what happens to the other learner, who then watches afterwards and checks. You'll find more suggestions in the teacher's notes for each lesson, and it's a good idea to vary the way you use the video material in class to keep it interesting.

2 Exploit the humour in the Language live clips

The *Language live* clips introduce functional language in a light-hearted way, which helps maintain learners' interest and make learning more enjoyable overall. A lot of the humour is visual and can be seen through the actors' expressions, but sometimes it will be useful to draw learners' attention to features in the clips, to get the most out of them. This is where it's important to watch the clip beforehand, and think about how you can draw learners' attention to these aspects with the use of guiding questions. For example, in Unit 2 you could ask *How is the man feeling?*, in Unit 4 you could ask *Why is the man nervous?*

3 Doing online research

The *World culture* lessons involve two opportunities for learners to do online research. Firstly, in the *Find out first* section where they collect background information on the topic of the video, and secondly after the *World view* section when they find out about further things related to the topic of the video. This is an important 21st century skill for learners to master in English, and so the following ideas may help:

- **Make the most of available technology:**
  If learners have smartphones, they can use them to do the research. If not, you can set it for homework: before the class for the *Find out first* sections and after class for the research later in the lesson.

- **Vary the way in which learners do research:**
  In one lesson learners can research alone then compare answers in pairs, and in the next lesson they could research in pairs, then pool ideas as a class or in groups. Vary the way in which learners research, too, so rather than just using the same search engine, different learners could enter the search terms into different encyclopedia sites, forums, etc., and compare results.

- **Be on hand to help:**
  Since there are very few limits as to what's available online, circulate and be available to help with language, and also to step in in the case of inappropriate search results.

- **Encourage learners to prioritise information:**
  Part of being a good researcher is not just obtaining results but also prioritising the most important points. Encourage learners to do this by asking them to find no more than three facts, for example, or only noting down facts which they can find on more than one website.

- **Encourage learners to be critical thinkers:**
  There is a lot of information available on the internet, and not all of it is always reliable! Encourage learners to question information they find, and corroborate it with other learners. How reputable is the website where they found the information? Whether they can prove what they've found clearly is perhaps not as important as encouraging them to question everything.

Using the *Study, Practice & Remember* sections

The *Study, Practice & Remember* sections are a new feature of *Cutting Edge Elementary Third Edition* and can be found at the back of the *Students' Book*. Each unit has a *Study* section which provides a summary of key language as well as review and extension exercises.

The *Study, Practice & Remember* sections have the following main aims:

- to ensure systematic consolidation of new language before learners move on to the next unit.
- to recycle vocabulary through recording and practice.

1 Use the *Study, Practice & Remember* sections to consolidate learning

The *Study* sections provide a comprehensive overview of each language point covered in the main unit. These can be used in different ways. For example:

- learners read the *Study* section before focusing on the *Grammar* box in the main unit.
- after clarifying the language in the lesson, give learners a few minutes to read the *Study* section to consolidate what they have learnt, and think of questions to ask you.
- learners read the *Study* section for homework, either before or after the class, and think of questions they would like to ask.
- if you think your learners need additional practice before attempting the more communicative activities in the main units, you could select one or two of the *Practice* activities to do in class first.

2 Use the different activities as warmers and fillers

The activities in the *Study, Practice & Remember* sections can be used when you have ten or fifteen minutes to spare. For example, you could do the *Study* section at the end of one lesson, and do the exercises in the Practice sections in another lesson.

3 Make the most of the Remember these words sections

These sections aim to provide learners with a list of the most important words and phrases from each unit. However, it is important for learners to 'take ownership' of these lists, by adding to them, providing translations, example sentences, definitions, etc. Encourage learners to experiment with different ways of doing this and finding out what works for them.

You can also use these lists towards the end of each unit to plan recycling activities (see *Teaching tips: Working with lexis* on page 21).

4 Set homework based on these sections

If you are short of time in class, the *Practice* section could easily be set as homework. If you do this, it might be useful to explain in class where learners should look in the *Study* section if they need to do further revision.

5 Set aside time for learners' questions

If you set the *Study* or *Practice* sections for homework, in the next lesson set aside some time for learners to ask any questions they have. You could encourage learners to discuss their questions in small groups before answering them with the whole class.

6 Encourage learners to take responsibility for their own progress

The approach in the *Study, Practice & Remember* section is to encourage learner independence and personal responsibility for progress. By using these sections frequently and in different ways, you will provide opportunities for learners to reflect on their learning and experiment with different ways of studying.

TEACHING TIPS

How to get the most out of Cutting Edge Elementary Third Edition

Teaching elementary learners

Teaching elementary learners comes with its own unique challenges and benefits. Learners at this level are still finding their feet, and the road ahead can seem a little daunting at times. However, they may also be surprised to discover that they already know quite a bit of English, but need the confidence to use it. Elementary learners need lots of support and encouragement, as well as a 'safe' environment in which to practice.

1 Give plenty of praise and support

When students so something well, or answer a question correctly, make sure you acknowledge it by saying, for example, *Well done* or *Good*. However, do not go too far here, for example, by saying *That was excellent!* unless it really was, as it might become a little patronising. Learners also need lots of support when you set up activities and when they do them. Learning another language can be a little daunting at first, but with the right level of support and praise you will be able to gradually build their confidence in using English.

2 Draw attention to what learners already know

Remind students that they already know a lot of English, whether it is the use of 'international' words related to computers or sport or well-known phrases for greetings, such as *Hi!* Or *How are you?* Once learners realise they already know quite a bit of English, the road ahead may feel less daunting. Also, make the aims of each lesson clear to learners at the start, and at the end of each lesson, recap what they have learnt. This will make it clear to learners that they are making good progress with English.

3 Teach useful classroom language

It can be useful to teach common classroom language at the start of a course, in order to lessen some of the burden of communication. Write the most common instructions you need to give, and the most common questions students might need to ask, on a poster and place it in clear sight of the class. Refer back to it when appropriate in the lesson until students are comfortable using the phrases in English. As you continue with the course, make a note of any common classroom language which comes up with your class, and adapt your poster to incorporate it.

4 Grade your language

At this level you need to adapt the language you use so that students can follow your instructions and feel comfortable interacting with you. Obviously you will need to speak a little more slowly, but there are other things you can do to grade the language you use with your students.

- **Use pauses:**
  Remember that students are not just listening to what you say, they are also processing it in order to understand it in their L1. Use clear pauses after key words in instructions and things you need to get across. This will give learners a chance to 'digest' what you are saying.

- **Use gestures:**
  There are many gestures you can use for different instructions, for example, *listen* (cup your ear), *work together* (move your fingers together), etc. The actual gestures you use are not so important, but if you use the same ones frequently, your students will come to understand what you want them to do.

- **Use imperatives:**
  Avoid using phrases such as *I'd like you to…* or *Now I want you to…* etc. At this level learners only need to hear imperatives for instructions. As long as you use them in a friendly way, they can be much more effective.

- **Use the board:**
  If you want to rearrange learners, for example, draw a simple plan on the board of how you would like the groups/class to look. This can be much easier for students to refer to.

5 Use realia and visuals

This is especially important if you are teaching nouns within a topic, for example, clothes or food. Trying to describe *banana*, for example, is quite difficult at this level. Showing a picture or (even better) a real banana will save time and make things clearer.

6 Monitor and check learners know what to do

Some learners, if they do not understand what you want them to do, will tell you. Others might not want to be 'difficult', and will just nod and pretend they understand when they do not. It is important at this level that you do not take anything for granted, especially when setting up activities. Here are some useful techniques for checking understanding.

- **Elicit an example:**
  If students are doing a practice exercise, do the first one together, and elicit the answer. This will tell you whether students know what *type* of answer they need to give, or even just if they are looking at the right exercise!

- **Demonstrate:**
  With a more complicated activity, demonstrate with a stronger student. It will make it much easier for learners to follow if they can *see* what they have to do.

- **Ask a question:**
  It can be useful to ask questions to check simple details about an activity, for example, *Are you speaking or writing? Can you show your partner your answer?* Bear in mind that questions are only really useful for small details like this.

- **Monitor:**
  After you have set up an activity, you will often need to quickly go round the class and check everyone knows what to do. Weaker students may need further help.

7 Correct errors sensitively

It is important to correct errors at appropriate times in class i.e. when you are focusing on accuracy or during controlled practice. This is something learners expect, even at this level, and will feel somewhat cheated if you do not correct them. However, it is important to do this sensitively, by giving the learners a chance to correct themselves or inviting other students to correct the error. Do not spend too much time focusing on the error, but aim to establish the correct answer as soon as possible and then establish this firmly as the correct form.

TEACHER'S NOTES INDEX

01 PEOPLE AND PLACES

OVERVIEW

PAGES 6–7

Speaking and listening: Introductions

Grammar: *be*: positive forms

Common European Framework: Students can introduce themselves and others.

PAGES 8–9

Vocabulary: Countries and nationalities

Grammar: *be*: positive and negative short forms

Pronunciation: Word stress

Common European Framework: Students can produce simple phrases about people and places.

PAGES 10–11

Vocabulary: Jobs

Grammar: Articles with jobs; *be*: personal questions

Pronunciation: Intonation and stress in questions and short answers

Common European Framework: Students can ask for and give personal information.

PAGES 12–13

Task: Find information from documents

Common European Framework: Students can understand short simple texts.

PAGES 14–15

World culture: Life in the Arctic

Common European Framework: Students can follow changes of topic of factual TV items, and form an idea of the main content.

Speaking and listening (PAGE 6)

1a 🎧 **1.1** As an introduction, ask students questions about the pictures, e.g. *Who are they? Where are they? What are they doing?* Encourage students as much as possible and don't worry about mistakes at this stage. Students then order the conversation. Play the recording for students to check their answers.

ANSWERS:

2, 3, 1, 4

b Focus students' attention on the conversation. Demonstrate the activity by performing the conversation with a volunteer from the class. Students work in pairs to practise the conversation.

2a Quickly check the pronunciation of the sentences in the box. Students then work in pairs to complete the conversations.

b 🎧 **1.2** Play the recording to check the answers. Students practise the conversations in pairs. Circulate and offer help and encouragement as necessary. In feedback, ask a couple of pairs to perform their conversations for the class.

ANSWERS:

1 I'm fine, thanks.　**2** Nice to meet you, May.　**3** Are you from the USA?　**4** Where are you from?

Grammar focus 1 (PAGE 7)

be: positive forms

See *Teaching tips: Working with grammar*, page 20.

GRAMMAR

be: positive forms

1 Write on the board: *I'm from (name of city)*. Elicit from students that *'m = am*. Draw a stick picture of a man and write: *He's from Rome*. Draw a stick picture of a woman and write: *She's from Rome*. Elicit that *'s = is*. Draw an arrow to both the man and the woman and write: *They're from Rome*. Elicit that *'re = are*. Students complete the gaps in the sentences using the board and the previous conversations to help them. During feedback, highlight:

- the change in word order, e.g. *you are → are you ... ?*
- the use of apostrophes for contracted forms.

ANSWERS:

1 am/'m　**2** Are　**3** is/'s　**4** is/'s　**5** are

Question words: *what/where*

2 Elicit the difference between *what*, used to ask for general information, and *where*, used to ask for information about places. Students complete the gaps. Highlight:

- the pronunciation of the *s* so students are not saying *Where he from?*
- the pronunciation of *Where are* /ˈweərɑː/.

ANSWERS:

1 What　**2** Where

You may want to ask students to read Study 1 on page 138 for a more detailed explanation of the positive forms of *be*.

PRACTICE

1a Students mingle, asking each other the questions.

┌───┐
Practice, exercise 1a: Alternative suggestion

If your students all come from the same country, encourage them to say which city they come from. If they come from the same city, then ask them to say which neighbourhood they are from.
└───┘

b Give an example in an open pair with one of the students. Students then work in pairs to talk about the people they spoke to in the previous exercise. Monitor to make sure students use *This is ...* instead of *He/She is ...* in the first sentence. In feedback, ask each student to tell the class about one of their classmates.

2 Quickly check the pronunciation of the countries, paying particular attention to word stress. Demonstrate the activity using a student as a partner. Students work in pairs to talk about the people in the photos.

ADDITIONAL PRACTICE

➡ **Study, practice & remember:** Practice 1

　Workbook: Grammar focus 1: *be: positive forms*, page 4

Vocabulary (PAGE 8)

Countries and nationalities

See *Teaching tips: Working with lexical phrases*, page 21.

1a Students match the countries to the nationalities.

b 🎧 **1.3** Students listen and check.

Country	Nationality
Spain	Spanish
China	Chinese
the USA	American
Brazil	Brazilian
Italy	Italian
Great Britain	British
Poland	Polish
Australia	Australian
Japan	Japanese
Vietnam	Vietnamese
Ireland	Irish
Russia	Russian

PRONUNCIATION

See *Teaching tips: Helping students with pronunciation*, page 22.

1 🎧 **1.4** Play the recording and check students can identify the stressed syllable by clapping or tapping.

2a Highlight the system used in the examples with the dots above the stressed syllable. Students mark the stress on the nationalities from Vocabulary, exercise 1a. Reassure students not to worry if they don't know.

b 🎧 **1.5** Students listen and check. Drill the pronunciation, paying attention to correct use of word stress.

ANSWERS:

British, American, Japanese, Chinese, Polish, Italian, Vietnamese, Russian, Irish, Spanish, Brazilian, Australian

ADDITIONAL PRACTICE

➡ **Resource bank:** Activity 1A *Nice to meet you!* (*be*: positive forms; Countries and nationalities)

Workbook: Vocabulary: *Countries and nationalities*, page 5; Pronunciation: *Word stress*, page 5

Reading and listening (PAGE 8)

1a When you set up the quiz, make sure you are enthusiastic and motivating as this will transmit itself to the students. Demonstrate the points system and put students into pairs or small groups to answer the questions. Check students understand *stamps* and *currencies*. You could do this by showing them realia or by drawing an envelope with a stamp on it and the symbols of different currencies on the board. Set a time limit of about five minutes, and circulate to see the groups are on-task.

b 🎧 **1.6** When the time is up, stop the quiz and elicit students' answers to each question before you play the correct answers on the recording. Students keep their scores and see who the winner is on points.

ANSWERS:

1 **a** Brazil, **b** China, **c** Poland, **d** Egypt
2 rupee: India, rouble: Russia, lira: Turkey, peso: Argentina
3 **a** Chinese, **b** Italian, **c** Russian, **d** Spanish, **e** Arabic
4 Samsung: Korean, Google: American, Honda: Japanese, M&S: British
5 Andrea Bocelli: Italian, Delta Goodrem: Australian, Luis Miguel: Mexican

---

Culture notes

Honda is a Japanese multinational company that is best known for producing cars and motorbikes.

Samsung is a Korean multinational company involved in many areas including shipbuilding, food production and insurance. The company is perhaps best known for its electronics division, which produces televisions and mobile phones.

M&S, also known as Marks and Spencer, is a British retail company. The company was the market leader in the UK until a crisis in the late 1990s. The company is best known for its clothes and food products.

Google is an American technology giant. The company first became famous due to its internet search engine, but has since expanded into other areas of technology, including maps, email and mobile phones.

Andrea Bocelli (b. 1958) is an Italian tenor, who also plays many musical instruments. When he was a child he had an accident while playing football that left him blind. He has recorded fourteen solo albums and has sold over 80 million records. He has had seven albums in the top ten in the USA, has won Grammies and been nominated for an Oscar.

Delta Goodrem (b. 1984) is an Australian singer, pianist and actor. She sprang to fame in the soap opera *Neighbours* in 2002 and a year later her first album had sold over 4.5 million copies. Five singles from the album were number one hits in Australia, the first time a debut album has had five hits.

Luis Miguel (b. 1970) is a Mexican singer. He recorded his first album when he was only 11 and won his first Grammy at the age of 15. He is famous not only for his records but also for his outstanding live shows. On his 1999–2000 tour he performed 105 concerts that were seen by 1.5 million people.

Grammar focus 2 (PAGE 9)

be: positive and negative short forms

See *Teaching tips: Working with grammar*, page 20.

1a Focus students' attention on the photos. Check students understand *married*, *businesswoman* and *holiday* by pointing to a wedding ring, talking about famous businessmen and businesswomen, and eliciting popular places to go on holiday. Do the first couple of sentences as an example. Students then continue to match the sentences to the photos.

b 🎧 **1.7** Students listen and check.

ANSWERS:

2 B	3 A	4 B	5 A	6 C	7 C	8 A	9 B	10 C
11 A	12 B	13 B	14 A	15 C				

Grammar focus 2, exercise 1b: Additional activity

You might like to take this opportunity to show students the audio scripts at the back of the book. Direct students to audio script 1.7 on page 166. Ask students to listen again and underline all of the examples of the verb *to be*. If necessary, remind students of the different forms of the verb in the present. This activity will make students aware that they have the audio script at the back of the book and it will also help raise awareness of the verb *to be* for the next activity.

GRAMMAR

be: positive and negative short forms

1 Elicit the answer for the first gap, *I'm*. Students complete the other gaps individually using the previous exercise to help. Students check in pairs. Circulate to help and make sure students are putting the apostrophe in the correct place.

ANSWERS:
Positive short forms: I'm, he's, she's, they're
Negative short forms: you aren't, he isn't, she isn't, it isn't, they aren't

You may want to ask students to read Study 2 on page 138 for a more detailed explanation of positive and negative short forms of the verb *to be*.

PRONUNCIATION

See *Teaching tips: Helping students with pronunciation*, page 22.

1a Direct students to audio script 1.8 on page 166. Ask students to underline all of the short forms.

  b 🎧 **1.8** Students listen and pay attention to the pronunciation of the short forms. Check students' pronunciation, particularly with the linking sounds in *you aren't* /juːwɑːnt/, *he isn't* /hiːjɪznt/ and *we aren't* /wiːjɑːnt/.

2 Drill the sentences chorally and individually.

PRACTICE

1a Demonstrate by writing some true and false sentences on the board, e.g. *Her name's Hanna. She's from Argentina.* Read them aloud and ask students if they are true or false and to correct the sentences if false. Students work individually to write their own sentences.

  b Ask a student to read out a couple of sentences and have the class correct them where appropriate. Students continue in pairs. Circulate and help as necessary.

2a This activity helps students to personalise the language. Write the two examples on the board and do them with one of the students in front of the class. Before students do the exercise, check the following: *school, classroom, small, the evening, at work*. Give students a few minutes to go through the sentences and rewrite the false ones. Circulate and help as necessary.

  b Students work in pairs to compare their sentences. At the end, do some quick class feedback on each sentence.

ADDITIONAL PRACTICE

💬 **Study, practice & remember:** Practice 2

Workbook: Grammar focus 2: *be: positive and negative short forms*, page 7

Vocabulary (PAGE 10)

Jobs

See *Teaching tips: Working with lexical phrases*, page 21.

Potential problem with jobs

In the following exercises we have used *actor* for a man or a woman. While some people still use *actress* for a woman, it is becoming increasingly common to use *actor* for both sexes. Likewise, *police officer* is more common than *policeman/woman*.

1 Students match the pictures to the words in the box.

ANSWERS:
A footballer **B** doctor **C** engineer **D** waiter
E police officer **F** businesswoman **G** shop assistant
H musician **I** actor **J** lawyer **K** businessman **L** singer

Vocabulary, exercise 1: Alternative suggestion

You could make this more competitive by putting students into pairs or small groups and asking them to race each other to complete the exercise.

PRONUNCIATION

See *Teaching tips: Helping students with pronunciation*, page 22.

1 🎧 **1.9** Remind students how to mark the word stress with a dot above the stressed syllable. Students then listen and mark the stress.

ANSWERS:
a <u>foot</u>baller, a mu<u>si</u>cian, an engi<u>neer</u>, a <u>law</u>yer, a po<u>lice</u> <u>of</u>ficer, a <u>sing</u>er, a <u>shop</u> as<u>sis</u>tant, a <u>doc</u>tor, an <u>ac</u>tor, a <u>wait</u>er, a <u>busi</u>nessman, a <u>busi</u>ness<u>wo</u>man

2 Drill the pronunciation of the words, paying attention to the word stress and the schwa /ə/ ending of *footballer* /ˈfʊtbɔːlə/, *lawyer* /ˈlɔɪjə/, *police officer* /pəˈliːs ˌɒfɪsə/, *singer* /ˈsɪŋə/, *doctor* /ˈdɒktə/, *actor* /ˈæktə/, and *waiter* /ˈweɪtə/.

Vocabulary: Alternative suggestions

a If you have a small class, put pictures of jobs on a table or the floor. Say a job and ask students to point to it. If no one knows the job, then teach it. After they've listened to you saying the jobs a few times, let them take it in turns to say a job and the others point to the correct picture. If you want to increase motivation, say a job and students try to pick up the picture before the others. The winner is the one with the most pictures at the end.

b Students do exercise 1, have one minute to memorise the words and then close their books and try to write all the jobs. The winning student is the one who remembers the most.

ADDITIONAL PRACTICE

💬 **Workbook:** Vocabulary: *Jobs*, page 7; Pronunciation: *Word stress*, page 7

Grammar focus 3 (PAGE 10)

Articles with jobs

See *Teaching tips: Working with grammar*, page 20.

1 Check with students which sentence is correct. Tell them that when we talk about jobs we use the articles *a/an*.

ANSWER:
Sentence 2 is correct.

GRAMMAR

Articles with jobs

1 Write on the board: *He's ___ musician.* and *She's ___ engineer.* Elicit the article to complete each gap. Teach the rule using the box in the book. Check students understand *vowel*.

You may want to ask students to read Study 3 on page 138 for a more detailed explanation of articles with jobs.

PRACTICE

1a Students complete the sentences with *a* or *an* then check in pairs.

b 🎧 **1.10** Students listen and check.

ANSWERS:

1 a   2 an   3 a   4 a   5 a   6 an   7 a   8 a

2a Demonstrate the activity by writing a couple of sentences on the board about the jobs of people in the class. Elicit corrections where appropriate. Give students a few minutes to write their own sentences. Circulate and help.

b Students work in pairs to correct each other's sentences.

ADDITIONAL PRACTICE

➥ **Study, practice & remember:** Practice 3

Workbook: Grammar focus 3: *Articles with jobs*, page 7

Grammar focus 4 (PAGE 11)

be: personal questions

See *Teaching tips: Working with grammar*, page 20.

1 Do the first question with the class as an example. Students continue to choose the correct answers then check in pairs. During feedback make sure students understand that @ is pronounced *at* and *.com* is pronounced *dot com*.

ANSWERS:

1 b   2 a   3 b   4 a   5 a   6 b

GRAMMAR

Questions and short answers with *be*

1 Work through the rules in the Grammar box. Make sure to highlight the following:

- the word order in the questions, using arrows to show the inversion of the subject and verb *you are → are you … ?*
- the negative short answers: *No, I'm not.* and *No, she isn't.* The students should be able to give you these.
- that we use short forms rather than repeating the full information in the question, for example *Yes, I am.* NOT *Yes, I am married.*
- that we don't contract the positive short forms, for example *Yes, she is.* NOT *Yes, she's.*

You may want to ask students to read Study 4 on page 138 for more information about questions and short answers with *be*.

2 Students work in pairs and practise the questions and answers in exercise 1. Monitor for pronunciation.

PRACTICE

1 Ask students to complete the questions and answers. Remind students to use the abbreviated forms.

ANSWERS:

1 A is/'s B is/'s   2 A job B is/'s   3 A Where B from

2 Focus students' attention on the photos and demonstrate the activity using one of the photos and a stronger student. Students work in pairs to ask and answer questions about the people in the other photos.

3a Students choose the correct answers, check in pairs, and then as a class. Drill the sentences with your students and, in anticipation of the next exercise, make sure students use a rising intonation pattern.

ANSWERS:

1 Are   2 Is   3 Are   4 Are   5 Is   6 Are

b Give students a few minutes to write their own answers to the questions.

PRONUNCIATION

See *Teaching tips: Helping students with pronunciation*, page 22.

1 🎧 **1.11** Write *teacher* on the board and elicit the word stress. Then write *I'm a teacher.* and say the sentence. Elicit the sentence stress and mark it on the board with a dot above the stressed syllable.

Direct students to audio script 1.11 on page 166. Students listen to the recording and mark the stressed words.

Write on the board: *Are you from France?* Ask the question with a rising intonation and mark the pattern on the board. Play the recording again and ask students to mark the intonation patterns.

2 Drill the questions and answers, paying particular attention to sentence stress and intonation patterns.

4 Students work in pairs to ask and answer the questions from exercise 3a. Circulate and monitor for correct intonation and sentence stress.

ADDITIONAL PRACTICE

➥ **Resource bank:** Activity 1B *The English class* (*be*: personal questions); Activity 1C *Short answer snap* (*be*: short answers to *Yes/No* questions)

Study, practice & remember: Practice 4 and 5

Workbook: Grammar focus 4: *be: personal questions*, page 8

Task (PAGE 12–13)

Find information from documents

See *Teaching tips: Making tasks work*, page 23.

Preparation (PAGE 12)

Reading

1 Focus students' attention on the photo of Deepa and her Employee Personal Information card. Do the first question with the whole class, showing where to find the answer. Check *emergency* if necessary, but otherwise discourage students from trying to understand every word on the card. The aim here is to practise reading to extract specific information. In feedback, encourage students to give you the correct answers and to identify where they found the information.

ANSWERS:

1 T   2 T   3 F   4 T   5 F   6 F   7 T   8 T   9 F

2a 🎧 **1.12** Focus students' attention on the Useful language box. Ask students to read the questions and quickly deal with any unknown vocabulary. Students listen to the conversation and tick the questions and answers they hear.

b Students compare their answers in pairs and then listen to the recording again to check their answers. If you have weaker students, or students who are lacking confidence, allow them to listen and read the audio script on page 166.

Task (PAGES 12–13)

Speaking

1 Divide the class into two groups, A and B. As look at Tom's documents on page 13 and Bs look at Michiko's documents on page 132. Each group completes the relevant profile card on page 12.

Students can work individually and then compare answers with another student in their group. Circulate and help as necessary. Help students with the pronunciation of *Brighton* /ˈbraɪtən/ and the email addresses: *Thomas B at Yahoo dot co dot UK* and *sato at family law dot com*.

ANSWERS:

Tom

Full name: Thomas J. Briggs

Age: 22 (at time of going to print – he was born in 1991)

Address: 44 Preston Road, Brighton, BN1 2PR

Job: university student

Where from?: Great Britain

Email address: thomasb@yahoo.co.uk

Telephone: 07744 345332

Michiko

Full name: Michiko Sato

Age: 31 (at time of going to print – she was born in 1982)

Address: 416 Water Street, New York, NY 10002

Job: family lawyer

Where from?: Japan

Email address: sato@familylaw.com

Telephone: 212 544 9887

2 Put students into A/B pairs. Check that they understand the task and remind them to look back at the Useful language box. Ask two stronger students to start asking and answering questions about Tom in front of the class. Tell the students to keep their written information 'secret' from their partner and to write down the new answers in the relevant profile card. Circulate, helping as necessary and collecting examples of any problems for error correction work later.

3 Students work in pairs to ask each other questions. This activity will help students to personalise the language and also change the pronouns from *his/her* to *your*.

Share your task

The idea here is to give students a chance to 'perfect' their speaking in this context and provide them with a recording of a 'polished' version. This will provide extra motivation for students, as well as extra practice. Students can either make an audio or video recording, depending on how comfortable they feel and what equipment is available. Students could even use their mobile phones to do this. If possible, they'll need a quiet place to make their recording. Students can either record themselves during the lesson, or as homework and bring the recordings to the next class.

World culture, Find out first:

To help your students prepare for the next class, go through the questions in exercise 1 on page 14. If necessary, discuss ideas for searching for this information on the internet, pointing out the search terms, and suggest other sources of information students could use. Encourage students to use English language websites as much as possible.

World culture (PAGES 14–15)

Life in the Arctic

Culture notes

The Inuit are a group of different indigenous peoples who live in Canada, Alaska, Greenland and Russia. While there are some marked differences between each group, the similarities, especially in their languages, are more important.

The Inuit people face a number of challenges to their way of life. Global warming has led to changes in the weather patterns in the Arctic which have had dramatic effects on how and when they can hunt. A side effect of global warming has also been to open up the Arctic to resource development. This 'invasion' poses a threat to the Inuit as countries and companies race to be the first to extract precious metals and oil from the region.

Another potential problem is that young people are caught between a traditional lifestyle and the possibility of a more Western way of life with all the luxuries and problems that entails. One indicator of these problems is the rise of myopia, or short-sightedness, in young Inuit. Myopia was virtually unheard of in the Inuit community until fairly recently. A different diet or western education are seen as two of the possible reasons for its appearance.

Find out first (PAGE 14)

1a Students work in pairs to try to guess the answers to the quiz. If some students have not done the research, try to put them with a student who has done it.

b If you have access to the internet and students haven't been able to find the answer to some of the questions, ask students to go online and do some further research. Highlight the search terms. Circulate and offer help with vocabulary and try to encourage people to use only English language websites. Otherwise, tell your students the answers.

ANSWERS:

1 b   2 a   3 b   4 b   5 c

View (PAGE 14)

See *Teaching tips: Using the video material in the classroom*, page 24.

2a Tell the students they are going to watch a DVD about life in the Arctic. Make sure students understand the key vocabulary by going through the words in the box, paying particular attention to the pronunciation of *igloo* /ˈɪgluː/ and the meaning and pronunciation of *mussels* /ˈmʌslz/, which are a small black shellfish.

b ▶ Students watch the DVD and tick the things from the box that they see.

ANSWERS:

the sun, snow, ice, igloo, mussels, tea

3 Tell students that this is the audio script for the DVD, but with some gaps that they have to fill in with words from the box. Give them time to read through the script so they know what they have to listen for. Students compare their answers in pairs.

Students then watch the DVD again to check their answers. Check as a class to make sure everyone heard the answers.

ANSWERS:
1 food **2** is **3** from **4** friends **5** cold **6** it's **7** ice **8** eat

World view (PAGE 15)

4a Demonstrate the activity by ticking one or two statements that you think are true for your country. Students work individually to read through the rest of the sentences and tick the ones that apply to their country.

World view, exercise 4a: Alternative suggestion

If your students come from the same country, write these sentences on the board as an alternative and ask students to tick the ones that are true for them. You might need to use mime or draw pictures to help students understand.

I like the cold.

I hate eating fish.

I love plants and trees.

I never saw snow.

b Students work in pairs to compare their answers.

Find out more ⓢ (PAGE 15)

5a Ask if students have ever heard of any of the indigenous people. If they have, encourage them to make a note of anything they know and share their ideas with the class.

b If you have access to the internet at school, students work in pairs to research the three groups of indigenous people. Focus students' attention on the search terms that they should use. Circulate and help with new vocabulary as necessary and encourage students to use English language websites.

ANSWERS:
the Degar: Live in Vietnam, where the weather is warm and wet. Eat meat and vegetables.
the Tuareg: Live in the Sahara, where the weather is hot and dry. Eat bread, milk, cheese and cereals.
the Yanomami: Live in the Amazon rainforest, where it is warm and wet. Eat fruit, meat and fish.

Find out more, exercise 5b: Alternative suggestion

Because this may be the first time your students have done an activity like this, you might like to ask them to research only one of the groups. Put students into pairs and tell them which group to research. When they have finished, reorganise students into bigger groups to exchange the information they found.

Write up your research

6 Show your students the example text about the Inuit. Encourage your students to use this as a model to write up the information they found in exercise 5b about the indigenous people. If you don't have time to do this in class, it can be done as homework.

Study, practice & remember
(PAGES 138–139)

See *Teaching tips: Using the Study, practice & remember sections*, page 25.

Practice 1

ANSWERS:
1 am/'m **2** is/'s **3** are/'re **4** are/'re **5** is/'s **6** are/'re

Practice 2

ANSWERS:
1
1 He's a student. **2** I'm Marta. **3** You're on holiday. **4** I'm not married. **5** We aren't from Madrid. **6** We're from Rome.
2
1 I'm from Poland. **2** He's at work. **3** You aren't English. **4** They're Italian. **5** I'm not a student. **6** She's 19 years old.

Practice 3

ANSWERS:
a: footballer, lawyer, doctor, police officer, musician, businessman
an: engineer, actor

Practice 4

ANSWERS:
1 How **2** What **3** Where **4** How **5** What

Practice 5

ANSWERS:
1 you, I **2** His, He's, he's **3** We, Our **4** His, They
5 she, Her **6** They, their

Remember these words

ANSWERS:
1
2 Great Britain, British **3** Russia, Russian **4** Italy, Italian
5 Spain, Spanish **6** China, Chinese **7** Poland, Polish
8 Japan, Japanese
2
1 a businessman **2** a lawyer **3** a doctor **4** an engineer
5 a waiter **6** a shop assistant **7** a musician **8** a footballer

OVERVIEW

PAGES 16–17

Vocabulary: Everyday objects

Grammar: *this/that, these/those*; Possessive *'s*

Common European Framework: Students can communicate in simple and routine tasks using simple phrases to ask for and get things.

PAGES 18–19

Grammar: *have got*

Reading and vocabulary: Family

Common European Framework: Students can ask and answer simple questions on familiar topics.

PAGES 20–21

Task: Talk about your five favourite people

Common European Framework: Students can exchange ideas and information on predictable topics.

PAGES 22–23

Writing: Completing a form

Speaking: Answering questions

Common European Framework: Students can provide personal information in written form.

Vocabulary (PAGE 16)

Everyday objects

See *Teaching tips: Working with lexical phrases*, page 21.

WARM UP

If possible, bring in realia of some of the items in the photos, plus other items that you think your students would like to know or need to know. Ask students to identify what the items are and categorise them according to whether they have them, want them or don't need them.

1 Focus students' attention on the photos and the vocabulary in the box. Students match the words to the pictures individually then check in pairs. Encourage students to use articles in front of the singular nouns.

2 Demonstrate the activity with things from your bag. Students then show each other things in their bags. Circulate and offer help as necessary, always remembering to encourage students to use articles.

PRONUNCIATION

See *Teaching tips: Helping students with pronunciation*, page 22.

1 🎧 **2.1** If necessary, remind students how to mark the stressed syllables. Students listen and mark the stress then check in pairs. Play the recording again if there are any doubts. In feedback, write the words on the board and mark the stress for later reference.

ANSWERS:

a <u>bott</u>le of <u>wa</u>ter, a <u>ca</u>mera, a <u>wa</u>llet, <u>tiss</u>ues, an i<u>den</u>tity card, a <u>cre</u>dit card, <u>keys</u>, <u>glass</u>es, a <u>mo</u>bile <u>phone</u>, a <u>dic</u>tionary, <u>pho</u>tos, a <u>bag</u>, a <u>pac</u>ket of <u>chew</u>ing gum, a <u>me</u>mory <u>stick</u>, <u>coins</u>, a <u>watch</u>

2 Drill the pronunciation chorally and individually. Pay particular attention to the silent syllables in *camera* /ˈkæmrə/ and *dictionary* /ˈdɪkʃənri/, as well as the sounds in *tissues* /ˈtɪʃuːz/, *mobile* /ˈməʊbaɪl/ and *coins* /kɔɪnz/.

3 Give students a minute to remember all of the items in the pictures. With books closed, students work in pairs to try to remember all of the items.

Vocabulary, exercise 3: Additional activities

a Arrange students into two teams. Ask the first team to write the name of an item on the board. Then ask the second team to do the same. The activity continues until one team cannot remember any more items. The other team is then the winner.

b If you have brought in some realia for the warm up activity, you can use it again to practise the vocabulary. Put all of the items on a tray and give students one minute to memorise everything and then cover it with a cloth or a towel. Take away one item without letting any of the students see what it is. Then show the tray again and ask students to write down which item is missing. Repeat until all the items have gone. In feedback, students read out their list in the order in which the items disappeared.

ADDITIONAL PRACTICE

➡ **Workbook:** Vocabulary: *Everyday objects*, page 9; Pronunciation: *Word stress*, page 10

Grammar focus 1 (PAGE 17)

this/that, these/those; Possessive *'s*

See *Teaching tips: Working with grammar*, page 20.

1a Focus students' attention on the two cartoons. Elicit a description of some of the things in the pictures. Students work individually to choose the correct word then check in pairs.

b 🎧 **2.2** Students listen and check.

ANSWERS:

1 This   2 these   3 Tina's   4 that's   5 those   6 Bono's

GRAMMAR

this/that, these/those; Possessive 's

Write *here* and *there* in two columns on the board and ask students where to put *this (book)* and *that (book)*. Then elicit the plural forms in the correct columns:

	here	there
singular	this	that
plural	these	those

Read through the examples in the book with your students. Give some examples using realia from your bag, and from students' bags.

Potential problem with the possessive 's

Some students might have a problem with the pronunciation of the possessive *'s*. The examples in the Grammar box are *Tina's cat.* and *Bono's friends.* In these cases the last sound of both names is a vowel and so is voiced. When the last sound is voiced, the pronunciation of the possessive *'s* is usually the voiced /z/. When the last sound is unvoiced, it is usually /s/. The exceptions to this rule are words that end in the sounds /s/, /z/, /ʃ/, /ʒ/, /tʃ/ and /dʒ/. In these cases, the possessive *'s* is pronounced as /ɪz/. This is especially important if your students have names which end in these sounds.

You may want to ask students to read Study 1 on page 140 for a more detailed explanation of *this/that, these/those* and possessive *'s*.

Grammar: Alternative suggestion

While the drawings in the book will be clear to most people, it would be helpful if you provided an exaggerated demonstration. Use some realia, for example a book and some keys, and put them on a desk near you and say *this book* and *these keys*. Then move away from the desk so there is about a metre between you and the items. Say *that book* and *those keys*. Then move as far away as you can from the desk and repeat *that book* and *those keys*. If possible, ask some of your students to then copy you.

PRONUNCIATION

See *Teaching tips: Helping students with pronunciation*, page 22.

1 🎧 **2.3** Play the recording and drill the four phrases chorally and individually. Pay particular attention to the /ð/ sound and to the difference between the singular /ðɪs/ and the plural /ðiːz/. Give some initial discrimination practice by saying *this, this, these, this, these, these*, etc. slowly and then more quickly. Then do the same in phrases (*this pen, these books*, etc.). Students have to indicate which they hear by holding up either their right or left hand. Then ask students to take your place and say the phrases.

2a 🎧 **2.4** Play the recording and students write the eight sentences.

> **ANSWERS:**
>
> **1** What's this in English? **2** Is this your wallet? **3** Is that your bag? **4** This is my friend Ben. **5** These are my parents. **6** That's my teacher over there. **7** Who are those children? **8** Are these your glasses?

b Students repeat the sentences. Help them to pronounce the /s/ in *What's this? What's that?* by back-chaining, i.e. *this → sthis → What's this?*

Pronunciation: Helping students with the /ð/ and /θ/ sounds

The /ð/ and /θ/ sounds can cause problems for many English language students. There are a number of things you can do to help students:

- Show your students that to make the /ð/ sound their tongue should just come out between the lips and touch the top teeth slightly. You can model this by standing with your profile towards the students and putting your index finger on your lips and showing how your tongue just touches your finger.
- For the /θ/ sound, ask students to make the /s/ sound. Then ask them to move their tongue slightly forward to touch the back of their top teeth.

Don't expect students to be able to produce the sounds perfectly at the first attempt. Reassure students that you will work on this in future classes and that they will eventually achieve it.

PRACTICE

1 Students work individually to choose the appropriate answer then check in pairs before checking answers as a class.

> **ANSWERS:**
>
> **1** this **2** Paola's **3** that **4** John **5** these **6** friend's **7** those **8** sister's

Practice, exercise 1: Additional activity

Ask your students to read the sentences aloud to focus on their pronunciation. Make sure students have read and understood the sentences and then give them a moment to prepare to read them aloud. Keep a brisk pace and don't let the activity go on for too long.

2 Demonstrate the activity by pointing to an object across the room and asking *What's that?* and seeing if students know the word in English. Then get them to ask you, to see if they can accurately reproduce the question. Check the plural form in the same way. Students work in pairs. Likely objects could include *a CD player, a DVD player, an overhead projector, a white/blackboard, pens, chalk, a computer, a light, coats, scarves, chairs, a noticeboard, a picture, a register, a door, a ceiling, a wall, windows* and anything that can be seen outside the windows. Circulate and provide the word if the students don't know it. Collect a list of the words, which you or the students could write on the board.

Practice, exercise 2: Alternative suggestion

If you have students who are lower elementary, they might be intimidated by all of the potential vocabulary in and around the classroom. To help with this, prepare some flashcards with the names of objects in the classroom on them. Distribute the flashcards randomly to students and ask them to put them on or next to the appropriate objects in the classroom. If students are not sure, encourage them to ask other students to help. Once all of the flashcards have been matched to the objects, check the pronunciation and then get students to ask and answer questions about the objects in pairs.

ADDITIONAL PRACTICE

➡ **Resource bank:** Activity 2A *What's this?* (*this/that, these/those*)

Study, practice & remember: Practice 1

Workbook: Grammar focus 1: *this/that, these/those*; Possessive *'s*, page 10; Pronunciation: *this/that, these/those*, page 10

Grammar focus 2 (PAGE 18)

have got

See *Teaching tips: Working with grammar*, page 20.

WARM UP

Revise the language covered in the last class by pointing to things around the classroom and asking the questions *What's that?* and *What are those?* Then put students into pairs and encourage them to ask each other. Allow them to get up and move around the class if they want to.

1 🎧 **2.5** Focus students' attention on the photo and the conversation. Students listen and complete the conversation.

> **ANSWERS:**
>
> **1** I haven't got **2** Have you got **3** I've got

Grammar focus 2, exercise 1: Alternative suggestions

a Introduce the structure by showing students what you have in your bag. Take out the items one by one and say *I've got …* . Make sure you have included some examples of the vocabulary from the last class, but don't be afraid to include new things as well.

b If you have a strong class, you could ask students to complete the conversation before they listen to the recording. This will help to challenge them more and you can check to see what they already know.

GRAMMAR

have got

1 Write the examples on the board or ask students to look at the exercise in the book. Ask students to complete the gaps. Encourage them to look back at the previous exercise to find the answers.

2 🎧 **2.6** Students listen and check. During feedback, highlight:
   - the use of *'s* or *has* for the *he/she* forms.
   - the short forms of *have* (*'ve*) and *have not* (*haven't*).
   - the word order in the questions.

> **ANSWERS:**
> + got, got, got
> − got, got, haven't got
> ? got, Has ... got, Have ... got

3 Write on the board: *He's Japanese.* and *He's got a Japanese car.* and ask students what *'s* means in each case.

You may also want to check short answer forms at this point. Elicit the short answer to the question *Have you got a dictionary?* Write up the short answers *Yes, I have.* and *No, I haven't.* and check the third person short answer forms *Yes, he/she has.* and *No, he/she hasn't.*

You may want to ask students to read Study 2 on page 140 for a more detailed explanation of *have got*.

PRONUNCIATION

See *Teaching tips: Helping students with pronunciation*, page 22.

1 Focus students' attention on the sentences in the Grammar box again. Tell students to listen to the recording again and pay attention to the pronunciation of *'s got* and *'ve got*.

2 Drill the sentences chorally and individually. Make sure students are using the short forms as well as using appropriate sentence stress and intonation patterns for the questions.

PRACTICE

1 Do the first one as an example. Students work individually to complete the sentences and then check in pairs. During feedback, make sure students have used the short forms.

> **ANSWERS:**
> 1 've got   2 haven't got   3 's got   4 've got   5 Have, got
> 6 's got   7 've got   8 Has, got

> **Practice, exercise 1: Alternative suggestion**
>
> If your students seem to be handling this language point with ease, ask them to complete this activity orally instead of in writing. Put students into pairs to say the sentences to each other, then check as a class. This procedure will change the focus of the activity to make it more authentic, as well as challenging the students more by giving them less time to think about their answers.

2a Match the first question to the answer as a class. Students work to match the other questions to the answers. If some students finish quicker than others, encourage them to practise the conversation in pairs. In feedback, nominate pairs to say questions and answers for the class.

> **ANSWERS:**
> 1 c   2 b   3 d   4 a

b Demonstrate the activity with a stronger student. Students work in pairs to ask and answer questions about the things in the box.

> **Practice, exercise 2b: Additional activity**
>
> Put students into groups and ask them to carry out a survey about some of the items from the box. In feedback, each group could present their findings to the class e.g. *Two people have got a cat.* or *One person's got a dictionary.*

ADDITIONAL PRACTICE

➡ **Resource bank:** Activity 2B *Who's got a Ferrari?* (*have got*)
   Study, practice & remember: Practice 2
   Workbook: Grammar focus 2: *have got*, page 11

Reading and vocabulary (PAGE 19)

Family

See *Teaching tips: Working with lexical phrases*, page 21.

1a Focus students' attention on the photo. Ask these questions: *Do you recognise her? What job do you think she does?* Focus on the family tree and make sure students are aware that there are a number of gaps in the tree. Then ask your students to read the article to complete the missing information. There is some unknown language in this text, but try not to pre-teach it. Instead, encourage students to complete as much of the task as possible despite not knowing some of the vocabulary. Most of the new words will be covered in exercise 2.

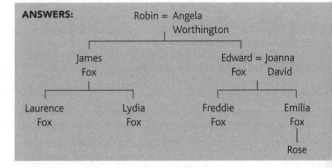

> **ANSWERS:**
>
> Robin = Angela Worthington
> — James Fox
> — Edward = Joanna Fox   David
> — Laurence Fox
> — Lydia Fox
> — Freddie Fox
> — Emilia Fox
> — Rose

b Give students a very limited amount of time to count the number of actors. This will encourage them to read quickly.

> **ANSWER:**
> Seven other people in her family are also actors.

2 Do the first one or two as an example. Students complete the rest of the table.

> **ANSWERS:**
> **Male:** father, son, uncle, husband
> **Female:** niece, sister, granddaughter, grandmother, girlfriend
> **Male and female:** children, grandparents, cousin

PRONUNCIATION

See *Teaching tips: Helping students with pronunciation*, page 22.

1a 🎧 **2.7** Students listen to the recording and identify the family words used in each sentence. Play the recording again and focus on the pronunciation of each word.

b Drill the pronunciation of the words and then the sentences chorally and individually. Pay attention to the sounds in *nephew* /ˈnefjuː/, *son* /sʌn/, *daughter* /ˈdɔːtə/, *niece* /niːs/ and *cousin* /ˈkʌzən/.

3 Students answer the questions referring to the family tree and the article.

> **ANSWERS:**
> 1 1   2 2   3 Angela Worthington   4 James Fox   5 He's an actor.
> 6 Laurence Fox   7 Lydia Fox   8 Joanna David and Edward Fox

4 Students work in pairs to ask and answer questions about their families.

Reading and vocabulary, exercise 4: Additional activities

a If your students have photos of their family and friends, for example on their phones, encourage them to show other students and describe them. Start by showing pictures of your family and friends and describing them as an example. Put students into pairs and ask them to do the same.

b Ask your students to write a paragraph describing their own family. You could ask them to use the text from exercise 1a as a model or, alternatively, you could provide them with a model of your own. The advantage of providing your own model is that students often like to learn something about their teacher and you can tailor it to meet the specific needs of your students. If possible, print out your description so students can take it home. This writing could be done in class or as homework.

Model answer:

My name's *Thomas*. I come from *Birmingham* in *England*. My father's name is *Stan* and he's a *bus driver*. My mother's name is *Kath* and she's a *nurse*. I've got *one brother and one sister*. My brother's name is *Noel* and he's a *doctor*. My sister's name is *Elizabeth* and she's a *maths teacher*. My *wife's* name is *Helena* and she's a *lawyer*.

ADDITIONAL PRACTICE

Resource bank: Activity 2C *The family* (Family; Possessive *'s*)

Workbook: Vocabulary: *Family*, page 11

Task (PAGES 20–21)

Talk about your five favourite people

See *Teaching tips: Making tasks work*, page 23.

Preparation (PAGE 20)

Listening

WARM UP

To set a context for this class and to revise the language from the previous one, ask students to talk about Emilia Fox and her family. Start by asking your students what they can remember without reading the text again. If necessary, give them a minute to read about her again, and then elicit more information. Pay attention to the pronunciation of the vocabulary for family members.

1a Focus students' attention on the photos. Ask students in pairs to guess which photo represents which favourite person.

Culture notes

George Clooney (b. 1961) is an American actor, director and screenwriter. He first came to fame when he was in the TV series *ER*, where he played a doctor on an emergency ward. Since then he has gone on to appear in numerous films and has won an Oscar and several Golden Globes. He has also been included in various lists of the sexiest men ever.

In recent years George Clooney has devoted himself to political activism and humanitarian work. He is most closely associated with trying to find a solution to the Darfur conflict as well as working for the survivors of the 2010 Haiti earthquake.

Sherlock Holmes is a fictional detective created by the Scottish writer Sir Arthur Conan Doyle. The books were written around the turn of the 20th century and describe how Sherlock Holmes, with the help of his assistant Dr Watson, was able to solve crimes that baffled the police by using his superior intellect.

The series of books is arguably one of the most famous collections of detective stories ever written and has led many people to believe that Sherlock Holmes was a real person. There is a museum at his fictional address, 221b Baker Street, devoted to all things associated with Sherlock Holmes.

b 🎧 **2.8** Students listen and check.

> **ANSWERS:**
> 1 Elaine   2 Emily   3 Sherlock Holmes   4 Anthony
> 5 George Clooney

c Students complete column A in the table then check in pairs. Check as a class.

> **ANSWERS:**
> **Emily:** Liz's niece
> **Elaine:** Liz's friend
> **George Clooney:** Liz's favourite actor
> **Sherlock Holmes:** Liz's favourite fictional character

2a Give students a minute to read through the information in the box. They then listen again and fill in column B. Students then check in pairs. If necessary, play the recording again. Check as a class.

> **ANSWERS:**
> **Anthony:** is 26 years old, has got two children
> **Emily:** is lovely
> **Elaine:** is a really good friend, has got a new job
> **George Clooney:** is fantastic, is from the USA
> **Sherlock Holmes:** is not a real person

Listening, exercise 2a: Additional activity

If your students have had problems processing all of the information, or haven't understood everything in the listening, ask them to look at audio script 2.8 on page 167. Play the recording again and ask them to underline all of the parts of the script that refer to the answers. Point out the phrases *Ah ...* and *Yeah ...* and ask if students use similar things in their language. You might also like to highlight the pauses that the speaker uses and show students that it is acceptable to pause sometimes to think about what you want to say.

---

b Students work in pairs to say two things about each person. Circulate and offer help. Encourage students to use the possessive *'s*. Elicit some of the ideas in feedback.

3 Focus on the Useful language box. Give students a moment to read through the sentences. Students then listen and tick the phrases they hear.

Task (PAGE 21)

Speaking

1a Give students a few minutes to decide who their favourite people are. Be flexible and allow students to choose more than one person from each category if they wish.

b Give students plenty of time to prepare this part and don't demand that they talk about all five people. It is better if they talk about two or three people well, rather than five people badly. Circulate and offer help and encouragement. Remind students to use the language from the Useful language box.

2 Students work in pairs to practise talking about their favourite people. Circulate and offer help. Encourage students to show photographs of the people they talk about if they have them.

3a Put students into small groups to talk about their favourite people.

b Encourage students to ask questions about their classmates' favourite people.

Task: Speaking: Additional activity

Write the names of your five favourite people on the board and show photographs of them if you have them available. Ask students which one they would like to hear about. Tell the students they have to listen to you and answer the questions from exercise 1b. This will give students something to focus on when they listen to you and provide an extra model for their speaking practice. Elicit the answers, and then ask if students have any questions about the person you spoke about. Tell students they are going to do the same thing and then follow the steps in the book.

Share your task

The idea here is to give students a chance to 'perfect' their speaking in this context and provide them with a recording of a 'polished' version. This will provide extra motivation for students, as well as extra practice. Students can either make an audio or video recording, depending on how comfortable they feel and what equipment is available. Students could even use their mobile phones to do this. If possible, they'll need a quiet place to make their recording. Students can either record themselves during the lesson, or as homework and bring the recordings to the next class.

Some additional ideas could include:

• Students talk about just one of their favourite people if they don't feel very confident or if they have a lot to say.

• Find out if the class as a whole has any favourite people in common and ask students to record a piece about each of those people. These recordings could be uploaded to a class blog or a social networking site for other classes or people to comment on.

Language live (PAGES 22–23)

Writing (PAGE 22)
Completing a form

1 Focus students' attention on the photo by asking questions about who is in it, where they are and what they are doing.

2 Students match the words/phrases to the examples. Some of this vocabulary will be new for students, but try to avoid giving definitions at this point. Instead, encourage students to do the ones they know and then try to guess the others. During feedback, check the pronunciation of *signature* /ˈsɪgnətʃə/ and the email address: *Richard Adison at your world dot com*.

ANSWERS:
1 b   2 g   3 i   4 e   5 f   6 a   7 c   8 j   9 k   10 d   11 h

---

Culture notes

Postcodes in the UK (and zip codes in the USA) are used to make the post office more efficient, because it allows computers to read the address more quickly.

In the UK, the postcode is split into two parts. The first part is made up of one or two letters followed by one or two numbers. The second part is made up of one number followed by two letters. The first letter or letters refer to the city, and then the numbers refer to the part of the city. The second half of the postcode refers to the specific road and a small group of houses.

The postcode is always written at the end of the address and the letters should be in capitals.

---

3 Complete the first couple of gaps about yourself as an example. Students continue on their own then check in pairs. Circulate and offer help as necessary.

Speaking (PAGE 23)
Answering questions

See *Teaching tips: Using the video material in the classroom*, page 24.

1 ▶ Check that students understand the words *receptionist* (the person who works in a doctor's surgery and makes appointments and welcomes people), *doctor* and *patient* (the person who visits a doctor because he or she is ill). Students watch the DVD and number the people in the order they hear them speak.

ANSWERS:
1 the receptionist   **2** the male patient   **3** the doctor
4 the female patient

2 Give students a minute to read through the information so they know what they have to pay attention for. Play the DVD for students to choose the correct answers then check in pairs. Play the DVD again if students are not sure. These questions are based on specific information, so pause the DVD at the appropriate point and repeat it if necessary.

ANSWERS:
1 c   2 b   3 a   4 c   5 a

3a Students decide who asked each question then check in pairs.

b ▶ Play the DVD to check the answers.

ANSWERS:
1 R   2 R   3 R   4 R   5 R   6 D   7 J   8 D

PRONUNCIATION

See *Teaching tips: Helping students with pronunciation*, page 22.

1 Students watch and listen to the key phrases. Focus on sentence stress and the intonation of the questions.

2 Drill the questions chorally and individually.

4 Students work in pairs to ask and answer questions. They can decide whether to use their own information or the information from the book.

ADDITIONAL PRACTICE

Workbook: Writing: *Completing a form*, page 13; Language live: *Answering questions*, page 13

Students can now do Progress test 1 on the Teacher's Resource Disc.

Study, practice & remember

(PAGES 140–141)

See *Teaching tips: Using the Study, practice & remember sections*, page 25.

Practice 1

ANSWERS:

1

1 this **2** that **3** those **4** these **5** This **6** Those

2

1 no apostrophe
2 That's Anna's bag.
3 She's got two sisters.
4 What's the matter?
5 He's Laura's cousin.
6 My father's name is Sam.
7 He's got three dogs.
8 What's your brother's name?

Practice 2

ANSWERS:

1

1 's got **2** have got **3** haven't got **4** hasn't got
5 haven't got **6** 's got

2

1 Are you **2** Have you got **3** are you **4** Have you got
5 Are you **6** Have you got **7** have you got **8** Have you got
9 Have you got **10** Are you

Remember these words

ANSWERS:

1

1 a brother, a nephew, a grandfather
2 an aunt, a mother, a niece
3 grandchildren, parents, cousins
4 a camera, a mobile phone, a DVD player

2

Money: coins, a credit card, a wallet
Food and drink: a bottle of water, a packet of chewing gum
Books: a dictionary

3

1 sister **2** father **3** wife **4** son **5** nephew **6** grandchildren
7 daughter **8** niece **9** parents **10** cousin

OVERVIEW

PAGES 24–25

Vocabulary: Common verbs

Grammar: Present simple: positive and negative (*I, you, we, they*)

Common European Framework: Students can provide information about where they live and people they know.

PAGES 26–27

Grammar: Present simple: questions and short answers (*I, you, we, they*)

Vocabulary: Telling the time

Pronunciation: Stress and weak forms: questions; telling the time

Common European Framework: Students can understand arrangements and routine habits.

PAGES 28–29

Reading and vocabulary: Places in a town

Listening: Life on a Scottish Island

Common European Framework: Students can understand what is said clearly on familiar topics.

PAGES 30–31

Task: Describe life in your favourite town

Common European Framework: Students can give a simple description or presentation about where they live.

PAGES 32–33

World culture: Indian Railway

Common European Framework: Students can identify the main point of TV news items reporting events, accidents, etc. where the visual supports the commentary.

Vocabulary (PAGES 24–25)

Common verbs

See *Teaching tips: Working with lexical phrases*, page 21.

1a Focus students' attention on the photos. As a class, ask for a description of the different things they can see, for example *fishing boat, trees, sea, people, men, nets, shops, cars, motorbikes, lights*. Are the students' homes similar or different?

b Give students a moment to read the words in the box. Check students can remember the meanings by asking questions like *Is her sister a man or a woman?* Students read the text very quickly to find which people are mentioned. To encourage students to read quickly, you might want to set a time limit, for example three minutes.

There are a number of new words in the text for students at this level. Try to avoid pre-teaching them before students read as they are not needed in order to answer the first question.

ANSWERS:

her friend, her father, her mother

2a Introduce key vocabulary for your students to understand the text enough to answer the questions. Check students understand *flat, get up, bus, dinner, parents, south, house*. You could introduce these words with pictures and mime. Do the first statement as an example, showing how it is either true or false. Students check in pairs.

Vocabulary, exercise 2a: Alternative suggestion

If you have strong elementary students, don't introduce the vocabulary before they look at the statements. Instead, encourage the students to do as many as they can and guess the meaning of any new words from context. Once they have finished the activity, introduce the pictures or do the mimes and ask students to suggest which words from the text they refer to.

b 🎧 **3.1** Students listen and check.

ANSWERS:

1 F (They live in a flat.)
2 F (They study at university.)
3 F (They go by bus.)
4 T
5 F (They live in a small village.)
6 T
7 F (They work for a small company.)
8 F (They have dinner at home.)

c Students work in pairs to practise saying the sentences. Circulate and monitor, particularly for sentence stress.

3 Students use the words in the box to complete the gaps. During feedback, use the vocabulary to ask students questions, e.g. *Do you live in a house or a flat? Do you go to bed early or late?* This will help students to personalise the language.

ANSWERS:

1 go   2 have   3 study   4 work   5 get up

ADDITIONAL PRACTICE

🔁 **Workbook:** Vocabulary: *Common verbs*, page 14

Grammar focus 1 (PAGE 25)

Present simple: positive and negative (*I, you, we, they*)

See *Teaching tips: Working with grammar*, page 20.

1 Write an example of a negative verb on the board. Give students time to read the text again and find three more examples from the text.

GRAMMAR

Present simple: positive and negative (*I, you, we, they*)

Notes on the approach to the Present simple

We have introduced the negative Present simple sentences here without talking about auxiliary verbs. At this stage we believe it isn't necessary for students to know the grammatical names for all the parts of language and so it has been introduced as a lexical form: to talk about negatives say *don't* or *doesn't*. If your students are interested in analysing the grammar, you can provide the names and talk about the grammar in more detail.

Write on the board a false sentence about where you live, e.g. *I live in New York*. Elicit that this is false and ask for a correction. Write on the board the negative form, e.g. *I don't live in New York*. Elicit that *don't* is the contracted form of *do not*.

1 Students complete the gaps individually then check in pairs. During feedback, make sure students use the contracted form *don't*.

> **ANSWERS:**
> + go, have, work
> − don't, don't, don't

You may want to ask students to read Study 1 on page 142 for a more detailed explanation of the Present simple: positive and negative (*I, you, we, they*).

PRACTICE

1 Do the first couple as examples. Give students a few minutes to complete the other sentences.

> **ANSWERS:**
> Students' own answers using:
> **1** (don't) get up   **2** (don't) have   **3** (don't) go   **4** (don't) have
> **5** (don't) go   **6** (don't) study   **7** (don't) go

> **Practice, exercise 1: Alternative suggestion**
>
> With stronger elementary students you might like to do this activity orally instead of in writing. Ask students to work together and complete the sentences without writing them down. In feedback, ask for suggestions and write them on the board.

2a Give students time to read through the ideas and deal with any new vocabulary, especially *have a big meal for lunch*. Circulate and offer help as necessary.

b Students work in pairs to compare their sentences. In feedback, ask students what they had in common with their partners.

ADDITIONAL PRACTICE

Study, practice & remember: Practice 1

Workbook: Grammar focus 1: *Present simple: positive and negative (I, you, we, they)*, pages 14–18

Grammar focus 2 (PAGE 26)

Present simple: questions and short answers (*I, you, we, they*)

See *Teaching tips: Working with grammar*, page 20.

1a 🎧 **3.2** Check that students know where Dublin, Ireland is. Give students time to read through the questions and deal with any language they have problems with. Students listen and tick the questions they hear.

> **ANSWERS:**
> **2** Do you live with your family or friends? ✓
> **3** Do you get up early? ✓
> **4** Do you have breakfast at home? ✓
> **7** Do you have lunch in a café? ✓
> **8** Do you have dinner early? ✓
> **10** Do you go to bed early? ✓

b Students listen again and make a note of the answers. Some students will find it challenging to listen and make notes, as this can be difficult even in a first language. If necessary, play the recording more than once and pause just after the relevant part so students can make their notes.

> **ANSWERS:**
> **2** I live with my family.
> **3** No, I don't. I get up at nine o'clock, or sometimes ten.
> **4** Yes, I do. I have a cup of coffee and some bread.
> **7** Yes, I do. I have lunch in this café ... but just a small lunch, like a sandwich or something.
> **8** I have dinner at different times ...
> **10** No, I don't. I go to bed about twelve o'clock ... or sometimes one or two o'clock in the morning.

GRAMMAR

Present simple: questions and short answers (*I, you, we, they*)

1 Write on the board: *I have breakfast early*. Underneath, write ___ ___ ___ *breakfast early?* Point explicitly to the question mark and elicit how the question can be completed (*Do you have breakfast early?*) Use arrows and/or different colours to highlight the changed position of the verb and the subject. Repeat this with a couple more sentences to show the pattern. Go back to the first question about breakfast. Ask a couple of students and elicit the short answers: *Yes, I do. / No, I don't.* Write these on the board and then repeat for the other questions you have used.

Highlight the meaning of the Present simple, i.e. something which is permanent or which is always true (and not only at the present time). This is particularly important if your students speak a language which only has one present tense, where English has two.

2 Students complete the questions and short answers in pairs.

> **ANSWERS:**
> **1** Do, do   **2** Do, don't

You may want to ask students to read Study 2 on page 142 for a more detailed explanation of the Present simple: questions and short answers (*I, you, we, they*).

PRACTICE

1a Students work individually to complete the questions and answers then check in pairs.

b 🎧 **3.3** Students listen and check.

> **ANSWERS:**
> **1** Do, don't   **2** Do, do   **3** go, do   **4** Do, don't   **5** work, don't
> **6** Do, don't

2 Focus students' attention on the questions in exercise 1a again. Students work in pairs to ask and answer the questions. Circulate and make sure students are using short answers. In feedback, ask students to tell everyone about their partner, e.g. *He lives in a flat. She works in an office.*

PRONUNCIATION

See *Teaching tips: Helping students with pronunciation*, page 22.

1 🎧 **3.4** Say the two words *do* and *you* slowly and separately and hold up two fingers to represent the two words. Bring the two words together and give the new pronunciation /djə/. Ask students if they do similar things in their first language (most languages do). Tell students that this is very important for understanding spoken English. Play the recording and ask students if the person says *do you* or /djə/. Play the recording again and ask students to identify which words are stressed. Tell students that the important words are usually stressed.

2 Drill the questions chorally and individually.

ADDITIONAL PRACTICE

➡ **Resource bank:** Activity 3A *Pick four cards* (Present simple: questions and short answers)

Study, practice & remember: Practice 2

Workbook: Grammar focus 2: *Present simple: questions and short answers (I, you, we, they)*, page 16; Pronunciation: *Sentence stress in questions*, page 16

Vocabulary (PAGES 26–27)

Telling the time

See *Teaching tips: Working with lexical phrases*, page 21.

1a Focus students' attention on the clocks and the time phrases below. Students match the times to the pictures individually then check in pairs before checking answers as a class.

ANSWERS:

1 B   **2** A   **3** F   **4** E   **5** C   **6** D

b Tell students there are two ways to tell the time. Students work to match the times in the box with the times in exercise 1a. In feedback, it is useful to have a clock with moveable hands available and check *past* and *to* with *5, 10, 20, 25* and *quarter past, half past* and *quarter to*. Demonstrate meaning very carefully for the students, whose way of telling time may be different in their language.

ANSWERS:

2 quarter past two (clock A)
3 half past one (clock F)
4 quarter to eight (clock E)
5 twenty past ten (clock C)
6 five to nine (clock D)

2a Do the first one as an example. Students work individually and then check in pairs.

b 🎧 **3.5** Students listen and check.

ANSWERS:

1 quarter past seven   **2** half past nine   **3** twenty to nine
4 quarter to seven   **5** five past twelve   **6** twenty past two
7 four o'clock

PRONUNCIATION

See *Teaching tips: Helping students with pronunciation*, page 22.

1 Either play the recording again, or say the times yourself, highlighting the stress. Drill, giving choral and individual repetition. Highlight the use of the schwa in *to* /tə/.

2 Students listen and repeat each of the times in exercise 2a.

3 Focus students' attention on the photos. Check the pronunciation of the city names and then do the first one or two as an example. Students then work in pairs to ask and answer questions about the times.

ANSWERS:

It's six o'clock in Berlin.
It's ten past ten / ten ten in Istanbul.
It's twenty to four / three forty in Paris.
It's quarter to two / one forty-five in Rio de Janeiro.
It's five to ten / nine fifty-five in San Francisco.
It's quarter past six / six fifteen in Canberra.
It's half past seven / seven thirty in Hong Kong.

4a Check students understand *weekdays*. Read through the first four questions with the students. Elicit another question from the class as an example and then ask students to write three more.

b With low elementary students you might want to give them the chance to think about their answers before they start talking. Students work in pairs to ask and answer the questions.

c Highlight the different preposition for *At weekends … .* Students work in pairs to ask and answer the same questions, but this time about weekends. In feedback, ask what things people do both on weekdays and at weekends.

ADDITIONAL PRACTICE

➡ **Resource bank:** Activity 3B *Time pelmanism* (Telling the time)

Study, practice & remember: Practice 3

Workbook: Vocabulary: *Telling the time*, pages 17–18

Reading and vocabulary (PAGES 28–29)

Places in a town

See *Teaching tips: Working with lexical phrases*, page 21.

1a Focus students' attention on the pictures and the vocabulary in the box. Check pronunciation of *beach* /biːtʃ/. Students match the vocabulary to the pictures individually and then check in pairs. Finally, check as a class.

ANSWERS:

A a park   **B** a swimming pool   **C** a street market   **D** a supermarket
E a block of flats   **F** a beach   **G** a restaurant   **H** small shops
I a cinema   **J** a shopping centre

b Students work individually to tick what things they have in the city or town they come from.

c Students work in pairs to compare the things in their cities. In feedback, find out what things all the students have got where they live.

Reading and vocabulary, exercises 1b &1c: Alternative suggestion

If your students all live in the same town or city, encourage them to talk about the different neighbourhoods they come from, the neighbourhoods they work in or the place where they grew up.

2a Focus students' attention on the photos in the article. Give students a minute to decide on their answers to the questions.

b Ask students to read the article quickly to find the answers. Encourage them not to worry about any unknown vocabulary; all they need to do is understand enough to answer the questions.

ANSWERS:

left: Dubai, a city in the United Arab Emirates
top right: Aurignac, a village in France
bottom right: Southwold, a town in the UK

3 Do the first one as an example. Students work individually to match the sentences to the places. Students check their answers in pairs before checking as a class. During feedback, encourage students to justify their answers before you confirm or correct them.

ANSWERS:

2 D   3 S   4 D   5 S   6 A

4a Students work individually to find similarities and differences to the places they live.

b Students work in pairs to compare their findings.

ADDITIONAL PRACTICE

Workbook: Vocabulary: *Places in a town*, page 18

Listening (PAGE 29)

Life on a Scottish Island

> **Culture notes**
>
> Stornoway is a town of about 9,000 people on the Isle of Lewis in the Outer Hebrides, which are a series of islands off the west coast of Scotland. The town itself is the biggest one on all the islands and is home to the council and various cultural bodies that celebrate the distinctive nature of the people of these islands.
>
> The majority of people in the Outer Hebrides speak Scottish Gaelic as well as English. Scottish Gaelic is from the Celtic family of languages that used to be prominent all over northern Europe, but can now be found in only a few isolated places.
>
> The weather can be particularly unforgiving with an average high temperature in summer of 16°C and an average low in winter of 2°C. The highest temperature ever recorded was a mere 26°C.

1 🎧 **3.6** Check that students know where Scotland is. If they seem interested, you could elicit things they know about Scotland and put them on the board. Focus students' attention on the photo and elicit a description. Ask your students if this looks like a good place to live. Give students a minute to read through the list, then play the recording for them to tick the things Sheena talks about.

ANSWERS:

She talks about all five things:
the journey from Ullapool to Stornoway ✓
the languages on the Isle of Lewis ✓
the shops in Stornoway ✓
summer sunsets ✓
weekends ✓

2 Check the meaning of *ferry*, *dark* and *light*. Give students time to read through all of the questions before they listen and choose the correct answers. Students check in pairs. Play the recording again if students are unsure, and then check as a class.

ANSWERS:

1 a   2 b   3 b   4 b   5 b

3a Give students a few minutes to complete the sentences. Offer help as necessary.

POSSIBLE ANSWERS:

1 ... it's very isolated. / ... all the shops are closed on Sunday. / ... it's light at 10.30 p.m. in summer.
2 ... it's very different to where I live.

b Students work in pairs to compare their ideas.

Task (PAGES 30–31)

Describe life in your favourite town

See *Teaching tips: Making tasks work*, page 23.

Preparation (PAGE 30)

Reading and listening

> **Culture notes**
>
> Melbourne is the biggest city in the state of Victoria in the south east of Australia. With a population of 4.1 million it is also the second most populous city in Australia after Sydney.
>
> Melbourne was founded in 1835 and was named after the British Prime Minister at that time. In the 1850s it briefly became the world's largest and wealthiest city due to the discovery of gold in the local area.
>
> Nowadays it is seen as the cultural capital of Australia. It is the home of the Australian film and television industries and has a long tradition in the arts, especially in music, dance and painting. *The Economist* magazine's Intelligence Unit ranked Melbourne as the world's most liveable city in 2011 and 2012. Since 2006 it has been in the top ten university cities in the world and is fast developing a reputation as a place to innovate and create new ideas.

1 Focus students' attention on the photos and elicit a brief description of what is in each one. Focus on the facts about Melbourne. Check students understand *Capital of the state* and *Average temperature*. Ask students if they think Melbourne looks like a good place to live. Encourage students to justify their answers.

2a 🎧 **3.7** Focus students' attention on the questionnaire. Give enough time for students to read and deal with any unknown vocabulary, especially *Do shops open late?* Ask students to guess what the answers might be before they listen. Students then listen and check their guesses.

b 🎧 **3.8** Students listen and check their answers.

ANSWERS:

1 a   2 c   3 c   4 b   5 b   6 a   7 a   8 a

3a Focus students' attention on part a of the Useful language box. Students listen to the first part of the interview again and tick the questions they hear.

ANSWERS:

Do most people live in houses or flats? ✓
What time do children start school? ✓
Where do most people have lunch? ✓
Do shops close at (lunchtime)? ✓
Do shops open on (Sunday)? ✓
What time do people have dinner? ✓

b Students listen to the second part of the interview again and identify phrases from part b of the Useful language box.

ANSWERS:

Most people live in houses. ✓

Children start/finish school at ... ✓

Most people don't go home ... ✓

Most people have lunch/dinner at ... ✓

Restaurants/Pubs open/close at ... ✓

Task (PAGE 31)

Speaking

1a Give students plenty of time to think of their answers. Encourage students to think of places they have visited, as well as the ones they have lived in. This will help if all your students come from the same place. Circulate and offer help as necessary.

b Students work in pairs to ask and answer the questions and note their partner's answers.

2 Students work in groups to describe their or their partners' favourite towns.

Share your task

The idea here is to give students a chance to 'perfect' their speaking in this context and provide them with a recording of a 'polished' version. This will provide extra motivation for students, as well as extra practice. Students can either make an audio or video recording, depending on how comfortable they feel and what equipment is available. Students could even use their mobile phones to do this. If possible, they'll need a quiet place to make their recording. Students can either record themselves during the lesson, or as homework and bring the recordings to the next class.

World culture, Find out first:

To help your students prepare for the next class, go through the questions in exercise 1a on page 32. If necessary, discuss ideas for searching for this information on the internet, pointing out the search terms, and suggest other sources of information students could use. Encourage students to use English language websites as much as possible.

World culture (PAGES 32–33)

Indian railway

Culture notes

Railways were first introduced to India in 1853 by the British colonial power as a way to quickly transport goods and the military around the country. In 1951, a few years after Indian Independence was achieved, the railways were nationalised into one state-owned company called Indian Railways.

Today, Indian Railways still plays an indispensable role in communications and trade in this vast country. The system comprises 115,000 km of track over a route of 64,000 km. In 2012 it transported 25 million passengers per day, or 9 billion per year. Income amounted to almost $19 billion, with $5 billion coming from passengers and the rest from freight. The company employs over 1.4 million people and, as such, is the ninth biggest employer in the world.

WARM UP

If possible, show a flag and/or a map of India and elicit the country. Ask students to look at the photos and describe some of the things they can see. Give students a minute or so to work in pairs to write down as many things they know about India as possible. If students need some prompting, you might like to get them thinking about *Gandhi*, *curry*, *cricket*, *the Taj Mahal*, *Mumbai*, *New Delhi* and *Bollywood*.

Find out first (PAGE 32)

1a Students work in pairs to try to guess the answers to the quiz. If some students have not done the research, try to put them with a student who has done it.

b If you have access to the internet and students haven't been able to find the answer to some of the questions, ask students to go online and do some further research. Highlight the search terms. Circulate and offer help with vocabulary and try to encourage people to use only English language websites. Otherwise, tell your students the answers.

ANSWERS:

1 a   2 b   3 c   4 c   5 b

View (PAGE 32)

See *Teaching tips: Using the video material in the classroom*, page 24.

2a Tell your students they are going to watch a DVD about an Indian family. Make sure students understand the key vocabulary by going through the glossary.

b ▶ Make sure students read the complete list of people who appear in the DVD. Students then watch to put the people in the order in which they see them. They check in pairs and then as a class.

ANSWERS:

1 Sanjay Geera   2 a porter   3 a British tourist on the train
4 Satna (Sanjay's wife)   5 Sanjay's son

3 Give students time to read through all of the sentences. If students can remember any of the answers, allow them to make a choice before they watch again. Play the DVD again for students to check their ideas or choose the correct answers. Students check in pairs and then as a class.

ANSWERS:

1 small   2 weather   3 Six   4 the station master   5 forty
6 Summerhill   7 office   8 8.30   9 school

World view (PAGE 33)

4a Students work individually to decide who said each sentence. They check in pairs and then as a class.

ANSWERS:

I am serious about my job – it's important. – SN, ST

My day is very long. – SN

We live in a big house. – A

I work in an office. – ST

I catch a train to work in the morning. – ST

We go to a private school. – C

b Students work individually to change the sentences so that they are true for them. Circulate and offer help as necessary.

c Students work in pairs to compare their ideas. In feedback, invite some of the pairs to tell you what they have in common.

Find out more ⟨signal icon⟩ (PAGE 33)

5a Write UNESCO on the board and see if students know anything about the organisation. Ask students to read the text quickly to check their ideas. Find out if they know about any UNESCO sites in their country.

Culture notes

UNESCO stands for the United Nations Educational, Scientific and Cultural Organization. It was created in 1921 as a specialist agency as part of the United Nations to promote peace and security through international collaboration in education, science and culture. The organisation pursues these goals in a number of different ways, for example by awarding prizes and giving grants.

UNESCO is probably best known for its role in designating cities, towns, areas and buildings as being important culturally or scientifically. This designation can be very important in preserving areas as it attracts international attention.

---

b Quickly check if students have heard of the UNESCO World Heritage Sites and if they know where they are.

c If you have access to the internet at school, students work in pairs to research the World Heritage Sites. Focus students' attention on the search terms that they should use. Circulate and help with new vocabulary as necessary and encourage students to use English language websites.

ANSWERS:

Great Barrier Reef: Near the coast of Queensland, Australia. It's the largest coral reef in the world.

Angkor Wat: In Cambodia. It's the largest Hindu temple in the world.

Rapa Nui: An island in Polynesia in the Pacific Ocean. Also known as *Easter Island*, it is famous for its gigantic statues.

Grand Canyon: In Arizona, USA. A huge valley cut through the rock by the Colorado River.

Stonehenge: In Wiltshire, UK. A Neolithic stone circle, the exact purpose of which is still cause of much debate.

Historic Cairo: In the centre of modern-day Cairo, Egypt. Has many mosques and other important monuments.

Find out more, exercise 5c: Alternative suggestion

If you are short of time, ask students to research just two of the sites. Then put students into groups so that there is at least one person who has researched each of the sites. Students then exchange their information and take notes.

Write up your research

6 Focus students' attention on the sentence prompts and elicit some information that could be used for one or two of the gaps. Tell students to use the prompts to write up their research. This could be done in class or as homework.

Study, practice & remember
(PAGES 142–143)

See *Teaching tips: Using the Study, practice & remember sections*, page 25.

Practice 1

ANSWERS:

1
1 go   2 aren't   3 don't have   4 work   5 're
6 don't get up   7 don't eat   8 don't study
9 don't work   10 don't drink

2
1 live   2 live   3 don't live   4 go   5 study
6 speak   7 go   8 finish   9 don't go   10 have

Practice 2

ANSWERS:

1
1 Do they live, do   2 Do you work, don't   3 Do they get up, don't   4 Do you have, do   5 Do you study, don't

2
1 Are, aren't   2 Do, do   3 Have, haven't   4 Do, do
5 Do, don't   6 Are, aren't

Practice 3

ANSWERS:

1
1 6.05   2 10.35   3 8.30   4 10.20   5 11.40   6 3.15
7 9.00   8 9.45

2
a half past three   b quarter past six   c ten past five   d eleven o'clock   e quarter to six   f twenty-five to ten   g five to four   h twenty past seven   i twenty to ten   j five past one

Remember these words

ANSWERS:

1
1 live   2 have   3 study   4 get up   5 go   6 work

2
1 at   2 on   3 at   4 at   5 in   6 on   7 in   8 at

OVERVIEW

PAGES 34–35

Vocabulary: Activities

Listening: A typical pop star?

Grammar: Present simple: positive and negative (*he/she/it*)

Common European Framework: Students can provide information on habits and routines.

PAGES 36–37

Reading and vocabulary: Phrases for time and frequency

Grammar: Present simple: questions and short answers (*he/she/it*)

Pronunciation: *does*

Common European Framework: Students can find simple, predictable information in everyday material.

PAGES 38–39

Task: Choose a holiday activity

Common European Framework: Students can agree and disagree with others.

PAGES 40–41

Speaking: Meeting people

Writing: Introducing a friend

Common European Framework: Students can write short, simple notes relating to matters in areas of immediate need and interest.

Vocabulary (PAGE 34)

Activities

See *Teaching tips: Working with lexical phrases*, page 21.

1   Focus students' attention on the photos. You could do this by asking quick questions about them, for example *How many photos show one person? How many photos show people doing exercise?* Check the pronunciation of *cycling* /ˈsaɪklɪŋ/ and the meaning of *spending time*. Students work in pairs to match the photos with the activities.

2   Get students to ask you about the pictures. Model possible replies: *Yes, I love it/them. / Yes, I do. / It's/They're OK. / No, I don't. / No, I hate it/them.* Remind students that we do NOT say *Yes, I like.* or *Yes, I like cooking.* Students work in pairs. Circulate and help, particularly with natural replies. In feedback, students could tell you one thing that they had in common and one thing that was different.

> **Vocabulary, exercise 2: Additional activity**
>
> Prepare a number of pieces of paper or cards with the name of an activity on each one. Put students into small groups. Students have one minute to draw a picture and get the other students to guess what the activity is. The student who is drawing cannot speak, but must only draw pictures.
>
> When a student guesses the activity then both the person drawing and the person who guessed get a point. The winner is the person with the highest number of points at the end of the activity.
>
> To avoid having to give complicated instructions, demonstrate the activity with a couple of stronger students. Reassure students that it doesn't matter if they don't have great drawing skills. You can prove this yourself by not drawing beautiful or perfect pictures.

ADDITIONAL PRACTICE

➡ **Workbook:** Vocabulary: *Activities*, page 21

Listening (PAGE 35)

A typical pop star?

WARM UP

Write some of your favourite bands and musicians on the board. Invite students to suggest other artists, or ask them to write the names on the board. Students then work individually to decide which of them they like or dislike. In feedback, find out which band or musician is the class favourite.

> **Culture notes**
>
> Adele, whose real name is Adele Laurie Blue Adkins, (b. 1988) is a famous singer-songwriter from London. One of her friends put a recording of one of her songs on the internet in 2006, and the next year she won a prestigious Brit award for new musicians. Her first album, *19*, was released in 2008 and won many awards and sold millions of copies. This success was surpassed by her second album, *21*, which won six Grammies and received excellent reviews from both critics and fans. This album was at number one in the UK and the USA for longer than any other album by a female solo artist. In 2013 she won an Oscar for her song *Skyfall*, which was the theme music for the James Bond film of the same name.
>
> Adele's voice is classed as a contralto. She sings soul, R&B and pop music and her many influences include Ella Fitzgerald, Etta James, the Spice Girls and Pink. Unusually for many vocalists she writes most of her own material.

1a   🎧 **4.1** Focus students' attention on the photo of Adele. Ask them what they know about her. Students listen to the first part of the podcast and answer the two questions. They check in pairs before checking answers as a class.

> **ANSWERS:**
> **1** the UK   **2** singer

b   🎧 **4.2** Give students time to read the list before listening to the recording and ticking the items they hear.

> **ANSWERS:**
> her house ✓
> her friends ✓
> her concerts ✓
> her clothes ✓

2   🎧 **4.3** Give students time to read through all of the sentences. If they can remember any of the answers, allow them to make a choice before they listen again. Play the recording again for students to check their ideas or choose the correct answers.

> **ANSWERS:**
> **1** London   **2** England   **3** dog   **4** mother   **5** big concerts
> **6** simple   **7** black

> **Listening, exercise 2: Additional activity**
>
> It can sometimes be a good idea to ask students to read the audio script and listen to the recording at the same time. This type of activity can help to improve listening skills, improve pronunciation and boost the confidence of weaker students.

3 Students work in pairs to discuss the question. In feedback, elicit different ideas.

Listening, exercise 3: Additional activities

a If students like Adele, or if they have shown an interest in her from this activity, play one of her songs. You could develop activities to examine the lyrics, or you could just play the song and ask students simple questions like *Do you like this song? What type of music is it? Do you often listen to music like this?*

b If you have access to the internet in class, you can find videos of many of Adele's songs online, often with the lyrics as part of the video.

c If students are interested in music, you could broaden the discussion. Ask questions like *What do you like listening to when you are in a car / working / doing exercise / on a romantic date … ?*

Grammar focus 1 (PAGE 35)

Present simple: positive and negative (*he/she/it*)

See *Teaching tips: Working with grammar*, page 20.

1 Direct students to audio script 4.2 on page 168. Identify the first verb as an example. Ask the class if it is positive or negative. Students continue individually to find the rest of the verbs and decide if they are positive or negative. They check in pairs before checking answers as a class.

ANSWERS:
Positive: lives, likes, loves, likes, loves, has, likes, loves, says, 's, hates, wears, likes, says, make
Negative: doesn't like, doesn't like, doesn't have, don't make

GRAMMAR

Present simple: positive and negative (*he/she/it*)

1 Ask students what they can remember about Adele and put it on the board, e.g. *She likes simple clothes.* Elicit more sentences that include different verbs. Students complete the gaps to provide examples for the rules.

ANSWERS:
+ wears
– doesn't

2 Work through the examples with your students. As you do, make sure you highlight:
- the third person *-s*.
- the use of *doesn't*.
- that we do NOT say *She doesn't likes*.
- the use of the plural noun form after *likes* and *hates*.
- the use of the *-ing* form for activities that people like or dislike.

You may want to ask students to read Study 1 on page 144 for a more detailed explanation of the Present simple: positive and negative (*he/she/it*).

PRONUNCIATION

See *Teaching tips: Helping students with pronunciation*, page 22.

1 🎧 **4.4** Direct students to audio script 4.4 on page 168. Show your students how to count the number of syllables for the first couple of verbs as an example. Students continue with the remaining verbs. This is important because some students will confuse the pronunciation because of the silent *e* and so introduce an extra syllable where it is not needed. You could also look at the pronunciation of the final *s*; /s/ or /z/. See the notes on pronunciation of the possessive *'s* on page 34 of this Teacher's Book for more information.

ANSWERS:

1	1	2	2	3	1	4	1	5	2	6	2	7	1
8	3	9	3	10	1	11	1	12	2				

2 Drill the verbs chorally and individually. Try to drill phrases as well as just the individual verbs as this will help students to put them into context.

PRACTICE

1a Do the first one as an example. Students continue to write four true and four false sentences about Adele. If they can't remember, encourage them to check with the audio script.

POSSIBLE ANSWERS:
1 She likes going for walks with her dog. (T)
2 She likes flying. (F)
3 She doesn't like her dog. (F)
4 She likes spending time with her mother. (T)
5 She doesn't like spending time with friends. (F)
6 She likes doing big concerts. (F)
7 She likes black clothes. (T)
8 She doesn't like the food on aeroplanes. (T)

b Do an example with the class. Read out a false sentence and encourage the class to correct you. Students work in pairs to share and correct their sentences.

ADDITIONAL PRACTICE

🔲 **Resource bank:** Activity 4A *Things you love and hate* (Present simple; likes/dislikes with nouns and *-ing*)

Study, practice & remember: Practice 1

Workbook: Grammar focus 1: *Present simple: positive and negative (he/she/it)*, pages 19–20

Reading and vocabulary (PAGE 36)

Phrases for time and frequency

See *Teaching tips: Working with lexical phrases*, page 21.

WARM UP

To revise the language from the previous class, ask your students some quick-fire questions, for example *Do you like going for walks? Do you like watching sport?* Get students to reply with the short answers *Yes, I do.* or *No, I don't.* Make sure you keep the tempo up to increase the energy levels. After you have asked a few questions, invite students to ask each other questions in open pairs.

1a Focus students' attention on the pictures. Ask some introductory questions, for example *What time is it in the first picture? Which person is positive and which negative? Do you like sleeping in the afternoon?* Students quickly read the article and match the statements to the pictures. They check in pairs before checking answers as a class. If there is some disagreement about the answers, encourage students to justify their answers before confirming or correcting.

> **ANSWERS:**
> **1** bottom left　**2** bottom middle　**3** top left　**4** bottom right
> **5** top right

b Students work in pairs to talk about the questions.

2a Students complete the gaps with an appropriate preposition.

b Students read the article again to check their answers.

> **ANSWERS:**
> **1** in　**2** in　**3** in　**4** at　**5** on

3 Students can work in pairs to place the adverbs on the line. Alternatively, you could draw the line on the board, write the adverbs on cards and invite the class to stick them in the correct place.

> **ANSWERS:**
> always, usually, often, sometimes, not often, never

4a Tell students a little bit about yourself using the statements, e.g. *I never go shopping at the weekend. I always check my email in the morning.* Students then work individually to complete the sentences with an adverb so that the sentences are true for them.

> **Potential problem with adverb position**
>
> These adverbs are usually located in mid-position; this means they normally come before the main verb and after the auxiliary. However, they come after the verb *to be* as in example sentence 6 in exercise 4a.
>
> *Sometimes* is a more flexible adverb as it can also be found at the beginning or end of a clause. There is no real difference in meaning, instead it is more a question of style and the speaker's preference.

b Students work in pairs to compare their sentences. In feedback, ask students to report to the class what their partner does, making sure they use the third person *s* appropriately.

ADDITIONAL PRACTICE

➡ **Resource bank:** Activity 4B *Always, sometimes, never* (Phrases for time and frequency)

Study, practice & remember: Practice 2

Workbook: Vocabulary: *Phrases for time and frequency*, pages 21–22

Grammar focus 2 (PAGE 37)

Present simple: questions and short answers (*he/she/it*)

See *Teaching tips: Working with grammar*, page 20.

WARM UP

Introduce the topic by quickly talking about the Olympics. Ask questions like *Do you like watching the Olympics? What is your favourite sport in the Olympics?*

1 Students quickly read the text and answer the two questions.

> **ANSWERS:**
> **1** seven　**2** London

2a Focus students' attention on the questions and the words in the box. Do the first one as an example. Students complete the questions and then check in pairs before checking answers as a class.

> **ANSWERS:**
> **1** come　**2** Does　**3** Who　**4** live　**5** like　**6** play　**7** Where
> **8** have

b Students work individually to answer the questions and then check in pairs. While checking answers as a class, encourage your students to justify their answers by giving evidence from the text.

> **ANSWERS:**
> **1** Yes, she does.
> **2** Yes, she does.
> **3** She works for British TV and radio, and a charity.
> **4** No, she doesn't.
> **5** Yes, she does.
> **6** She plays tennis and golf.
> **7** She lives in London.
> **8** She has three children.

GRAMMAR

Questions and short answers with *he/she/it*

1 Write the following question about Denise Lewis on the board: ___ ___ ___ *in Birmingham?* Point explicitly to the question mark and elicit how the question can be completed (*Does she live in Birmingham?*) Use arrows and/or different colours to highlight the changed position of the verb and the subject. Repeat this with a couple more sentences to show the pattern. Go back to the first question about Denise living in Birmingham. Ask a couple of students and elicit the possible short answers: *Yes, she does. / No, she doesn't.* Write these on the board and then repeat for the other questions you have used. Elicit that *doesn't* is the contracted form of *does not*.

Remind students of the meaning of the Present simple, i.e. something which is permanent or which is always true (and not only at the present time).

Students complete the question and short answer.

> **ANSWERS:**
> Does, doesn't

Wh- questions

Ask students how many possible answers there are for the previous questions in this Grammar box about Denise Lewis. Elicit that there are two (or three): *Yes, she does. / No, she doesn't.* (or *I don't know.*).

Write on the board: *Where does Denise Lewis live?* Show students that with a question starting with *Where* the possible answers are open, while questions starting without *Where* have a closed set of possible answers. Repeat the procedure for *What*. Write on the board: *Does she swim?* and elicit the answer *Yes, she does.* or *No, she doesn't.* Then write the question *What sports does she do?* and elicit a list of sports.

You may want to ask students to read Study 3 on page 145 for a more detailed explanation of the Present simple: questions and short answers (*he/she/it*).

PRONUNCIATION

See *Teaching tips: Helping students with pronunciation*, page 22.

1 🎧 4.5 Model the two possible pronunciations of *does*: /dʌz/ and /dəz/. Play the recording and check students can identify the difference by raising their right hand for /dʌz/ and their left hand for /dəz/.

2 Drill the questions. Encourage students to take the part of the teacher by asking them to ask the question and have other students raise their right or left hands depending on what they hear.

PRACTICE

1 Students match the answers to the questions then check in pairs before checking answers as a class.

ANSWERS:

1 From Birmingham.   **2** Yes, she does.   **3** She also does charity work.   **4** She likes dancing.   **5** No, she doesn't.   **6** Her family.

2 Do the first couple of questions as an example. Students complete the questions individually. During feedback, make sure students pronounce *does* correctly.

ANSWERS:

1 What   **2** does   **3** Where   **4** Does   **5** does   **6** Does
7 What   **8** Does

3 Students work in pairs. Direct student A to page 133 and student B to page 134. Give students a few minutes to read their text. Students then ask and answer each of the questions from exercise 2 about the texts.

Culture notes

Denise Lewis (b. 1972) had been a top athlete in the heptathlon for a number of years but had only managed a couple of silver medals in the World Championships and a bronze at the 1996 Olympics in Atlanta. However, in the Sydney Olympics in 2000 she won gold by the relatively small margin of only 53 points. Although the Sydney Olympics were relatively successful for Great Britain, this was one of only two gold medals won in athletics and this helped to propel Denise to national fame. She tried to defend her title in the 2004 Athens Olympics but injuries prevented her from competing past the long jump. She retired after the 2004 games but remains a popular figure in broadcasting.

Tom Daley (b. 1994) has been diving since he was a child. When he was 10 he won a competition for under 18s and it was quickly recognised that he had a lot of potential. When he was 13 he won the British Championships and, in the same year, he also started to win international medals. He has won a gold medal in the European and World Championships in the 10-metre platform, but only won a bronze at the London Olympics in 2012. Since that time he has started to work in TV, but he says he remains focused on his diving.

Victoria Pendleton (b.1980) is currently the most successful British female cyclist and one of the most successful female cyclists ever. She won a string of European, World and Olympic gold medals between 2005 and 2012. Her main discipline was the sprint, which she totally dominated until her retirement after the London Olympics in 2012. Since her retirement she has written a controversial autobiography and appeared on the hit TV show *Strictly Come Dancing*.

Practice, exercise 3: Alternative suggestion

If you have weaker elementary students, or students who don't have much confidence, make sure to give them more time to read through and check their answers. Put students into pairs to read the same text. Half of the pairs should read about Tom Daley on page 133 and the other half should read about Victoria Pendleton on page 134. Students check the answers to the questions in exercise 2 with their partners. When they are sure they have got the right answers, make new pairs with a person who has read the other text. The new pairs then ask and answer the questions from exercise 2 about the text they didn't read.

ADDITIONAL PRACTICE

⮕ **Resource bank:** Activity 4C *Three people I know* (Present simple: questions and short answers)

Study, practice & remember: Practice 3

Workbook: Grammar focus 2: *Present simple: questions and short answers (he/she/it)*, pages 22–23; Pronunciation: *Strong and weak forms of* does, page 23

Task (PAGES 38–39)

Choose a holiday activity

See *Teaching tips: Making tasks work*, page 23.

Preparation (PAGES 38–39)

Reading and listening

WARM UP

Introduce the topic by asking students about their holidays, e.g. *Where do you like going? Who do you usually go with?* Don't worry about correcting grammar or vocabulary; just get students thinking about the topic of holidays.

1a Students match the words in the box to the photos.

ANSWERS:

A sailing   **B** preparing dinner   **C** playing music
D taking a photograph

b Check the meaning of *guitar* and *violin*. In some languages these words are very similar. Students quickly match the courses to the photos. You could give a time limit of one minute to encourage students to do this very quickly by just reading the headings.

ANSWERS:

A Course 3   **B** Course 4   **C** Course 1   **D** Course 2

2 Ask students to read the advert again, but this time in more detail and taking more time. Students answer the questions individually and then check with a partner before checking answers as a class. Ask students to justify their answers before confirming or correcting.

ANSWERS:

2 1   **3** 4   **4** 2   **5** 3   **6** 3   **7** 4   **8** 1

3 🎧 4.6 Focus students' attention on the photos and the quotes. Play the recording of the first person and ask students to check their ideas with a partner. Check as a class. If your students need support with their listening skills, repeat this procedure for each of the following three speakers. If your students are comfortable with listening, play the final three together without pausing.

ANSWERS:

Lucy: Likes: being in the fresh air, swimming, being near water, scenery; Doesn't like: being inside

Cassia: Likes: working with other people to create something, dancing

Juan: Likes: music, painting, being alone, looking at beautiful scenery; Doesn't like: being with a lot of other people

Tom: Likes: meeting people, learning new things, going out with friends, good food; Doesn't like: cooking

4a 🎧 **4.7** Make sure students know that they are going to be listening to two new people talking about one of the people from the previous exercise. Students listen and answer the two questions. Check as a class.

ANSWERS:

1 Lucy   **2** the sailing course

b Focus students' attention on the Useful language box. Give them a minute to read through the sentences and deal with any doubts. Students listen and tick the phrases they hear.

ANSWERS:

Maybe the (painting) course is good for … ✓
What do you think? ✓
I think the (sailing course) is good for her … ✓
… because she likes being outside. ✓
I'm not sure. ✓
Yes, you're right. ✓
Yes, I agree. ✓

Task (PAGE 39)

Speaking

1a Give students a few minutes to read through the advert again and the information about the remaining three people. If your students lack confidence, you could ask them to quickly check their ideas with a partner.

b Put students into small groups. Encourage them to discuss which holiday would be best for each person. Circulate and offer help as necessary.

2 Ask one person from each group to report back to the class on the decisions they came to.

Task: Additional activity

Ask students to write a paragraph about the holiday course they would choose to go on. This writing can be done in class or as homework.

Share your task

The idea here is to give students a chance to 'perfect' their speaking in this context and provide them with a recording of a 'polished' version. This will provide extra motivation for students, as well as extra practice. Students can either make an audio or video recording, depending on how comfortable they feel and what equipment is available. Students could even use their mobile phones to do this. If possible, they'll need a quiet place to make their recording. Students can either record themselves during the lesson, or as homework and bring the recordings to the next class.

Some additional ideas could include:

- Students record themselves talking about which holiday course they would choose for a friend or family member and why.
- Students talk about a dream holiday course they would like to go on.

Language live (PAGES 40–41)

Speaking (PAGE 40)

Meeting people

See *Teaching tips: Using the video material in the classroom*, page 24.

1a Ask the class how they feel about meeting people for the first time. Students might have difficulties with vocabulary so be prepared to offer substantial help and don't let this part go on for too long. Write on the board any suggestions from students. You might also like to introduce vocabulary such as *nervous*, *shy*, *confident*, *relaxed*, *excited*.

b ▶ Students watch the DVD and answer the question.

ANSWER:

Robert feels quite nervous.

2 Give your students enough time to read through the statements. Students watch again and decide if the statements are true or false. Students check in pairs and then as a class.

ANSWERS:

1 T
2 F (He gives Mrs Wicks some flowers.)
3 F (Mr Wicks makes some tea.)
4 T
5 F (He likes coffee.)
6 F (He doesn't really like it.)
7 T
8 T

3a Do the first one as an example. Students work individually to choose the correct answers.

b ▶ Students watch and check.

ANSWERS:

1 to see   **2** This   **3** to meet   **4** These   **5** lovely   **6** Would
7 please   **8** fine   **9** working

PRONUNCIATION

See *Teaching tips: Helping students with pronunciation*, page 22.

1 Students watch and listen to the key phrases. You could ask students to pay attention to which words are stressed.

2 Drill the phrases chorally and individually.

4 Students complete the conversation with the words in the box. They check in pairs and then check as a class. When checking the answers, ask students to read the whole sentence and not just the correct word. This will help students improve their connected speech, including sentence stress.

ANSWERS:

1 lovely   **2** fine   **3** Scotland   **4** meet   **5** These   **6** drink
7 running   **8** love

Speaking, exercise 4: Additional activity

If you think your students need to gain some confidence before writing their own conversation, you could ask them to roleplay the conversation from the DVD. Tell students they are going to try to copy the actors in the DVD from exercise 1b and then play it again. Put students into groups of four and ask them to select a role. Give them a few minutes to practise the roleplay and then ask one or two groups to perform it for the class. Ask the class if they think it was similar to the original.

This activity will allow weaker students to practise the conversation without worrying about whether they are making language mistakes. It will also make the next activity easier as they will have had more interaction with the language.

5a Brainstorm different alternatives for the conversation, e.g. *the guest could bring chocolates or a drink, the guest might be asked about his job.*

 b Students work in groups of three to rewrite the conversation in exercise 4 and then act it out. You could ask for volunteers to perform their conversations for the class.

Writing (PAGE 41)

Introducing a friend

1 Focus students' attention on the photos. Ask students if they recognise the city (*London*). As a class, match the first question to an answer as an example. Students complete the rest individually.

ANSWERS:
1 c   2 g   3 f   4 a   5 b   6 h   7 e   8 d

2 Elicit answers for the first gap as an example. Students complete the rest of the gaps using the information in exercise 1. They check in pairs before checking answers as a class.

ANSWERS:
1 Okinawa in Japan   2 London   3 musician   4 living
5 the weather   6 very nice

3 Give students time to complete their notes about a person they know or someone they have invented. Circulate and offer help and encouragement as necessary.

4 Tell students they should use the email from exercise 2 as a model. Students write a description of their friend using their notes from exercise 3. If you are short of time, this could be done as homework.

ADDITIONAL PRACTICE

Workbook: Language live: *Meeting people*, page 23; Writing: *Introducing a friend*, page 23

Students can now do Progress test 2 on the Teacher's Resource Disc.

Study, practice & remember
(PAGES 144–145)

See *Teaching tips: Using the Study, practice & remember sections*, page 25.

Practice 1

ANSWERS:
1
    1 knows   2 studies   3 listens   4 watches   5 does
    6 hates   7 goes   8 works   9 has   10 likes
2
    1 hates   2 doesn't have   3 doesn't like   4 loves
    5 doesn't watch   6 does   7 wears   8 finishes
3
    1 playing   2 cooking   3 hates   4 getting   5 going
    6 likes   7 going   8 watching

Practice 2

ANSWERS:
1 You never listen to me.
2 I am always at school at 9 o'clock.
3 He often catches the bus to work.
4 My sister sometimes visits me on Sunday.
5 She is often late for class.
6 I never watch football on television.
7 They sometimes speak English at home.
8 My children are never at home.
9 We don't often go out at the weekend.
10 My flat is often cold in the evenings.

Practice 3

ANSWERS:
1
    1 Do, don't   2 does   3 Do, do   4 does   5 Does, doesn't
    6 does
2
    1 d   2 f   3 e   4 a   5 c   6 b

Remember these words

ANSWERS:
1
    1 going   2 spending   3 playing   4 spending   5 cooking
    6 cycling   7 watching   8 going
2
    1 morning   2 always   3 check   4 fresh   5 relax   6 free
    7 have   8 weekend

OVERVIEW

PAGES 42–43

Vocabulary and reading: Transport

Pronunciation: Weak forms: prepositions and articles

Common European Framework: Students can identify specific information in simpler texts such as short newspaper articles.

PAGES 44–45

Vocabulary: Travelling

Grammar: *can/can't*: possibility and ability

Pronunciation: *can/can't*

Common European Framework: Students can get simple information about travel options.

PAGES 46–47

Grammar: Articles: *a/an*, *the* and *no article*

Common European Framework: Students can exchange information about familiar topics such as work and family.

PAGES 48–49

Task: Do a transport survey

Common European Framework: Students can communicate in simple tasks requiring direct exchange of information related to routine matters.

PAGES 50–51

World culture: Race across London

Common European Framework: Students can understand a native speaker when the speech is clear and relatively slow.

Vocabulary and reading (PAGES 42–43)

Transport

See *Teaching tips: Working with lexical phrases*, page 21.

WARM UP

Either write the names of common means of transport on the board or prepare a collection of pictures. Useful items would include *car*, *bus*, *motorbike*, *bicycle*, *taxi*. Read out the following sentences one by one: *I come to school by … . I go to work by … . I go out at night to a restaurant by … . I visit family and friends by … .* After each sentence, elicit how people travel for each of the activities and develop a list of advantages and disadvantages for each one.

1 Students work in pairs to find the types of transport in the photos. Explain that they will not find all of them. Check the pronunciation of *motorbike* /ˈməʊtəbaɪk/, *scooter* /ˈskuːtə/, *bicycle* /ˈbaɪsɪkl/ and *underground train* /ˈʌndəɡraʊnd treɪn/.

ANSWERS:

a bus, a train, a tram, a taxi, a bicycle, a scooter, a motorbike, a ferry

2a Write *fast* at the top of the board and *slow* at the bottom. Check students understand and then ask them where to put *plane*. Write it at the top and number it 1. Then ask them for number 11 at the bottom (*bicycle*). Students work individually to put the rest of the words in order.

b Students compare their answers with a partner.

POSSIBLE ANSWERS:

1 plane	**2** train	**3** underground train	**4** ferry **5** motorbike
6 car	**7** taxi	**8** tram	**9** bus **10** scooter **11** bicycle

3 Ask a student: *How do you usually travel to school/work?* Check that he/she uses the correct preposition: *by bus*, *by train*.

Highlight the use of *by* for all the types of transport and the use of *on foot* when we walk. Students work in pairs to talk about how the various people travel.

4a Tell students that 74% of Americans drive a car compared to 59% of Japanese people. Get students to guess what the percentage of Germans who drive a car might be. Students then decide which number from the box could go in the first gap. They then work individually and put the numbers in the other gaps. Encourage them to guess the meaning of unknown words. Check how to say numbers with *million* and *percent*.

b 🎧 **5.1** Play the recording for students to check their answers.

ANSWERS:

1 53 **2** 2 **3** 9 million **4** 45 **5** 1 million **6** 160 **7** 270 **8** 5 **9** 60 million

5a Do the first one as an example, but don't give the correct answer at this point. Students then work individually to choose the correct answers.

b Identify the answer for the first question using the text. Students then use the article to check the rest of their answers.

ANSWERS:

1 drive **2** ride **3** ride **4** take **5** to **6** for **7** on **8** off **9** to

PRONUNCIATION

See *Teaching tips: Helping students with pronunciation*, page 22.

1 🎧 **5.2** Write the words *a*, *the*, *to* and *for* on the board. Elicit the pronunciation. Students will probably give you the strong version /eɪ/, /ðiː/, /tuː/, /fɔː/. Tell them this is fine, but usually we don't say the words like this. Model the weak pronunciation and make sure students can pronounce the schwa in /ə/, /ðə/, /tə/, /fə/. Tell students that, while we stress the important words, we don't put any stress on these words because they are not as important. Play the recording and ask students to decide if the speakers use the strong or the weak pronunciation.

2 Drill the phrases. It is much better to drill phrases rather than individual words because it allows students to put the stress in the right place.

6a First check the meaning of *a lot of* and *not many*. Do the first one on the board and ask students if it is true for their town or city. If it is false, show students how to change it. If it is true, choose another example which is false and correct that one instead.

b Students work in pairs to compare their answers.

ADDITIONAL PRACTICE

➡ **Workbook:** Vocabulary: *Transport*, page 24

Vocabulary (PAGE 44)

Travelling

See *Teaching tips: Working with lexical phrases*, page 21.

> **Culture notes**
>
> Hong Kong is situated on China's south coast and is famous for its skyline of skyscrapers and bright lights. The name means *fragrant harbour* in Cantonese, although in recent years the smell from the harbour has not always been so pleasing.
>
> Hong Kong became a British territory after the first Opium War in 1842 between Britain and China. After another war in 1860 the land granted to Britain expanded to take in all of Kowloon. It remained a part of the British Empire until 1997 when China resumed sovereignty.
>
> Today Hong Kong has a largely separate system of government from mainland China. This has enabled it to retain its place as one of the world's financial centres and an important world city.

1 Focus students' attention on the photos of Hong Kong. Students work in pairs to answer the questions.

ANSWERS:

In the photos there's a ferry, a plane and two double-decker trams. It's probably not easy to travel about in Hong Kong.

2a Students discuss the questions in pairs.

b If you have a strong class, do the first couple of sentences together and then ask your students to continue with the rest. If you have a lower elementary class, check the meaning of the words in bold, especially *board*, *book your ticket online*, *luggage*, *gate number*.

c 🎧 5.3 Students listen and check.

ANSWERS:

b, d, h, e, g, a, j, f, c, i

3 Students work in pairs to discuss the questions.

ADDITIONAL PRACTICE

➡ **Resource bank:** Activity 5A *Transport crossword* (Transport; travelling)

Workbook: Vocabulary: *Travelling*, page 26

Grammar focus 1 (PAGES 44–45)

can/can't: possibility and ability

See *Teaching tips: Working with grammar*, page 20.

1a Students work in pairs to discuss the question. Get people's ideas and put them on the board.

b Check the meaning of *stopover*. Ask students to read the webpage quickly and see which of the ideas from the board are mentioned. After reading you might also want to check the meaning of *advice* (information to help people), *facilities* (services and infrastructure available for people to use) and *leisure* (things to do to relax and enjoy yourself in your free time).

GRAMMAR

can/can't: possibility and ability

> **Notes on *can/can't***
>
> We have introduced *can* and *can't* for both possibility and ability because often it is difficult to separate the two aspects. Most students will accept this, but if somebody has a problem and you want to be explicit about the difference, substitute *it is possible* or *know how to* for *can*.

Write on the board: *It is possible to fly direct to more than 160 destinations.* → *You ___ fly direct to more than 160 destinations.* Elicit *can* to fill the gap. Change the number to *350* in the second sentence and elicit the negative sentence using *can't*.

Go through the sentences and rules in the Grammar box. Highlight:

* that after *can* we use the base form of the verb and we don't change it for *he/she/it*.
* that *can't = can not*.
* that we make questions by inverting *can* and the subject.

You may want to ask students to read Study 1 on page 146 for a more detailed explanation of *can/can't*: possibility and ability.

PRACTICE

1a Students work individually to complete the sentences then check in pairs.

> **Practice, exercise 1a: Alternative suggestion**
>
> If you have stronger elementary students, ask them to complete this exercise orally in pairs instead of in writing. It will give them more of a challenge and will force them to think more quickly.

b 🎧 5.4 Students listen and check.

ANSWERS:

| 1 can | 2 can't | 3 can | 4 can't | 5 Can, can |
| 6 Can, can't | | | | |

PRONUNCIATION

See *Teaching tips: Helping students with pronunciation*, page 22.

Remind students about the strong and weak forms that they looked at in the Pronunciation boxes on pages 37 and 43. Model the strong and weak forms of *can*, i.e. /kæn/ and /kən/. Contrast this with the negative form of *can't* /kɑːnt/.

1 Students listen and identify which of the pronunciation forms above are used.

2 Drill the sentences chorally and individually.

2 🎧 5.5 Give students a moment to read the sentences before listening. Students listen and tick the things that you can do in Hong Kong and cross the things you can't do. Students check in pairs and then check as a class.

ANSWERS:

You can: travel by tram, find a seat easily on the underground trains, use a special travel card on all public transport, buy food and drink with the special travel card

You can't: eat and drink on the underground trains, find a taxi quickly

3 Give students a couple of minutes to think of two more questions. Remind students that they don't have to talk about where they live, but a place that they know. Students work in pairs to ask and answer the questions.

ADDITIONAL PRACTICE

➡ **Resource bank:** Activity 5B *The perfect holiday* (*can/can't*: possibility and ability)

Study, practice & remember: Practice 1

Workbook: Grammar focus 1: *can/can't*: possibility and ability, pages 26–27; Pronunciation: *can/can't*, page 28

Grammar focus 2 (PAGES 46–47)

Articles: *a/an*, *the* and *no article*

See *Teaching tips: Working with grammar*, page 20.

Culture notes

Mexico City, also known as Mexico D.F. (Federal District), is the capital of Mexico. The city itself has a population of around nine million people, but the metropolitan area has a population of around 21 million people, making it the fifth biggest metropolitan area in the world.

Mexico City was founded on an island in Lake Texcoco by the Aztecs in 1325. The lake today is only a fraction of the size it was before. The Aztecs called the city Tenochtitlan. The Spanish destroyed it in 1521 in a siege and then rebuilt it in 1524 according to contemporary Spanish designs.

Mexico City faces a number of problems today. The fact that it was built in a natural bowl means that pollution from the huge population tends to linger. Transport can be difficult and fear of crime is high. The city is also located on a natural fault line and so earthquakes are common.

The larger photo shows the Cathedral of the Assumption of Mary of Mexico, the oldest and biggest cathedral in the Americas. The taxi is a Volkswagen Beetle and they are everywhere in Mexico City; it is estimated that there are over 100,000 in the city. Although nowadays most of them are green it is still possible to see the old colours as shown in the photograph.

---

1 Focus students' attention on the photos. Ask for a quick description of the things they can see. They then quickly read the text and answer the three questions. Check as a class.

ANSWERS:
1 In Mexico City.   2 He's an engineer.
3 He plays football with his friends.

GRAMMAR

Articles: *a/an*, *the* and *no article*

1 Ask students to underline all of the articles in the text. Students then complete the rules by filling in the gaps with *a/an*, *the* or *no article*.

ANSWERS:
1 a/an   2 the   3 – (no article)

Potential problem with articles

The use of *no article* is important for languages that have articles but use them differently to English. For example, some languages use an article before people's names, but English usually doesn't. There is no quick fix to solve this problem, just lots of patient correction and awareness-raising activities.

You may want to ask students to read Study 2 on page 146 for a more detailed explanation of *a/an*, *the* and *no article*.

PRACTICE

1a Do the first one as a class as an example. Students complete the rest of the exercise individually. If students have problems, encourage them to use the Grammar box to help them.

b 🎧 **5.6** Students listen and check. In feedback, ask students which of the rules from the Grammar box applies to each of the answers.

ANSWERS:
1 –, the, –   2 –, an   3 the, the   4 –, –, –, –   5 a, –, –, the
6 –, the

2a Do the first one as an example, giving as much information as possible, e.g. *I live in a flat in Copacabana in Rio de Janeiro*. Give students enough time to write their answers. Circulate and offer help as necessary.

b Encourage students to use the Grammar box as a checklist to correct their writing.

Practice, exercise 2b: Alternative suggestion

Put students into pairs and ask them to correct each other's work. It can be difficult to spot your own mistakes, but spotting other people's is often easier. Be sure to handle this with sensitivity so as not to embarrass people.

---

c Students work in pairs to ask and answer the questions.

3a Ask students some general questions about Mexico, e.g. *What do you know about Mexico? Have you ever been to Mexico? What is Mexico famous for? Do you like Mexican food?* Students read the quiz and complete it with *a*, *an*, *the* or – (no article). Students check answers in pairs and then as a class.

ANSWERS:
1 –, –, the   2 –, –   3 –   4 a, –, –   5 –, the   6 the, the
7 a, a, an

b Look at the first sentence. Ask students if they think it is true that Mexico has a border with Costa Rica. Elicit that it isn't true, and show students a map if you have one to hand. Students work in pairs to decide if the rest of the sentences are true or false.

c Direct students to page 133 to check their answers. Give students a minute to decide which fact is the most surprising. In feedback, find out what the class thinks is the most surprising.

Practice, exercise 3: Additional activity

Ask your students to write a similar quiz about their city or country. If all your students come from the same place, ask them to work in pairs or small groups and to find challenging questions. If your students come from different places, group students together from their home cities or countries where possible and encourage them to ask relatively easy questions. This could be done in class or as homework. When the quizzes are ready, distribute them to other members of the class to answer.

ADDITIONAL PRACTICE

➡ **Study, practice & remember:** Practice 2

Workbook: Grammar focus 2: *Articles: a/an, the and no article*, page 28

Task (PAGES 48–49)

Do a transport survey

See *Teaching tips: Making tasks work*, page 23.

Preparation (PAGE 48)

Reading and listening

1a Answer the two questions as a class, making sure you clarify the meaning of *cycle-sharing scheme*.

> **ANSWERS:**
>
> The second photo from the top shows a cycle-sharing scheme.
> The photos are of London.

b If possible, check what the exchange rate is for pounds sterling to your local currency so that you can tell students the approximate cost per hour for a bike in London. Give students a couple of minutes to read the text and answer the questions.

> **ANSWERS:**
>
> **1** over 8,000   **2** Boris Bikes   **3** after the Mayor of London at that time, Boris Johnson   **4** nothing – it's free   **5** 47,000

2 Students work in pairs to discuss the questions. During feedback, ask students if they think the price is expensive and how much they would be willing to pay for a service like this in their own town/city.

3a Focus students' attention on the transport survey. Complete the first question with the class as an example. Students work individually to complete the rest of the questions. Circulate and offer help as necessary.

> **ANSWERS:**
>
> **1** How do you travel to school or work every day?
> **2** How long does your journey take?
> **3** How far do you walk every week?
> **4** Which of these things can you do?
> **5** How often do you travel by car?
> **6** How often do you use public transport?
> **7** What do you think of public transport in your town?

b Encourage students to think of their own final question.

4a 🎧 **5.7** Students listen and note the speaker's answers. Tell students they should also listen to see if the speaker answers their eighth question.

> **ANSWERS:**
>
> **1** e (bike)   **2** b   **3** a   **4** a, b, c   **5** c   **6** c   **7** e

b Focus students' attention on the Useful language box, parts a and b. Students listen again and tick the phrases they hear.

> **ANSWERS:**
>
> How do you travel to school/work/university (every day)? ✓
> How long does your journey take? ✓
> How far do you walk … ? ✓
> Can you drive a (car)? ✓
> Can you ride a bike? ✓
> How often do you use public transport? ✓
> I go by (bike). ✓
> I haven't got a car. ✓
> I don't use public transport (much / very much). ✓

Task (PAGES 48–49)

Speaking

1 Give students a few minutes to choose their answers. Circulate and offer help as necessary.

2a Students work in pairs to ask and answer the questions. Make sure students make a note of their partner's answers.

b Focus students' attention on the language in part c of the Useful language box. Put students into groups for them to report on their original partner's answers.

> **Task: Speaking: Additional activity**
>
> Use the same questions to carry out a class or group survey. Students work in groups of four to eight and find out everyone's responses. Review numbers and percentages and direct students to part c of the Useful language box. The group then gives a mini-presentation about their travel habits.

> **Share your task**
>
> The idea here is to give students a chance to 'perfect' their speaking in this context and provide them with a recording of a 'polished' version. This will provide extra motivation for students, as well as extra practice. Students can either make an audio or video recording, depending on how comfortable they feel and what equipment is available. Students could even use their mobile phones to do this. If possible, they'll need a quiet place to make their recording. Students can either record themselves during the lesson, or as homework and bring the recordings to the next class.

> **World culture, Find out first:**
>
> To help your students prepare for the next class, go through the questions in exercise 1b on page 50. If necessary, discuss ideas for searching for this information on the internet, pointing out the search terms, and suggest other sources of information students could use. Encourage students to use English language websites as much as possible.

World culture (PAGES 50–51)

Race across London

> **Culture notes**
>
> **The River Thames** is the traditional highway and soul of London. The city's location was originally chosen because this was the first place that the river could be crossed. The river brought trade, originally from Europe and then from all over the world. For a long time, if you wanted to travel any meaningful distance in London, you did so by river. It had a reputation for being dirty and polluted, but nowadays, even though it is still brown and muddy, it is actually a very clean river.
>
> **Kew Bridge** (pictured top left) is a low bridge with three arches that spans the River Thames at Kew, pronounced /kjuː/, in the west of London. There has been a bridge at Kew since 1759, but the current bridge dates from 1903. The bridge holds a road which is nearly always blocked with traffic.
>
> **Tower Bridge** (pictured top centre) is one of the iconic buildings of London and is often featured on postcards and advertising for the city. It was built in 1894 near the Tower of London, from which it gets its name. The road over the bridge can be raised up to allow ships to pass underneath.

Canary Wharf (pictured top right) is the second financial centre of London. The area is in Tower Hamlets in the East End of London. It used to be busy due to the docks that were there, but all business to the docks had dried up by the 1970s and left a very poor area. In the 1980s the government tried to regenerate the area and relieve the demand for space in the City by developing Canary Wharf. Although Canary Wharf is now prosperous, and over 90,000 people work there, the area surrounding it is still very poor.

London City Airport (pictured bottom) is located in the east of London, quite close to Canary Wharf. It is a relatively small airport with only one runway. Most of its passengers are travelling between the two financial centres in London and destinations in Europe and the UK.

Top Gear is a BBC TV programme about cars and motoring which holds the honour of being the world's most widely watched factual show. It first started in 1997 and has been through a number of format changes but only seems to have gained in popularity. It can be seen on TV all over the world as the BBC has exported it and it now has its own magazine available in many different languages. It has often been criticised for not being politically correct, for not taking global warming seriously and for encouraging people to break the law while driving.

Find out first (PAGE 50)

WARM UP

Ask students what they know about London. Students work in pairs to brainstorm everything they can think of. Ideas will probably include *rainy, cold, fog, bad food, expensive*, etc. In feedback, collect ideas and put them on the board or invite students to write them on the board.

1a Focus students' attention on the photos and ask them to match them to the names of the places. Elicit other famous places and put them on the board. Some examples might include *Big Ben, Buckingham Palace, the Houses of Parliament, Sherlock Holmes' house (at 221b Baker Street)*, etc.

ANSWERS:

top left: Kew Bridge and the River Thames
top centre: Tower Bridge and the River Thames
top right: Canary Wharf
bottom: London City Airport

b Students work in pairs to try to guess the answers to the quiz. If some students have not done the research, try to put them with a student who has done it.

c If you have access to the internet and students haven't been able to find the answer to some of the questions, ask students to go online and do some further research. Highlight the search terms. Circulate and offer help with vocabulary and try to encourage people to use only English language websites. Otherwise, tell your students the answers.

ANSWERS:

346 km, 110, Tower of London, business centre, small

View (PAGE 50)

See *Teaching tips: Using the video material in the classroom*, page 24.

2a Tell your students they are going to watch a DVD about a race across London. Make sure students understand the key vocabulary by going through the glossary. You might want to check students have understood by asking questions like: *What time is rush hour in your town/city? What is the speed limit in your country?*

b ▶ Give students time to read through the table and the vocabulary in the box. Students then watch the DVD to match the transport with the presenter and put the presenters in the order in which they finished the race. Students check in pairs and then as a class.

ANSWERS:

James: car, 4
Richard: bicycle, 1
the Stig: public transport, 3
Jeremy: speedboat, 2

3 Quickly check the pronunciation of the numbers and then give students time to read through all of the sentences so they know what they have to listen for. Students then watch to complete the sentences. Check in pairs and then as a class.

ANSWERS:

1 28   **2** 14   **3** 80   **4** 20 ... 25 ... 18

World view (PAGE 51)

4a Students work individually to tick the statements that are true for them.

World view, exercise 4a: Alternative suggestion

If your students all come from the same country or city, change the sentences and either write them on the board or read them out for students to tick on a piece of paper. Some example sentences might be:

I like cycling.

I love Formula One racing.

I always watch camel racing.

I want to run a marathon.

I never watch horse racing.

I always use public transport because it is cheap and efficient.

I sometimes go to work by bicycle.

b Students work in pairs to compare their answers.

Find out more ⓢ (PAGE 51)

5a Focus students' attention on the five famous races in the box. Students work individually or in pairs to brainstorm everything they can think of about them.

b If you have access to the internet at school, students work in pairs to research the famous races. Focus students' attention on the search terms that they should use. Circulate and help with new vocabulary as necessary and encourage students to use English language websites.

ANSWERS:

Tour de France: bicycle race, France, July
University Boat Race: rowing race, River Thames, March or April
New York City Marathon: running race (26 miles), New York, November
Dubai World Cup: horse race, Dubai, March
Monaco Grand Prix: motor race, Monaco, May

Write up your research

6 Students use the information from their research into one of the races to complete the description.

7 Students write about another race, either one from Exercise 5a or a different one they are interested in. This could be done in class or as homework.

Study, practice & remember

(PAGES 146–147)

See *Teaching tips: Using the Study, practice & remember sections*, page 25.

Practice 1

ANSWERS:

1 (Possible answers)
  1 You can study other languages, not only English.
  2 You can't park your car in the school car park.
  3 You can come to evening classes.
  4 You can study on computers.
  5 You can't use the library at the weekend.
  6 You can't speak to the teachers at any time.
  7 You can eat lunch in the school.
  8 You can't write in the textbooks.

2
  1 She can't drive a car.
  2 Can you play the guitar?
  3 I can't understand you.
  4 Can they get tickets for us?
  5 Can he cook Indian food?
  6 He can't speak Japanese but he can write it. / He can speak Japanese but he can't write it.
  7 You can't go to work by bus.
  8 Can they speak English?

3
  1 can't   2 can   3 can't   4 can   5 can't   6 can't   7 can
  8 can't

Practice 2

ANSWERS:

1
  1 –, an, the   2 a, the   3 the, –   4 –, –   5 –, the
  6 –, –, a, –   7 –, –   8 –, an, –   9 a   10 a, a, –

2
  1 ~~The~~ Bangkok is in Thailand.
  2 I'm a businessman and I usually work from ~~the~~ Monday to Friday.
  3 Marie finishes school at ~~the~~ 3 o'clock.
  4 Chris goes to ~~the~~ work at 4 o'clock in the afternoon.
  5 ~~The~~ Mr William's office is on the right.
  6 Sam's a teacher in ~~the~~ Ireland.
  7 He usually travels by ~~an~~ underground to the city centre.
  8 I usually have ~~a~~ breakfast at 9 o'clock at the weekend.
  9 Giovanna comes from ~~the~~ Italy, but now she lives in the UK.
  10 I've got a bicycle, but I usually go to work by ~~the~~ train.

3
  1 the   2 an   3 the   4 –   5 a   6 a   7 the   8 –
  9 the   10 –   11 –   12 a   13 –

Remember these words

ANSWERS:

1
  1 rides   2 off   3 ride   4 ferry   5 drives   6 take
  7 wait   8 on

2
  1 book   2 luggage   3 desk   4 gate   5 delayed
  6 board   7 through   8 pass

OVERVIEW

PAGES 52–53

Vocabulary: Food: countable and uncountable nouns

Grammar: *there is* and *there are; some* and *any*

Common European Framework: Students can order everyday goods and services.

PAGES 54–55

Reading: Healthy diets around the world

Vocabulary: Food pairs

Grammar: *how much* and *how many*

Common European Framework: Students can find simple, predictable information in everyday material.

PAGES 56–57

Task: Describe a favourite place to eat

Common European Framework: Students can describe a place or situation that is common and familiar.

PAGES 58–59

Writing: Describe a place to eat

Speaking: Ordering food and drink

Common European Framework: Students can order food.

Vocabulary (PAGE 52)

Food: countable and uncountable nouns

See *Teaching tips: Working with lexical phrases*, page 21.

WARM UP

Prepare a number of anagrams of simple words that are used for food. A good idea is to use international food words like *pizza*, *pasta*, *burger*, *cola*, *cornflakes*, etc. and also to use some local food. These words can either be written on the board or on a handout. Put students into groups and ask them to unscramble the anagrams. Once they have finished, ask students to categorise them into typical *breakfast*, *lunch* or *dinner* food, or ask them which ones they like and don't like.

1   Focus students' attention on the photos. Ask students if there is anything there that they particularly like or don't like. Students match the photos to the words in the box. They check in pairs and then as a class.

2a Draw the table on the board. Point to the picture of the tomatoes and elicit how many there are. Do the same with the olive oil and show how you can count the bottle, but you can't count the oil. Add *tomatoes* to the countable column and *olive oil* to the uncountable column. Students continue individually to complete the table and then check in pairs.

> **Vocabulary, exercise 2a: Alternative suggestion**
>
> Put the names of the foods on cards or have pictures of each. Students, in small groups, categorise them into countable and uncountable nouns.

b   🎧 **6.1** Students listen and check. Add the words to the appropriate columns on the board. Point out that uncountable nouns do not have a plural form.

ANSWERS:

Countable nouns: grapes, an apple, a banana, eggs, tomatoes, a sandwich, biscuits

Uncountable nouns: water, bread, chicken, cheese, olive oil, salad, orange juice, fruit

c   Drill the pronunciation of the words, especially *cheese* /tʃiːz/, *sandwich* /ˈsænwɪtʃ/ and *biscuits* /ˈbɪskɪts/.

3   Elicit one or two more food words and ask the class which column they should go in. Students work individually to add more words to the columns. They check in pairs and then as a class. Add the words your students suggest to the columns on the board. Alternatively, you could ask the students to come to the board themselves and add the words.

ADDITIONAL PRACTICE

➡ **Workbook:** Vocabulary: *Food: countable and uncountable nouns*, page 29

Grammar focus 1 (PAGE 53)

there is and *there are; some* and *any*

See *Teaching tips: Working with grammar*, page 20.

1   🎧 **6.2** Students listen to the sentences and decide if they are true or false, according to the photos.

ANSWERS:

1 T	2 F	3 T	4 F	5 T	6 F	7 F	8 F

GRAMMAR

there is and **there are**

1   Elicit from your students the different forms of the verb *to be* in the present. Write the first two example sentences from the Grammar box on the board. Ask students which one is singular and which one plural. Elicit which form of the verb *to be* is the correct one. Write on the board: *There ___ some water.* and remind students that *water* is uncountable. Show students that we use the singular verb *is* when the noun is uncountable.

ANSWERS:

There's, There are, There's

some and **any**

> **Notes on the approach to some and any**
>
> In the following exercise we have chosen to present *some* and *any* by saying that *some* is usually found in positive sentences and *any* is usually found in negative sentences and questions. While this is generally true there are some exceptions, including:
>
> • when we offer something to someone we often use *some*, for example *Would you like some tea?*
>
> • if we expect or want the answer to be *yes* we often use *some*, for example in the question *Did you do some homework last night?* The speaker is expecting, or hoping, that the answer will be *Yes, of course I did!*

2   Write the example sentences on the board. Ask if students can remember which words were used in the listening. Students choose the correct option.

ANSWERS:

some, any, some, any

3 Show how we normally use *any* in questions.

> **Potential problems with countable and uncountable nouns**
>
> For students who speak languages that differentiate between countable and uncountable nouns the concept is not difficult to grasp. The problem is with internalising the language and being able to manipulate it when needed.
>
> If students speak a language that doesn't differentiate between countable and uncountable nouns, then they not only have the problem of manipulating the language but also of understanding the concept.
>
> Reassure students that, over time and with practice, they will both understand and be able to use this language point. Make sure you correct students sensitively whenever they make a mistake and encourage students to experiment with the language.

You may want to ask students to read Study 1 on page 148 for a more detailed explanation of *there is* and *there are*; *some* and *any*.

PRONUNCIATION

See *Teaching tips: Helping students with pronunciation*, page 22.

1 Direct students to audio script 6.2 on page 169. Model *There's* in isolation and then *an* in isolation too. Next, say the two words together, without a pause or break between them, so that it sounds like the /z/ from *there's* has been dragged to the beginning of *an*. The result is /ðeə zən/. Play the same part of the audio script for students to hear it. Repeat the process with *There are a* so that it sounds like /ðeə rərə/.

2 Drill the phrases chorally and individually.

PRACTICE

1 Students work individually to choose either *some* or *any*. They check in pairs and then as a class. During feedback, ask students to use the rules in the Grammar box to justify each answer.

> **ANSWERS:**
>
> **1** any   **2** some   **3** any   **4** some   **5** any   **6** any
> **7** some

2a Give a couple of examples of true and false sentences about the photos and ask students to correct the false ones. Students then write their own true or false sentences.

b Model the conversation with a stronger student. Students then work in pairs to test each other.

3a Direct students to page 135. Tell students that a woman called Heather is having a picnic with her friends. Check students understand *picnic* (an informal meal held outside). Give students two minutes to remember as many things as possible, without taking notes.

b Model the conversation with a stronger student. Students work in pairs to try to remember the food items. Circulate and encourage students to ask *yes/no* questions.

c Students work in pairs or small groups to talk about their favourite picnic foods. If students aren't used to having picnics, choose a different context, e.g. *birthday party food*.

> **Practice, exercise 3: Additional activities**
>
> **a** Most supermarkets around the world produce free brochures to advertise their latest special offers. Using realia like this is excellent for students as it makes the activity seem more authentic. You can make use of these to revise this vocabulary in a number of ways:
>
> - If you have access to English language material, students can use it to find more vocabulary to describe food and drink.
> - Even if the material is not in English, you can still use the pictures. Put students into A/B pairs. Student A looks at the brochure while student B asks questions, for example *Are there any oranges? How much are they?*
> - If you have brochures from a variety of supermarkets, or the same supermarket from different times, ask students to compare them. For example, *This brochure has apples for 90p but there aren't any apples in that brochure.*
> - If the brochure is not in English, ask students to find translations for ten items of food vocabulary and present it in the next class.
> - If you have access to the internet, you can usually find the same material online.
> - If you have brochures from a different country, give them to your students to take to their local supermarket and ask them to compare the prices. They may need to take into account the exchange rate, but you can help them with this by checking on the internet before the class.
>
> **b** For homework, ask students to keep a diary of the food and drink they have. Give an example of your own so that students know what you expect, and make sure students use *some* where appropriate.
>
> For example:
>
> **Monday**
>
> *Breakfast*
>
> *Some cereal and some orange juice*
>
> *Lunch*
>
> *Some rice and beans, some salad, some chicken and an apple*
>
> *Dinner*
>
> *Two cheese sandwiches and some milk*

ADDITIONAL PRACTICE

Resource bank: Activity 6A *Food battleships* (Food; *there is* and *there are*; *some* and *any*); Activity 6B *The recipe game* (Food; *some* and *any*)

Study, practice & remember: Practice 1

Workbook: Grammar focus 1: *there is* and *there are*; *some* and *any*, page 30; Pronunciation: *there is* and *there are*, page 30

Reading (PAGE 54)

WARM UP

To revise the language from the previous class describe some of the things you have for breakfast, for example *I usually have some bread, coffee and fruit*. In pairs, ask students to talk about what they usually have. Repeat for lunch and dinner. In feedback, find out if there is any food that the whole class usually has for breakfast, lunch or dinner.

1a Focus students' attention on the photos. Remind students of the language for giving opinions from page 39 of the Students' Book. Students work in pairs to answer the questions. In feedback, get some ideas and put them on the board.

b Check the meaning of the word *diet*. In this article it is used to talk about the food we eat regularly, not a special food plan designed to help lose weight. Students read the article quickly to check if their ideas are mentioned. If your students have problems reading quickly, give them a time limit of three minutes and stress they only have to check if their ideas were correct.

ANSWERS:
top: Japan, people eat a lot of fish, fruit and vegetables
centre: a Mediterranean country, people eat a lot of olive oil, fruit and vegetables
bottom: India, people eat a lot of fruit and vegetables, and herbs and spices

2 Do the first one as an example. Students then work individually to match the rest of the statements with the diets. They check in pairs and then as a class. When checking as a class, ask students to justify their answers with information from the text.

ANSWERS:
1 A   2 B   3 C   4 B   5 A   6 C   7 A   8 B

3 Students work in pairs to discuss the questions. In addition, ask students if they would like to eat or try the diets mentioned in the text.

Vocabulary (PAGE 55)

Food pairs

See *Teaching tips: Working with lexical phrases*, page 21.

1a Introduce the language topic by writing on the board *rock and ___*. Elicit *roll* to fill the gap. Ask students if they have ever heard anybody say *roll and rock*. Tell students that English has a lot of phrases like this made up of _A_ *and* _B_ and that they can't be said the other way around.

Elicit a word in box B to go with *fruit*. Explain that all of the words from the first box can be paired with a word from the second box with *and* in the middle. Students work individually to complete the rest of the word pairs then check in pairs.

b 🎧 6.3 Students listen and check. Stress the importance of using these word pairs in this order and NOT, for example, *vegetables and fruit*.

ANSWERS:
fruit and vegetables, herbs and spices, knife and fork, salt and pepper, bread and butter, fish and chips, sweet and sour, tea and coffee, food and drink

PRONUNCIATION

See *Teaching tips: Helping students with pronunciation*, page 22.

1 Refer back to the example of *rock and roll*. Ask students if the pronunciation is *rock AND roll* /ænd/ or *rock 'n' roll* /ən/. Tell students that it is so common to say /ən/ that in this case it is often even written as *'n'*. Focus on the Pronunciation box, model the example and ask students where the main stress falls. Play the recording from exercise 1b again and ask students if the pattern is the same in all the word pairs.

2 Drill the word pairs chorally and individually.

2 Read aloud one of the words from the first box and invite the class to provide the complete word pair. Students work in pairs to test each other in the same way.

Vocabulary, exercise 2: Additional activity

Use Pelmanism (also known as 'concentration', 'memory' or 'pairs') to practise the language from this exercise. Prepare cards with either pictures of the vocabulary from exercise 1a or the words. Each card should have just one item on it.

Place the cards face down on the table and turn one over and say the word. Then turn another card over and say the word for this card. If the two cards form a pair, for example *knife and fork*, the student should say them in the correct order and with the correct pronunciation. If the student can do this, he or she keeps the cards and has another turn.

If the student does not turn over a pair or cannot say the phrase correctly, he or she has to turn the cards back over so that they are face down in the same place.

The winner is the person with the most cards at the end of the game.

ADDITIONAL PRACTICE

➡ **Workbook:** Vocabulary: *Food pairs*, page 31

Grammar focus 2 (PAGE 55)

how much and *how many*

See *Teaching tips: Working with grammar*, page 20.

Culture notes

British food has something of a bad reputation. It is often associated with boiled potatoes and vegetables, and is perceived as being very bland and boring.

In recent years things have changed considerably in the UK with an explosion in the variety and quality of food available in restaurants. While it is true that there are still a lot of fast food restaurants around, you can also find cuisine from all over the world, even in the smallest cities. Indian food is amongst the most preferred types of dish nowadays.

And it is not just in restaurants that habits are changing, but also in the home. Supermarkets sell a lot of exotic herbs and spices and the range of goods available is considerable. There is still a long way to go, but things are improving.

1a If appropriate, ask students what they know about British food. Students then work in pairs to complete the quiz. You could do this as a competition to see which pairs know the most about British people and their food.

b Direct students to page 134 to check their answers. Ask your students if there was anything from the quiz that they found particularly surprising.

GRAMMAR

how much* and *how many

1 Students choose the correct answers by referring to the quiz.

ANSWERS:
1 countable   2 uncountable

You may want to ask students to read Study 2 on page 149 for a more detailed explanation of *how much* and *how many*.

PRACTICE

1a Do the first one as an example. Students complete the rest of the questions with *how much* or *how many* individually. They check in pairs and then as a class.

ANSWERS:

1 How much	**2** How many	**3** How much	**4** How much
5 How much	**6** How much	**7** How many	**8** How much
9 How many	**10** How many	**11** How much	**12** How many

b Students work in pairs to ask and answer the questions. In feedback, find out what the pairs had in common.

Practice, exercise 1: Additional activities

a Tell students they are going to organise a class party and they are in charge of buying the food and drink. Put students into pairs to write a shopping list for all the things they need, and what they think each should cost. Make sure both students have a copy of the shopping list. Circulate and offer help when necessary.

When students have completed their list, ask half of them to sit down and tell them they are shop assistants. Tell the other half they need to buy all of the things on their list. Teach the phrase *Do you have any ___?* The students who are shopkeepers use their list as their inventory, and the price is what they need to sell their goods for. Give the customers a few minutes to try to buy as many things as possible. When they have finished, swap roles.

b To practise *how much* and *how many* and revise language from the previous units, ask students to work in pairs and write five questions about the class and the people in it. For example, *How many people have got black hair? How much homework do we have?* Once they have finished their questions, distribute them to other pairs for them to answer.

ADDITIONAL PRACTICE

Resource bank: Activity 6C *Sports stars* (*how much* and *how many*)

Study, practice & remember: Practice 2

Workbook: Grammar focus 2: *how much* and *how many*, page 32

Task (PAGES 56–57)

Describe a favourite place to eat

See *Teaching tips: Making tasks work*, page 23.

Preparation (PAGE 56)

Listening

WARM UP

In order to practise the vocabulary introduced so far in this unit, play Hangman. Draw a gallows on the board and dashes under it that correspond to the number of letters in the word you have chosen. Tell students it is a competition between you and the class. Invite them to call out letters that they think are in the word. If students need help with the letters, invite other students to help before you do.

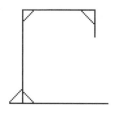

If the letter they have called out is in the word, write it over the appropriate dash. If it isn't, draw a part of the person who is to be hanged and write the letter on a different part of the board so that it isn't repeated.

Do this for a couple of words and, if your students like the activity, allow them to play it in groups.

1 Focus students' attention on the photos. Ask for a quick description of the different things they can see, including the type of food/cuisine. Students work in pairs to answer the questions.

2a 🎧 **6.4** Give students a minute to read through the sentences. Deal with any unknown vocabulary, e.g. *noodles*. Students listen and note the people next to the sentences. They check in pairs. Play the recording again if you think students would benefit from it.

ANSWERS:

1 J	**2** K	**3** T	**4** T	**5** K	**6** J

b Focus students' attention on the Useful language box. Give students a couple of minutes to read through the phrases. Students then listen to the recording again and tick the ones they hear.

ANSWERS:

The name of my favourite restaurant is … ✓
I like it because (I love fish and chips). ✓
It's a great place to go with (your friends). ✓
My favourite place to eat is/isn't … ✓
I love eating there because … ✓
You can sit outside and the view is really nice. ✓
It's always busy. ✓
It's very friendly. ✓
It's (not) expensive. ✓
The speciality is (*bun cha*). ✓
A typical dish is (*lomo saltado*). ✓
It's made with fish and vegetables. ✓

Task (PAGE 57)

Speaking

1a Give students enough time to think about their answers. Circulate and offer help as necessary.

Task: Speaking: Alternative suggestion

Give students a minute to read the points in the list in exercise 1a. Tell them you are going to talk about your favourite place to eat and they have to make notes for each of the points. Describe your favourite place, making sure you cover all of the points and use as many of the phrases from the Useful language box as possible. Ask students to work in pairs and compare the notes they made. Students then carry on with the activity as described.

This is a useful exercise because it serves as another model for students to follow and students often like to know more about their teacher's life outside the classroom.

---

b Remind students to use the phrases from the Useful language box when preparing their talk.

2 Students work in small groups to tell each other about their favourite place to eat. You might like to encourage students to take notes as they listen to help them in the next task.

3 Students work with a partner from a different group and report on what the people from their original group said.

Language live (PAGES 58–59)

Writing (PAGE 58)

Describe a place to eat

1a Focus students' attention on the restaurant card and the photo. Students work in pairs to discuss the questions.

ANSWER:

It's an Italian restaurant.

b Students complete the table using information from the restaurant card, the menu and the review. They check in pairs and then as a class.

ANSWERS:

Restaurant name: Giuseppe's
Address: 15 Market Street, Cardiff
Type of food / Typical dishes: pizza and pasta
Days/times open: Open Tuesday to Saturday, from 12–2 p.m. and 6–10.30 p.m.
Words to describe food/atmosphere: delicious, lively, busy, friendly, cheap

2 Complete the first gap with the class as an example, highlighting the information from the table in exercise 1b. Students work individually to complete the rest of the email then check as a class.

ANSWERS:

1 Giuseppe's	**2** Cardiff	**3** Italian	**4** £8.95	**5** busy
6 friendly	**7** efficient	**8** lively	**9** five	**10** 12–2
11 6–10.30				

3a Give students a few minutes to make notes. If they talked about a restaurant for the Speaking activity on page 57, they could think about the same restaurant again here to save time and give them more confidence.

b Tell students that they should use the email in exercise 2 as a model to follow. If you don't have time to do this in class, it can be done as homework.

Writing, exercise 3b: Additional suggestion

Instead of asking students to hand in their work to you, you could display it around the classroom and ask students to walk around and read each other's emails. As they read, they should decide which of the restaurants they would like to visit.

Speaking (PAGE 59)

Ordering food and drink

See *Teaching tips: Using the video material in the classroom*, page 24.

1 Focus students' attention on the menu and the photo. Use the picture to check the meaning of *muffin*. Review the pronunciation of the prices. Ask students if they drink coffee and what type they drink. Students quickly answer the two questions.

ANSWERS:

1 three   **2** three

2 ⏵ Students watch the DVD and answer the questions. They check in pairs.

ANSWERS:

1 Customer A orders a medium cappuccino and a chocolate muffin. It costs £3.95.
2 Customer B orders a large cappuccino and a banana muffin. It costs £4.20.

3a Students complete the phrases with one word. Tell students all of the phrases were in the DVD.

ANSWERS:

1 like	**2** Would	**3** else	**4** Can	**5** in	**6** That	**7** would
8 medium	**9** Thank	**10** welcome	**11** that	**12** change		

b ⏵ Students watch the key phrases and check their answers.

PRONUNCIATION

See *Teaching tips: Helping students with pronunciation*, page 22.

1 Write the sentences on the board. Play the first key phrase again and draw the intonation pattern above it. Play the second key phrase and ask students to do the same in their books, or ask one to come to the board and do it. Continue like this for the rest of the phrases. Elicit what type of intonation patterns are polite and friendly, and which ones are not. Generally, the intonation pattern should rise towards the end of the sentences to be polite and friendly. Demonstrate this by saying some of the phrases with a flat intonation pattern or with one falling towards the end. If you have a monolingual class, ask them if the pattern is the same or different in their language.

2 Drill the sentences chorally and individually, making sure to use polite, friendly intonation patterns.

Pronunciation: Helping students with intonation patterns

If students have difficulties repeating the intonation patterns, it might be useful to them to physically act out the pattern. Ask students to stand up when the intonation pattern rises and sit down when it falls. This serves to distract students from focusing too much on what they are saying and allows their voice to follow their bodies. If students are uncomfortable with standing up, you could ask them to move their hands up and down or even just their eyebrows.

4 Show the students how the flow chart works by roleplaying it with a stronger student. Students work in pairs to practise a conversation. When they have finished, they can swap roles. Circulate and monitor, especially for polite intonation patterns. You could ask a couple of pairs to perform their conversations for the class.

Speaking, exercise 4: Additional activity

If you have stronger students, you might want to develop this activity and make it more challenging by doing a roleplay of ordering food in a restaurant. Pre-teach *I'd like the bill, please.* and *Here you are, sir/madam*. Put students into groups of three and give students a menu or ask them to look at the menu for Giuseppe's on page 58. One student takes the role of waiter and the other two are customers. Students then work together to roleplay ordering food and eventually paying for it.

ADDITIONAL PRACTICE

Workbook: Writing: *Describe a favourite place to eat*, page 33; Language live: *Ordering food and drink*, page 33

Students can now do Progress test 3 on the Teacher's Resource Disc.

Study, practice & remember

(PAGES 148–149)

See *Teaching tips: Using the Study, practice & remember sections*, page 25.

Practice 1

ANSWERS:

1

1 There is(n't) an   2 There is(n't) a   3 There are(n't)
4 There is(n't) a   5 There are(n't)   6 There are(n't)

2

1 Is there any water in that bottle? Yes, there is.
2 Are there any beaches in your town? No, there aren't.
3 Is there any milk in the fridge? Yes, there is.
4 Are there any olives in the salad? No, there aren't.

3

1 some   2 any   3 some   4 any   5 any   6 some
7 any   8 any

Practice 2

ANSWERS:

1

1 many   2 many, are   3 much   4 many   5 much
6 much, is

2

1 many   2 plates   3 much   4 is   5 chicken
6 are   7 orange juice   8 there

Remember these words

ANSWERS:

1

1 sandwich   2 chicken   3 cheese   4 tomato
5 biscuit   6 juice

2

1 fish and chips   2 salt and pepper   3 tea and coffee
4 sweet and sour   5 knife and fork   6 bread and butter
7 food and drink   8 herbs and spices

OVERVIEW

PAGES 60–61

Grammar: Past simple: *was/were*

Pronunciation: Weak forms of *was/were*

Common European Framework: Students can participate in short conversations in routine contexts on topics of interest.

PAGES 62–63

Reading and vocabulary: Life events

Grammar: Past simple: regular and irregular verbs

Pronunciation: Regular past tense endings

Common European Framework: Students can talk simply about past times in familiar contexts.

PAGES 64–65

Listening: Jackie Kennedy Onassis

Vocabulary: Past time phrases

Common European Framework: Students can ask and answer questions about pastimes and past activities.

PAGES 66–67

Task: Tell a life story

Common European Framework: Students can provide a simple narrative.

PAGES 68–69

World culture: The Information Age

Common European Framework: Students can understand the main points in TV programmes that are clear and familiar.

Grammar focus 1 (PAGE 61)

Past simple: *was/were*

See *Teaching tips: Working with grammar*, page 20.

WARM UP

If your students are more or less the same age and come from the same country, elicit different TV programmes they used to watch as children. If your students are different ages, write a number of TV programmes on the board from different eras. Ask students: *Which ones did you like? Which ones did you hate? Why? What were they about?*

The aim of this warm up is to raise students' awareness of the need to be able to talk about the past, even if they don't know how to do it yet. Provide models of the Past simple but don't actively teach it yet.

1 Focus students' attention on the photos. Students work in pairs to discuss the questions then check as a class.

> **ANSWERS:**
>
> **top:** a footballer
> **centre (from left to right):** twins, a pop group, an ice skater
> **bottom (from left to right):** an actress, a composer

Culture notes

Wolfgang Amadeus Mozart (1756–1791) was born in present day Austria and soon showed himself to be a child prodigy. He was famous as a composer from the age of five and also played the piano and violin to the royalty of Europe. He is credited with revolutionising the way classical music was played.

The Jackson 5 were a band made up of five siblings from the Jackson family. They performed from 1964 through to 1990, but it was during the 1970s with Motown that they became phenomenally successful. Michael Jackson was the most famous member of the family, but Janet Jackson also enjoyed considerable solo success.

Mary-Kate and **Ashley Olsen** (b. 1986) are American actresses, fashion designers and businesswomen. The first show they starred in was called *Full House*, but the twins appeared in numerous TV shows during their childhood and teenage years and became amongst the wealthiest in their profession at a very young age.

Tara Lipinski (b.1982) is still the youngest person ever to win gold in figure skating at the Winter Olympics. She was only fifteen when she won in Nagano, Japan. She went on to win many more titles before she turned professional. She eventually retired from the sport due to injury. Nowadays, she is a sports commentator.

Pelé (b. 1940) was originally named Edison Arantes do Nascimento but took the nickname Pelé at school. He was born in Brazil and went on to become one of the best footballers ever. He won three world championships with Brazil and numerous titles with his club, Santos. He retired in 1977 after playing for several years with New York Cosmos.

Tatum O'Neil (b. 1963) is, to date, the youngest person ever to win an Oscar. At the age of ten she won Best Supporting Actress for her role in the film *Paper Moon*. She went on to appear in many more films both as a child and an adult. In 1986 she married the tennis star John McEnroe. However, the couple divorced in 1994 and since then Tatum has had drug problems.

2 🎧 **7.1** Students work individually to answer the questions in the quiz. They check in pairs before listening to the recording and checking as a class.

> **ANSWERS:**
>
> 1 a   2 b   3 b   4 b   5 a   6 a

Grammar focus 1, exercise 2: Alternative suggestion

Do this activity as a team quiz. Students keep their books closed and listen to you read the questions out one by one with the multiple-choice answers. Each team makes a note of its answers. Before listening to the recording, give all the teams the chance to read the questions just to make sure they have understood them properly. The team with the most correct answers is the winner.

GRAMMAR

be: past forms

1 Write the examples on the board or focus students' attention on the Grammar box. Refer students to the examples from the quiz.

2 Show students the use of *was/were born*. While this is an important language point, and one that students often have problems with, don't worry about the reasons for this construction. Simply teach it as a lexical phrase.

3 Students complete the gaps. Check as a class.

You may want to ask students to read Study 1 on page 150 for a more detailed explanation of the Past simple: *was/were*.

PRACTICE

Work through the example and do the first sentence with the class to make sure they know what to do. Students work individually to write sentences using the prompts. They check in pairs and then as a class.

ANSWERS:
1 Michael Jackson and his four brothers weren't in a jazz group. They were in a pop group.
2 The Olsen twins weren't born in 1976. They were born in 1986.
3 Tara Lipinski wasn't a gold medal winner at the Summer Olympics. She was a gold medal winner at the Winter Olympics.
4 Pelé wasn't the youngest player in the 1962 World Cup. He was the youngest player in the 1958 World Cup.
5 Tatum and Ryan O'Neal weren't in a film together in 1983. They were in a film together in 1973.

Practice, exercise 1: Additional activity

If you have a strong group of students, you might want to quickly introduce students to contrastive stress. Model the example *Mozart wasn't a singer. He was a composer.* Use exaggerated sentence stress to show the contrast between the false and true information. Students then work in pairs to correct the sentences in exercise 1 with appropriate stress patterns.

2a Students work individually to complete the questions. If they have any problems, refer them to the Grammar box.

b 🎧 **7.2** Students listen and check.

ANSWERS:
1 were   2 were   3 was, were   4 Were, were
5 was, were   6 was   7 were, were   8 Were, were

PRONUNCIATION

See *Teaching tips: Helping students with pronunciation*, page 22.

1 Remind students of some of the strong and weak forms you have looked at before, e.g. *does* on page 37 of the Students' Book. Elicit or model the strong form of *was* and *were* /wɒz/ and /wɜː/. Then model the weak forms /wəz/ and /wə/. Play recording 7.2 again and get students to decide which one is used.

2 Drill the sentences chorally and individually.

3 Students work in pairs to ask and answer the questions from exercise 2a. Circulate and monitor, paying attention to appropriate use of *was* and *were*.

ADDITIONAL PRACTICE

⇨ **Study, practice & remember:** Practice 1

Workbook: Grammar focus 1: *Past simple: was/were*, pages 34–35

Reading and vocabulary (PAGE 62)

Life events

See *Teaching tips: Working with lexical phrases*, page 21.

1a Check that students understand that *life events* means important things that happen in a person's life. Check the meaning of *meet someone, get married, leave school* and *start a business*. Give students a moment to put the life events in a logical order, but stress there is more than one correct answer.

b Students work in pairs to compare their orders.

POSSIBLE ANSWERS:
start school, study maths/history, leave school, go to university, graduate from university, get a job, move to a different town/country, meet someone, get married, have children, start a business

2 Students work in pairs to discuss the questions. In feedback, find out how many people like sharing information on social networking sites and how many like reading about other people.

3a Focus students' attention on the photos and the title of the article. Students work in pairs to discuss the questions.

b Students read the article quickly to check their ideas. They check in pairs and then as a class. After you have checked the answer, ask your students if they have heard of Pinterest or ever used it. If possible, it would be a good idea to have the website available to show students.

ANSWERS:
Ben Silbermann is interested in collecting things. He started Pinterest.

4 Elicit the answer for the first question as an example. Students continue to complete the information using the text. Check in pairs and then as a class.

ANSWERS:
1 1982   2 Iowa, USA   3 collecting stamps, leaves and insects
4 chemistry and political science at Yale University   5 moved to California   6 at Google in 2006   7 2008

5 Students work in small groups to discuss the questions. In feedback, ask each group to summarise what they spoke about.

ADDITIONAL PRACTICE

⇨ **Workbook:** Vocabulary: *Life events*, pages 36–37

Grammar focus 2 (PAGE 63)

Past simple: regular and irregular verbs

See *Teaching tips: Working with grammar*, page 20.

1 Focus students' attention on the four example sentences. Give students a moment to answer the two questions. They check in pairs and then as a class.

ANSWERS:
1 a, d   2 b, c

GRAMMAR

Regular verbs

1 Do the first one as an example, being very explicit about finding it in the article. Students find the other past forms of the verbs in the text.

> **ANSWERS:**
> loved, studied, graduated, moved, wanted, worked, decided, started

2 Elicit the answer from the class and write it on the board. Although there is a pronunciation section later on this page, it is a good idea to present the pronunciation of these verbs now.

> **ANSWER:**
> We add -ed to the infinitive.

Irregular verbs

3 Again, do the first one with the class as an example. Show how the construction is very different to the regular verbs. Students then continue to find the irregular past tense of the verbs. During feedback, check the pronunciation of both the present and the past forms. Direct students to page 175 for a list of irregular verbs.

> **ANSWERS:**
> felt, became, went, got, met, left, made, had, took

You may want to ask students to read Study 2 on page 150 for a more detailed explanation of the Past simple: regular and irregular verbs.

PRACTICE

1a Go through the example and do the first sentence with the class. Students work individually to write sentences about Ben Silbermann, using the article as a reference.

> **ANSWERS:**
> **1** As a child he loved collecting things.
> **2** He went to Yale University.
> **3** At university he studied chemistry and political science.
> **4** When he was 24, he moved to California.
> **5** He worked for Google for two years.
> **6** He left his job in 2008.
> **7** He got an apartment with two friends in 2009.
> **8** He started the online company Pinterest in 2010.

b Students work in pairs to try and remember six things about Ben's life.

2a Students work individually to write sentences about their own life events. Circulate and offer help as necessary.

b In pairs students ask and answer questions about their sentences.

PRONUNCIATION

See *Teaching tips: Helping students with pronunciation*, page 22.

1 🎧 **7.3** Focus students' attention on the audio script on page 169 or write the first two examples on the board. Play the first two words and get the students to count the number of syllables and mark these on the board. Play the recording and students count the syllables. Stop after each word, if necessary.

> **ANSWERS:**
> arrived = 2   loved = 1   needed = 2   waited = 2
> believed = 2   lived = 1   wanted = 2   liked = 1
> decided = 3   invented = 3   walked = 1   started = 2
> died = 1

2 Write on the board *wanted*, *waited*, *needed* and *decided*. Underline the final /t/ or /d/ sound and highlight that this is the only case in which we pronounce an extra syllable in the Past simple.

3 🎧 **7.4** Do the first two sentences with the whole class. Then play the recording and students write *a* or *b* to indicate in which sentence they hear the Past simple.

> **ANSWERS:**
> **1** a   **2** b   **3** b   **4** a   **5** b   **6** a   **7** b   **8** a

4 Drill the Past simple sentences chorally and individually.

3a Students work in pairs. Direct student A to page 134 and student B to page 136. Give students a few minutes to read and complete their information. Monitor and check the Past simple verb forms.

b In pairs, students then tell each other about the person.

ADDITIONAL PRACTICE

➡ **Resource bank:** Activity 7A *The history quiz* (Past simple: regular and irregular verbs); Activity 7B *Past tense bingo* (Past simple: irregular verbs)

Study, practice & remember: Practice 2

Workbook: Grammar focus 2: *Past simple: regular and irregular verbs*, page 37–38; Pronunciation: *Regular Past simple forms*, page 38

Listening (PAGE 64)

Jackie Kennedy Onassis

1 Focus students' attention on the photos. As a class, elicit a description of each one and suggestions for who is depicted. They then read the book extract to check their ideas.

Some students, especially younger ones, may not know who Jackie Kennedy Onassis was. If this is the case, just tell them she was a very famous American woman from the 1960s onwards.

> **ANSWERS:**
> **top:** Jackie and John Kennedy
> **centre:** Jackie Kennedy with Aristotle Onassis
> **bottom:** Jackie Kennedy

> **Culture notes**
> Jackie Kennedy Onassis (1929–1994) was also known as Jackie Kennedy and Jackie O, but was born Jacqueline Bouvier. She was married to President John F. Kennedy and so was the First Lady of the USA from 1961 to 1963. When JFK was assassinated in Dallas, she was in the car with him.
>
> During her time as First Lady she changed the way the role was perceived and became something of a fashion icon.
>
> Five years after JFK's death she married Aristotle Onassis, a Greek shipping magnate and one of the wealthiest men of his time. They remained married until he died in 1975.

2a Check the meaning of *fall* and *joke*. Students work individually to complete the sentences, but stress that they shouldn't worry if they don't know the answers. They check ideas in pairs.

b 🎧 **7.5** Students listen and complete the sentences or check their answers.

> **ANSWERS:**
> **1** was   **2** spent   **3** studied   **4** began, met   **5** fell, got
> **6** travelled, joked

3a 🎧 **7.6** Give students a minute to read through the sentences before they listen and put them in order. Play a second time if necessary. Check answers as a class.

ANSWERS:

a, b, f, d, g, h, e, c

b Students listen again for the date of each event from exercise 3a. They check in pairs and then as a class. Students might benefit from listening again and reading audio script 7.6 on page 170.

ANSWERS:

b 1968	**c** 1994	**d** 1968	**e** 1975	**f** 1968
g 1975	**h** 1975			

4 Give students a few minutes to think about a suitable person and to make notes about them. If you are short of time, this could be done as homework.

Vocabulary (PAGE 65)

Past time phrases

See *Teaching tips: Working with lexical phrases*, page 21.

1a Students work in pairs to complete the time phrases then check as a class. Make sure they understand they can use the words in the box more than once if necessary.

ANSWERS:

1 this summer / morning / afternoon / Tuesday / weekend / year
2 last summer / night / Tuesday / weekend / year
3 on my last birthday / Tuesday
4 yesterday morning / afternoon
5 when I was 12 years old / a child
6 20 years / ten minutes ago

Vocabulary, exercise 1a: Alternative suggestion

Write the beginnings of the six phrases on the board. Write the time phrases on large cards, which students can put on the board. Students work together to put the phrases in the correct place.

You could then use the same cards to put all of the phrases in order, as in exercise 1b.

---

b Students put the time phrases in the table in the correct category. Make sure students write the whole time phrase, for example *this morning*, and not just *morning*. Check in pairs and then as a class.

ANSWERS:

More than a year ago: last summer, last year, when I was 12 years old, when I was a child, 20 years ago

Less than a year ago but not this week: this summer, this year, on my last birthday

This week / Today: this morning, this afternoon, this weekend, this Tuesday, last night, last Tuesday, last weekend, on Tuesday, yesterday morning, yesterday afternoon, ten minutes ago

2a Give students a few minutes to read the questions in the quiz and think of two of their own. You could also use this time to let students prepare their answers.

b Students work in pairs to ask and answer the questions. In feedback, find out if anybody thought their partner said anything surprising.

ADDITIONAL PRACTICE

⟳ **Study, practice & remember:** Practice 3

Workbook: Vocabulary: *Past time phrases*, page 38

Task (PAGES 66–67)

Tell a life story

See *Teaching tips: Making tasks work*, page 23.

Preparation (PAGE 66)

Listening

WARM UP

In order to revise the language from the last class, take a few minutes at the beginning of this class, and future ones, to ask students questions about what they did yesterday, last weekend, last week, etc. Don't let this go on for too long and try not to let one person dominate unless they have a particularly interesting story to tell.

1 Focus students' attention on the photos. Students work in pairs to answer the two questions.

ANSWERS:

A a girl looking at a letter **B** people carrying a canoe **C** a man on a motorbike **D** a girl riding a bicycle **E** teenagers in school uniform **F** New York in winter

2a 🎧 **7.7** Students listen to the recording and put the photos in the correct order. Check in pairs and then as a class.

ANSWERS:

1 D	**2** B	**3** C	**4** E	**5** A	**6** F

b Give students enough time to read through the headings so they know what they have to listen for. Students listen and make notes then check in pairs. Play the recording again if necessary before checking answers as a class.

ANSWERS:

place/year of birth: London, 1972
hobbies as a child: playing sports
first job (what/where): teaching sports to children at a summer camp in America
travelling (who with/how): with her boyfriend on his motorbike
age graduated from university: 22
second job (what/where): teacher in a secondary school in the UK
when see Todd again: 13 years later
third job (what/where): nurse in a hospital in New York

3 Give students a few minutes to read through the phrases in the Useful language box. Students listen and tick the phrases they hear.

ANSWERS:

He/She was born in (London) in (1972). ✓
He/She didn't study very hard at school. ✓
He/She didn't go to university. ✓
As a child, (Alice) loved (sports). ✓
When he/she was 18, he/she left school. ✓
He/She graduated (from university) at the age of 22. ✓
In the end, he/she got a job (in a hospital). ✓

Preparation: Listening: Additional activity

Let students look at the Useful language box, then put up on a projector phrases with the prepositions or other words missing, for example *I was born ___ 1987. ___ a child, I liked playing tennis.* and see if students can complete them. Drill the phrases you think are most useful.

Task (PAGES 66–67)

Speaking

1 Give students a few moments to decide who they would like to talk about.

2 Students might need lots of preparation time for this activity. Circulate and offer help and encouragement as necessary. Suggest that students should use some photos if they have them available. Remind students to use the phrases from the Useful language box.

3 Students work in pairs to talk about the life story. Circulate and make a note of good language to praise later, as well as language that might need correcting.

Task: Speaking: Additional activity

Choose a strong student to start talking to you about his/her life. Pretend that you are bored and give no encouragement to the student. Stop and ask the students if you are a good listener, and why not.

Start again and this time keep eye contact, look interested and say things like *Mmm*, *Right*, and *Really?* Stop and have a discussion on the effect of showing interest. Ask students if this is different in their own cultures, and what sort of sounds or words they use to show that they are interested. Students then work on being an encouraging listener during the activity.

Share your task

The idea here is to give students a chance to 'perfect' their speaking in this context and provide them with a recording of a 'polished' version. This will provide extra motivation for students, as well as extra practice. Students can either make an audio or video recording, depending on how comfortable they feel and what equipment is available. Students could even use their mobile phones to do this. If possible, they'll need a quiet place to make their recording. Students can either record themselves during the lesson, or as homework and bring the recordings to the next class.

Additional idea:

• Students tell their own life stories.

World culture, Find out first:

To help your students prepare for the next class, go through the questions in exercise 2a on page 68. If necessary, discuss ideas for searching for this information on the internet, pointing out the search terms, and suggest other sources of information students could use. Encourage students to use English language websites as much as possible.

World culture (PAGES 68–69)

The Information Age

Culture Notes

Mark Zuckerberg (b.1984) is a computer programmer and internet entrepreneur. He is most famous for starting Facebook with his roommates while at university. Facebook has since become a worldwide phenomenon and has netted Zuckerberg an estimated wealth of over $10 billion.

Facebook started as a way for university students in the USA to connect with each other, but it quickly spread around the world. It has received a lot of criticism due to its privacy settings because a lot of people are worried about who can see information about them.

Find out first (PAGE 68)

1 Elicit some examples of social networking sites and put them on the board. Some examples might include *Facebook*, *Google +*, *Instagram*, *LinkedIn* and *Twitter*. Students then work in pairs to discuss the questions. In feedback, find out who in the class uses social networking sites the most/least.

2a Students work in pairs to try to guess whether the statements are true or false. If some students have not done the research, try to put them with a student who has done it.

b If you have access to the internet and students haven't been able to find the answer to some of the questions, ask students to go online and do some further research. Highlight the search terms. Circulate and offer help with vocabulary and try to encourage people to use only English language websites. Otherwise, tell your students the answers.

ANSWERS:

1 T	2 F	3 F	4 F	5 F

View (PAGE 68)

See *Teaching tips: Using the video material in the classroom*, page 24.

3a ▶ Check students understand the importance of *Harvard University* (one of the top universities in the USA) and *Silicon Valley* (an area where there are lots of IT companies). Students then watch the DVD and put the things in the order in which they see them.

ANSWERS:

1 Mark Zuckerberg with Barack Obama
2 the Queen of England's Facebook page
3 Harvard University
4 Mark Zuckerberg's first website
5 Silicon Valley, California
6 a magazine cover

b Give students time to read through all of the information in the box and the fact file so they know what they have to watch for. Stress to students that some of the information in the box is not needed. Students then watch the DVD and complete the fact file. If you feel students would benefit from it, play the DVD again. Students check in pairs and then as a class.

ANSWERS:

PERSONAL DETAILS
Name: Mark Zuckerberg
Born: 1984 in White Plains, New York
Studied **psychology** and computer science at **Harvard** University
Moved to Silicon Valley in **2004**
FACEBOOK FACTS
First website: thefacebook.com. It had **1 million** users after a few months.
Number of users worldwide: **800 million**
Number of users in UK: **30 million**
Most famous user in UK: **the Queen of England**
Yahoo tried to buy Facebook for $1 billion.
Microsoft tried to buy Facebook in 2007 for **$15 billion**.

World view (PAGE 69)

4a Do the first couple of sentences with the class as an example. Students then work individually to decide which of the statements they agree or disagree with.

b Students work in pairs to compare their answers.

Find out more ⓢ (PAGE 69)

5a Students work in pairs to make notes of any information they already know about the people in the box.

b If you have access to the internet at school, students work in pairs to research the people associated with the Information Age. Focus students' attention on the search terms that they should use. Circulate and help with new vocabulary as necessary and encourage students to use English language websites.

ANSWERS:
Tim Berners-Lee: Born in 1955 in London, UK. Studied physics at Oxford. Inventor of the World Wide Web.
Bill Gates: Born in 1955 in Seattle, USA. Studied at Harvard but left to found Microsoft.
Jimmy Wales: Born in 1966 in Alabama, USA. Studied at Auburn University. Co-founder of Wikipedia, the free online encyclopedia.
Sergey Brin: Born in 1973 in Moscow, Russia. PhD at Stanford University. Co-founder of Google.
Ashley Qualls: Born in 1990 in Michigan, USA. Founder of the website whateverlife.com.

Write up your research

6 Complete the first gap with the class as an example. Students then work individually to complete the rest of the gaps then check in pairs before checking answers as a class.

ANSWERS:
1 psychology and computer science   **2** Harvard   **3** 2003
4 facebook.com   **5** 2004

7 Students work individually to write up the research they did in exercise 5b using the template from exercise 6 as an example. This could be done in class or as homework.

Students can now do the Mid-course test on the Teacher's Resource Disc.

Study, practice & remember
(PAGES 150–151)

See *Teaching tips: Using the Study, practice & remember sections*, page 25.

Practice 1

ANSWERS:
1
  1 was, was   **2** was, was   **3** were, were   **4** weren't, was, was
  5 was, was   **6** were, was, wasn't, was
2
  1 Wolfgang Amadeus Mozart   **2** The Jackson 5
  3 Mary-Kate and Ashley Olsen, from the USA
  4 Tara Lipinski   **5** Pelé   **6** Tatum O'Neal
3
  1 was   **2** weren't   **3** were   **4** was   **5** was   **6** wasn't
  7 was   **8** was   **9** was   **10** was   **11** was   **12** weren't
  13 were

Practice 2

ANSWERS:
1
  1 arrived   **2** went   **3** made   **4** began   **5** had   **6** wanted
  7 became   **8** left   **9** got   **10** decided   **11** took   **12** died
2
  1 lived   **2** met   **3** went   **4** left   **5** wanted   **6** had
  7 studied   **8** stopped

Practice 3

ANSWERS:
1 The concert started half an hour **ago**.
2 I phoned Jim **yesterday** morning.
3 We were in class together **last** year.
4 She came to Spain **in** 2008.
5 We took this photo **when** we were on holiday.
6 My birthday is **on** 20th May.

Remember these words

ANSWERS:
1
  1 got   **2** studied   **3** left   **4** met, got   **5** started   **6** worked
2
  1 on   **2** ago   **3** at   **4** for   **5** on   **6** last   **7** ago   **8** on

OVERVIEW

PAGES 70–71

Vocabulary: Adjectives to describe stories

Grammar: Past simple: negative form

Common European Framework: Students can use simple expressions to talk about likes and dislikes.

PAGES 72–73

Vocabulary: Entertainment

Listening: *We Will Rock You* – a song and a musical

Grammar: Past simple: question form

Pronunciation: Linking of *did you* and *did your*

Common European Framework: Students can understand and extract the essential information from short recorded passages.

PAGES 74–75

Task: Talk about an evening in or out

Common European Framework: Students can describe events and say why they liked them or not.

PAGES 76–77

Speaking: Arranging an evening out

Writing: Arranging an evening out

Common European Framework: Students can communicate in simple tasks to get information and to discuss what to do next.

Vocabulary (PAGE 70)

Adjectives to describe stories

See *Teaching tips: Working with lexical phrases*, page 21.

WARM UP

To set the context, write *CINEMA* on the board and then underneath draw two columns with *advantages* and *disadvantages* at the top of each. Put students into groups and ask them to think of advantages or disadvantages of going to watch a film at the cinema. Some examples might include:

Advantages: a night out, comfortable, popcorn, good sound, big screen

Disadvantages: expensive, people talking, can't stop the film, boring

After a few minutes, ask students to write their ideas on the board in the two columns. Ask students if they prefer to go to the cinema or watch a film at home.

1a Quickly check the pronunciation of the film genres, especially the word stress in *comedy* /ˈkɒmədi/ and the sounds in *sci-fi* /ˈsaɪ faɪ/ and *historical* /hɪsˈtɒrɪkəl/. Students match the genres to the photos then check as a class.

> **ANSWERS:**
> **top:** action/adventure
> **centre (from left to right):** romance, historical
> **bottom:** action/romance/historical

b Elicit the names of example films for each genre.

Culture notes

Quantum of Solace (pictured top) was the 22nd James Bond film. It starred Daniel Craig as James Bond and was markedly less reliant on gadgets and more on life-like action scenes. There were also fewer humorous one-liners than in previous Bond films.

The film was well-received at the box office, breaking a number of records in the UK. The critics were more lukewarm to the film, but overall it was seen as more of a success than a failure.

Casablanca (pictured centre left) is an all-time classic that was released in 1942. It starred two of the biggest actors of its day in Humphrey Bogart and Ingrid Bergman and continues to be included on many people's list of all time best films.

As one of the characters says, the film is about choosing between 'love and virtue'. Rick Blaine, the main character, is forced to choose between the woman he loves and helping her husband continue to fight against the Nazis.

Elizabeth (pictured centre right) is a biographical film about Queen Elizabeth I (1533–1603). Cate Blanchett plays the role of Elizabeth and there are appearances by many other famous actors including Geoffrey Rush, Joseph Fiennes and Sir John Gielgud. The film was a critical success with numerous awards, including a nomination for Best Actress and Best Film at the Oscars.

The film tells the story of Elizabeth from the time she inherited the throne through to the beginning of England's Golden Age. This was a difficult time for Elizabeth as she contended with a divided nation and international competitors in France and Spain.

Titanic (pictured bottom) was released in 1997 and became an immediate critical and commercial success. It jointly holds, along with *Ben Hur* and *The Lord of the Rings: The Return of the King*, the record for the number of Oscars awarded to one film: 11. It was also the first film to gross over $1 billion and is the second highest grossing film of all time after *Avatar*.

The film is a fictionalised account of the sinking of the *Titanic* which, at the time, was the biggest ship ever and ironically had been dubbed 'unsinkable'.

2a Use gestures to show *sad*. Using the box, elicit the opposite of *sad* (*happy*). Students work individually to see how many other pairs of opposites they can find. They check in pairs and then as a class. During feedback, check the pronunciation of *frightening* /ˈfraɪtnɪŋ/, *exciting* /ɪkˈsaɪtɪŋ/ and *enjoyable* /ɪnˈdʒɔɪəbl/.

> **POSSIBLE ANSWERS:**
> sad / happy
> fast-moving / slow
> boring / exciting
> frightening / happy
> funny / serious

b Describe a film that you have seen recently using some of the adjectives in the box. Students work in pairs to talk about films they have seen. In feedback, find out what films your students would recommend and why.

> **Vocabulary, exercise 2b: Additional activity**
>
> Ask students to write a short paragraph for homework about a film they have seen recently.

ADDITIONAL PRACTICE

➡ **Workbook:** Vocabulary: *Adjectives to describe stories*, page 39

Grammar focus 1 (PAGE 71)

Past simple: negative form

See *Teaching tips: Working with grammar*, page 20.

1a Focus students' attention on the picture of Queen Cleopatra. Students work in pairs to answer the two questions. Elicit students' ideas and put them on the board. Take this opportunity to introduce some key vocabulary, e.g. *beauty, take a bath in milk, snake* and *poison*. If students don't mention these things, put them on the board and ask them if they know how they relate to Cleopatra.

b Students quickly read the text and check their ideas.

> **ANSWERS:**
> **1** more than 2,000 years ago   **2** beautiful, courageous, rich

GRAMMAR

Past simple: negative form

Go through the rules with the students. As you do, make sure to highlight:

- that we use *didn't* + the infinitive without *to*, i.e. *didn't live* NOT *didn't to live*.
- the short (contracted) form: *didn't*.
- that it is the same for all persons.

Point out that the structure is similar to the present simple:

he lives → *he doesn't live*

he lived → *he didn't live*

You may want to ask students to read Study 1 on page 152 for a more detailed explanation of the Past simple: negative form.

> **Grammar: Additional activity**
>
> Ask your students to go through the text on Cleopatra and underline all the examples of negative verbs in the past tense.

PRACTICE

1 Do the first one or two with your students as an example. Students work individually to write the sentences using the rest of the prompts. They check in pairs and then as a class.

> **ANSWERS:**
> People had baths, wore clothes, got married and wrote poems and plays. People didn't make phone calls, listen to the radio, drive cars or go to the cinema.

2a Do the first one or two with your students as an example. Students work individually to write sentences that are true about themselves. If your students are unsure what the irregular verb forms are, remind them to use the Verb list on page 175.

> **ANSWERS:**
> **1** I went out / didn't go out last night.
> **2** I watched / didn't watch a film last weekend.
> **3** I went / didn't go to the gym yesterday.
> **4** I saw / didn't see the TV news yesterday.
> **5** I listened / didn't listen to the radio this morning.
> **6** I read / didn't read a newspaper yesterday.
> **7** I played / didn't play a computer game yesterday.
> **8** I bought / didn't buy a magazine yesterday.
> **9** I drove / didn't drive a car yesterday.
> **10** I spoke / didn't speak English yesterday.

b Students work in pairs to compare their answers. In feedback, find out what students have in common.

> **Practice: Additional activity**
>
> Many countries have legendary or semi-legendary historical figures, for example King Arthur and Robin Hood from the UK. Ask students to do some research into such a figure from their country and to write a paragraph about him or her.

ADDITIONAL PRACTICE

➡ **Study, practice & remember:** Practice 1

  Workbook: Grammar focus 1: *Past simple: negative form*, page 40

Vocabulary (PAGE 72)

Entertainment

See *Teaching tips: Working with lexical phrases*, page 21.

1 Check students understand the phrases in the list, especially *to a musical* and *to a concert*. Students complete the phrases individually and check in pairs before checking answers as a class. Make sure to model the pronunciation with appropriate weak forms, e.g. *go to a musical* /gəʊ tuːwə ˈmjuːzɪkl̩/.

> **ANSWERS:**
> **1** cook   **2** go   **3** watch   **4** go   **5** go   **6** play
> **7** play/download   **8** go   **9** read   **10** go   **11** go   **12** go

2a Do the first two phrases as examples. Students work individually or in pairs to divide the phrases into the two categories.

> **ANSWERS:**
> **Evening in:** 1, 3, 6, 7, 9
> **Evening out:** 2, 4, 5, 8, 10, 11, 12

b Students think of more activities for an evening in or out. Elicit their suggestions and make sure they have used an appropriate verb.

> **POSSIBLE ANSWERS:**
> **Evening in:** play cards, talk to friends on Skype, watch TV
> **Evening out:** go to a pub/bar, go to a sports game, go to a shopping centre

3a Write on the board your five favourite activities. Give students a moment to do the same, with 1 being the activity they like most.

b Quickly tell your students about a couple of your favourite activities. Students work in pairs to compare their lists. In feedback, ask students to tell you about their partner's favourite activities.

> **Vocabulary, exercise 3b: Additional activity**
>
> Tell students about the last time you did one of these activities. Include extra information like who you did it with and if you had a good time. Ask students to tell each other about the last time they did some of the activities. This could lead into a writing exercise if you have time.

ADDITIONAL PRACTICE

➡ **Workbook:** Vocabulary: *Entertainment*, page 40

Listening (PAGES 72–73)

We Will Rock You – a song and a musical

WARM UP

Find a copy of the song *We Will Rock You* to play to your students. If you have access to the internet in class, you can find videos of the song online for students to watch. Tell students not to worry about the meaning of the song, just ask them general questions like *Do you like the song? Describe the song using the adjectives on page 70.* If students are interested in the lyrics, ask them to get them from the internet in their own time.

Culture notes

The West End is an area of London to the west of the historical centre. It has long been a favourite area of the rich and the elite with many important galleries, museums, bookshops, bars and clubs. Since the 19th century it has also been home to many theatres and so *West End theatre* has become a popular phrase to describe professional theatre staged in *Theatreland*. Along with New York's Broadway it is one of the two most important locations for theatre in the world. The area is often associated with big, blockbuster productions, especially long-running musicals like *The Lion King*, *Mamma Mia* and *Les Misérables*.

---

1 Introduce the topic by quickly asking students what types of music they like and what bands/artists they listen to. Find out when the last time they went to a concert or bought a CD was.

Focus students' attention on the photos and the short text. Check the meaning of *hit*. Give students a couple of minutes to answer the questions then check as a class.

ANSWERS:

1 Britain **2** Freddie Mercury **3** Brian May and Roger Taylor
4 Bohemian Rhapsody, We Are The Champions, We Will Rock You

2a 🎧 **8.1** Give students enough time to read through the topics before they listen. Stress to students that the listening is about a musical that uses Queen songs, not the band itself. Students check in pairs. If necessary, play the recording again before checking as a class.

ANSWERS:

b, f, g, e, c, h, d, a

b Ask your students to read the sentences to see if they can remember which ones are true or false. Students listen and check.

ANSWERS:

1 F (It came out in 1977.)
2 T
3 T
4 T
5 F (It's set in the future – 300 years from now.)
6 T
7 F (It's still playing in the same theatre in London.)
8 F (It went to Japan in 2005.)

Listening, exercise 2: Additional activities

a Direct your students to audio script 8.1 on page 170. Ask your students to listen again and underline all the past simple verb forms. Don't focus on the question forms yet, but if students do notice them, it will help raise awareness for the next grammar activity. During feedback, check the present form of the verbs, especially the irregular ones and remind your students of the Verb list on page 175. Make sure students pronounce the regular *-ed* past forms correctly.

b If your students are interested in music, encourage them to find information about their favourite bands or artists and present it to the class. You could also ask students to bring in the lyrics of their favourite songs and put them on the walls around the classroom.

3 Students work in pairs to discuss the questions.

Grammar focus 2 (PAGE 73)

Past simple: question form

See *Teaching tips: Working with grammar*, page 20.

1a Do the first question with the class as an example. Students work individually to order the words then check in pairs.

b 🎧 **8.2** Students listen and check.

ANSWERS:

1 When did the song come out?
2 Why did he write the song?
3 Did Brian May write the musical?
4 When did the musical come out?
5 Did the musical get good reviews?
6 Where did the musical first go on tour?

GRAMMAR

Past simple: question form

Read through the rules with your students using the example sentences in the Grammar box and the sentences from the previous exercise. Make sure you highlight:

- that we don't use the past form of the verb in questions, i.e. NOT *When did he died?*

- we use short answers when we answer *yes/no* questions, for example *Yes, they did.* and NOT *Yes, they made a lot of money.*

Point out that the structure is similar to the Present simple:

he lives → Does he live?

he lived → Did he live?

You may want to ask students to read Study 2 on page 152 for a more detailed explanation of the Past simple: question form.

PRACTICE

1a Show the example to the class and do the first question together. Students work individually to add *did* to the rest of the questions then check in pairs.

b 🎧 **8.3** Students listen and check. During feedback, make sure you model the pronunciation of *did* and *you/your* correctly.

ANSWERS:

1 Where did you live when you were a child?
2 Did you read a lot of books when you were a child?
3 Did your parents read books to you when you were a child?
4 When did you start learning English?
5 Did you watch a lot of TV last weekend?
6 When did you last go to a concert?
7 What music did you last listen to?
8 Did you go for a walk last weekend?
9 When did you last see a really good show?

PRONUNCIATION

See *Teaching tips: Helping students with pronunciation*, page 22.

1 Model the strong pronunciation of *did*, *you* and *your*: /dɪd/, /juː/ and /jɔː/. Then model the weak form of *did you* and *did your*: /dɪdʒə/. The pronunciation is the same in both cases but it is the context that makes it clear. Play the recording of the questions again and ask students to identify which pronunciation is used.

2 Drill the questions chorally and individually.

2a Model the activity with a stronger student by asking and answering the first couple of questions and giving extra information in your answers. Students work in pairs to ask and answer the questions in exercise 1a. Circulate and monitor for correct pronunciation.

b Students report back to the class on what their partner said. If students make mistakes with the past forms, encourage others in the class to help correct them instead of just correcting them yourself.

Practice, exercise 2: Additional activity

This activity can be done at the end of this class to activate the language, or at the beginning of the next class to set a context and review language.

Class survey. Write on the board: *When did you last ... ?* Elicit different ways to complete the question in the context of entertainment, for example *go to a concert*, *go to the cinema*, *play a computer game*, *eat at a restaurant*, *read a great book*. You should aim to have about five questions on the board. Then elicit a number of responses and write them on the board, e.g. *today*, *last night*, *yesterday*, *last week*, *last month*, *last year*, *a long time ago*.

Put students into groups with the same number of people as there are questions, i.e. if there are five questions, the groups should have five people. The groups allocate one question per person, and then all the students should ask as many people in the class as possible their question, and make a note of the answer.

After a few minutes of asking and answering questions, the groups get back together again and share their results with each other. For example, *Two people went to a concert last week, three people went to a concert last month and one person went to a concert a long time ago.*

If the class is interested in this activity, you could ask them to present their findings with graphs and tables.

ADDITIONAL PRACTICE

Resource bank: Activity 8A *Looking back* (Past simple: question form); Activity 8B *John Wayne* (Past simple: question form); Activity 8C *Safe, at last!* (Past simple: question form)

Study, practice & remember: Practice 2

Workbook: Grammar focus 2: *Past simple: question form*, pages 41–42; Pronunciation: *Linking*, page 42

Task (PAGES 74–75)

Talk about an evening in or out

See *Teaching tips: Making tasks work*, page 23.

Preparation (PAGE 74)

Listening

1a Work as a class to describe the photos. Make a note of interesting vocabulary and ideas to put on the board. Students quickly identify the activities in the box they can see in the photos.

b Students categorise the activities into *an evening in* or *an evening out*.

ANSWERS:

an evening in: stay in and read a book, watch a film on TV, have a dinner party
an evening out: go to the cinema, go to a restaurant, go to the theatre, go for a walk, go to a concert

c As a class, students brainstorm other activities to add to the lists.

2a 🎧 8.4 Students listen and decide if each person is talking about an evening in or out.

ANSWERS:

Lauren: evening out   **Daniel:** evening in   **Karl:** evening out

b Focus students' attention on the table. Give students time to read the table and identify the missing information so they know what to listen for. Play the recording again for students to complete the table.

ANSWERS:

	Lauren	Daniel	Karl
What?	jazz concert	dinner party	cinema
Who with?	friend (Kate)	four friends from work	girlfriend
Where?	small café in the centre of town	at home	local cinema
Good or bad?	really good	good (fun)	really bad

3a Elicit a word to complete the first question from the class as an example. Students complete the rest of the questions individually then check in pairs.

b Focus students' attention on the Useful language box. Students check their answers to exercise 3a with the phrases in the box.

ANSWERS:

1 last   2 with   3 get   4 Was   5 did   6 there
7 think   8 did

4 Students listen to the recording from exercise 2a again and write L, D or K next to the phrases in the box that they hear.

ANSWERS:

a Questions
When did you last have a really good/bad evening – in or out? – L, D, K
What did you do/cook? – L, D, K
Who did you see? – L
Who did you go with? / Who was there? – L, D, K
How did you get there? – L
What did you think of it? / Was it good? – L, K
Where did you see it? / Where was it? – L, K

b Answers
I went to (a fantastic concert). – L
I saw a band (called The Ravens). – L
It was brilliant / funny / sad / exciting / good. – L
I had a dinner party. – D
I didn't really enjoy it. – K
It was awful/terrible/boring – K

Task (PAGES 74–75)

Speaking

1   Give students a few minutes to think about a good or bad evening they have had. Encourage students to use the phrases from the Useful language box. Circulate and offer help and encouragement.

2a Students work in pairs to ask and answer questions about their good or bad evening. Monitor for examples of good language to praise and language that needs correcting.

b   Students work in different pairs to report what their original partner said.

Task: Speaking: Additional activity

If students have enjoyed talking about a good or a bad evening, you might like to extend this activity into a writing exercise. Ask students to write about their experiences as homework.

Share your task

The idea here is to give students a chance to 'perfect' their speaking in this context and provide them with a recording of a 'polished' version. This will provide extra motivation for students, as well as extra practice. Students can either make an audio or video recording, depending on how comfortable they feel and what equipment is available. Students could even use their mobile phones to do this. If possible, they'll need a quiet place to make their recording. Students can either record themselves during the lesson, or as homework and bring the recordings to the next class.

Language live (PAGES 76–77)

Speaking (PAGE 76)

Arranging an evening out

See *Teaching tips: Using the video material in the classroom*, page 24.

1   Students work in pairs to discuss the questions. In feedback, find out if the class has a favourite place to go to.

2a ▶ Tell students that they are going to watch Andy arranging an evening out at a pizza restaurant. Make sure students read the questions before they watch the DVD. Students check in pairs and then as a class.

ANSWERS:

1 Friday
2 Each person says yes then changes their mind and says no.

b   Check students remember how many people said no (3). Students watch again and make a note of the reasons why the people said no. Ask them if they think these are the real reasons why people can't go.

ANSWERS:

First woman: very busy
Man and second woman: dance class, birthday
These are probably *not* the real reasons for people saying they can't go. Each person only says no when they find out that their boss Peter is also going!

3a Remind students of the pronunciation of *can't* /kɑːnt/. Complete the first two sentences with the class as examples. Students complete the rest individually then check in pairs.

b   ▶ Students watch and check.

ANSWERS:

1 free   2 about   3 good   4 can't, busy   5 time   6 Would
7 go   8 idea   9 love   10 sorry

PRONUNCIATION

See *Teaching tips: Helping students with pronunciation*, page 22.

1   Students listen to the key phrases and focus on the pronunciation.

Pronunciation, exercise 1: Alternative suggestion

Instead of asking students to listen and think about the pronunciation, give students something specific to focus on. This will depend on your students' strengths and weaknesses, but you could ask them to focus on sentence stress, intonation patterns, weak forms or certain individual sounds.

2   Drill the key phrases chorally and individually.

4a Elicit some phrases that could be used for the first couple of steps in the flow chart. Give students a few minutes to prepare the rest of the conversation. Circulate and help as necessary.

b   Students work in pairs to practise their conversations. In feedback, ask some pairs to perform their conversations for the class.

Writing (PAGE 77)
Arranging an evening out

Culture notes

Until the 1950s, restaurants in the UK were very traditional and conservative. There were roughly four different types: expensive places serving quality meat and vegetables, cheap places for single working men, tea houses that served tea and snacks, and fish-and-chip shops that were especially popular on Fridays due to religious traditions that stated you shouldn't eat meat on that day.

Although other types of restaurant existed, for example the first Indian restaurant opened in 1809 and the first Chinese one in 1907, they were usually only popular with immigrants. From the late 1950s onwards there were more and more immigrants arriving in the UK who wanted a taste of home. There were also more British people travelling abroad on holidays who enjoyed different types of cooking when they were back home. In 1969 Pizza Express was the first restaurant to bring pizza to the UK. The late 1960s and early 1970s saw Chinese restaurants popping up all over the UK, and in the late 1970s these were followed by Indian restaurants. It turned out that British people liked the different, spicy foods available and so many other types of restaurant soon followed in their wake.

Today, the most common type of restaurant to be found in almost any town is Indian and Chicken Tikka Masala is reputed to be the most popular dish in the country.

In response to the competition, there has also been an improvement in food served in pubs, known as *pub grub*. You can find traditional fish and chips, and many other types of traditional British food. Some pubs have chosen to specialise in their food and have become known as *gastropubs*.

1 To set the scene, ask students: *Do you like sending text messages? How many text messages do you send a day? Do you think you send too many text messages? Do you prefer to send a text message or make a call?* Tell students they are going to read some text messages between Ahmed and Bianca, who are two English students. They are trying to arrange an evening out with their class. Students work individually to put the messages in the correct order then check in pairs before checking answers as a class.

ANSWERS:

b, e, a, d, g, f, c

2 Students use the information from the text messages to complete the email.

ANSWERS:

1 Friday   2 Viva Italia   3 Bold   4 7   5 in front of

3a Ask students about good restaurants in their local area. Focus students' attention on the three adverts for restaurants. Ask them if they would prefer to go to a real local restaurant or one of the ones in the adverts.

b Students work individually to write an email inviting their classmates to an evening out. Encourage them to use the model in exercise 2 and the example language provided in the box in this exercise. They should also feel free to use their imagination and make up any information they are not sure of.

ADDITIONAL PRACTICE

Workbook: Language live: *Arranging an evening out*, page 43, Writing: *Arranging an evening out*, page 43

Students can now do Progress test 4 on the Teacher's Resource Disc.

Study, practice & remember
(PAGES 152–153)

See *Teaching tips: Using the Study, practice & remember sections*, page 25.

Practice 1

ANSWERS:

1
1 didn't play   2 didn't listen   3 didn't drive   4 didn't eat
5 didn't watch   6 didn't wear   7 didn't drink   8 didn't go

2
1 He didn't want to go out for dinner.
2 I didn't walk to work yesterday morning.
3 She didn't play the piano when she was a child.
4 I didn't work all day yesterday.
5 He didn't talk to me on the phone.
6 They didn't start the class at 6 o'clock.
7 She didn't listen to the radio at breakfast.
8 We didn't finish work early yesterday.

3
1 Tina didn't read the letter this morning.
2 Jillian didn't leave school last year.
3 Sebastian didn't go to work last night.
4 They didn't give me a present.
5 We didn't drive here.
6 They didn't have breakfast this morning.
7 I didn't write that email.
8 Stacey didn't do her homework last night.

Practice 2

ANSWERS:

1
1 Did you walk to work this morning?
2 When did your parents buy their house?
3 Where did your father work?
4 What did you do last night?
5 Did John go swimming today?
6 Did you have a good weekend?
7 Where did she go to university?
8 Did your sisters go to school with you?
9 When you were ten did you like sport?
10 Did the book get good reviews?

2
1 was your last holiday?   2 did you go?   3 did you go with?
4 did you get there?   5 did you stay?   6 did you see?
7 did you think of it?   8 did you buy?

3
1 b   2 b   3 a   4 b   5 c   6 a

Remember these words

ANSWERS:

1
1 sad   2 exciting   3 frightening   4 funny   5 fast-moving
6 boring   7 enjoyable   8 romantic

2
1 went   2 went   3 went   4 downloaded   5 watched
6 went   7 played   8 read   9 cooked

3
1 historical   2 comedy   3 drummer   4 reviews
5 performance   6 sci-fi   7 audience   8 guitarist

OVERVIEW

PAGES 78–79

Vocabulary: Describing objects

Grammar: Comparative adjectives

Common European Framework: Students can use simple descriptive language to make brief statements about and compare objects and possessions.

PAGES 80–81

Grammar: Superlative adjectives

Common European Framework: Students can use simple structures correctly.

PAGES 82–83

Vocabulary: Shops and services

Reading: Top five unusual shops

Common European Framework: Students can understand short texts on everyday subjects and respond appropriately.

PAGES 84–85

Task: Choose souvenirs from your country

Common European Framework: Students can perform and respond to basic language functions, such as information exchange, and express opinions and attitudes in a simple way.

PAGES 86–87

World culture: Famous markets

Common European Framework: Students can follow changes of topic of factual TV news items, and form an idea of the main content.

Vocabulary (PAGE 78)

Describing objects

See *Teaching tips: Working with lexical phrases*, page 21.

WARM UP

Tell students that you have a problem and you need their help. All of your family and friends have a birthday in the next two weeks and you can't think of anything to get them as a present. Write a list of your friends and family on the board (to save time you might like to do this before the class) with basic information, for example: *Dad, 52, likes sport, hates TV; Sarah, sister, 30, has a new house; Helena, 24, best friend, reads, loves films*. In pairs or small groups, students suggest appropriate birthday presents for each of your family and friends. In feedback, decide what would be the best present for each one.

1a Focus students' attention on the photos. Check students know the names of each of the items and the pronunciation, especially *jewellery* /ˈdʒuːəlri/.

Look at the adjectives in the box and check the pronunciation, especially *fashionable* /ˈfæʃnəbəl/ and *uncomfortable* /ʌnˈkʌmftəbəl/.

Look at the photo of the car as a class and elicit adjectives that could be used to describe it. Students work individually to match the adjectives to the other photos.

POSSIBLE ANSWERS:

The jewellery is expensive, old and unusual.
The shoes are pretty, stylish and uncomfortable.
The bag is expensive, fashionable and unusual.
The watch is cheap, fashionable and easy to use.
The scooter is easy to use, economical and stylish.

b Students work in pairs to compare their answers. Check ideas as a class.

2 Students work in pairs to discuss the questions.

Vocabulary, exercise 2: Additional activity

Provide the model question: *Which one do you want for your birthday?* Drill the pronunciation of the question. Ask students to talk to everyone in the class to do a class survey to find out which item is the most popular.

ADDITIONAL PRACTICE

➡ **Workbook:** Vocabulary: *Describing objects*, page 44

Grammar focus 1 (PAGE 79)

Comparative adjectives

See *Teaching tips: Working with grammar*, page 20.

WARM UP

To set the context, ask students about their online shopping habits. Ask questions like *Do you often buy things online? What do you buy online? Is there anything you would never buy online? What was the last thing you bought online? Is it safe to buy things online?*

1 Check the meaning of *leather* /ˈleðə/ and *faux leather* /fəʊ ˈleðə/. Tell students to look at the two jackets and decide which one they would prefer. During feedback, ask for reasons.

2 Students work in pairs to answer the questions. Check as a class.

ANSWERS:

1 A   2 A   3 Students' own answers   4 B
5 Students' own answers

GRAMMAR

Comparative adjectives

1 Write the sentences on the board and ask students to complete the gaps, using the language from the activity they have just done. Check that they understand the meaning of the comparative form.

ANSWERS:

2 more   3 A/B, more, A/B

2 Write *new* on the board and elicit how many syllables the word has. Elicit the comparative form *newer*. Ask students to find another one syllable word and its comparative form from the previous exercise (*big → bigger*). Write *expensive* on the board and then go through the same process. Finally, write *easy* and elicit the comparative form. Try to elicit other adjectives from students that end in *-y*. Point out the irregular adjectives for *good* and *bad*.

You may want to ask students to read Study 1 on page 154 for a more detailed explanation of comparative adjectives.

See *Teaching tips: Helping students with pronunciation*, page 22.

1 🎧 **9.1** Play the recording or model the phrases and sentences yourself. Then write the phrases and sentences on the board and mark the stress.

2 Drill the phrases chorally and individually.

PRACTICE

Do the example on the board with the class. Students then work individually to write sentences to compare the items in the photos. Circulate and monitor.

POSSIBLE ANSWERS:

1
Dress B is more unusual than dress A.
Dress A is prettier than dress B.
2
Car D is faster than car C.
Car D is more expensive than car C.
Car C is more stylish than car D.
3
Camera E is smaller than camera F.
Camera E is easier to use than camera F.
Camera E is cheaper than camera F.

Practice: Alternative suggestion

If possible, bring in some real items that students can see and touch, for example two mobile phones, two pairs of trainers, two watches, two books. Provide labels with basic information, similar to the information in exercise 1. Students then walk around the room, look at the items and write their sentences. This will provide a different focus for the activity and will seem more authentic to the students.

Practice, exercise 1: Additional activities

In a strong elementary class, students can compare their sentences from exercise 1 in pairs. Alternatively, they can talk about other topics as a follow-up, for example *tablets* and *PCs*, *two different TV channels*, *vegetables* and *French fries*, *two famous actors*, *two local football teams*, etc.

ADDITIONAL PRACTICE

➡ **Resource bank:** Activity 9A *New Year's Eve* (Comparative adjectives)

Study, practice & remember: Practice 1

Workbook: Grammar focus 1: *Comparative adjectives*, pages 44–45; Pronunciation: *Stressed syllables*, page 45

Grammar focus 2 (PAGES 80–81)

Superlative adjectives

See *Teaching tips: Working with grammar*, page 20.

Culture notes

Harrods is one of the most famous department stores in the world. It was opened in 1851 on its current site in Knightsbridge in London by Charles Henry Harrod. Today it is the biggest shop in Europe with 90,000 m² of floor space. The next biggest shop in Europe is the KaDeWe in Berlin with 60,000 m² of floor space.

The motto of Harrods is *Omnia Omnibus Ubique – All Things for All People Everywhere* and they claim to be able to get anything you want in the world, so long as it is legal. The shop itself is a popular tourist attraction with many people visiting and buying one of the shopping bags with the famous Harrods logo.

Macy's opened in New York in 1858, but in 1902 moved its flagship store to 34th Street and Broadway where it remains today. Since that time it has grown to be a New York and American institution. Unlike Harrods, most major cities in the USA have a branch of Macy's, but it is still the original one in New York which is the most iconic.

As well as its mid- to up-market stores, Macy's is famous for its Thanksgiving Parade, which has been running since 1924. It is well known for its huge balloons of famous children's characters that parade around New York at the end of November each year.

1a Set the context by asking how many people like shopping. Check the meaning of *department store*. Ask if anybody has heard of or been to any of the shops. Students then work in pairs to look at the photos and discuss the three stores.

b Students quickly read the article and find out why the Shinsegae department store is famous. They check in pairs and then as a class.

ANSWER:

It's the biggest department store in the world.

2 Check the pronunciation of the numbers. Students then read the article again to find out what the numbers refer to. They check in pairs and then as a class.

ANSWERS:

a the number of shoppers who visited it on its opening day
b the square metres of shopping space
c the difference between Macy's in New York and Shinsegae
d the number of floors

3 Students work in pairs to discuss the questions.

GRAMMAR

Superlative adjectives

1 Write the sentences on the board and ask students to complete the gaps. They can look back at the article to find the language. Check they understand the meaning of the superlative form.

ANSWERS:

1 biggest   **2** most expensive

2 Write *fast* on the board and elicit how many syllables the word has. Elicit the superlative form *the fastest* and write it on the board next to *fast*. Write *expensive* on the board and elicit *the most expensive* and write this on the board also. Finally, write *easy* and elicit the superlative form *the easiest*.

Students complete the superlative adjectives, from memory if possible, and then check in pairs.

3 Refer students to the text to check their answers. Point out the irregular superlative for *good* and ask students if they know the superlative for *bad* (*the worst*).

ANSWERS:

2 the newest   **3** the busiest   **4** the most beautiful
5 the best

> **Potential problem with the pronunciation of *the***
>
> There can be a temptation among some students to stress
> the definite article *the* when using superlatives. Point out to
> students that we normally only use the weak form /ðə/, unless
> we are trying to be emphatic.

You may want to ask students to read Study 2 on page 154 for a
more detailed explanation of superlative adjectives.

PRACTICE

1a Focus students' attention on the quiz. Complete the first question
with the class as an example. Point out that they shouldn't worry
about the answers yet, they just need to complete the questions.
Students check in pairs.

b 🎧 **9.2** Students listen and check.

> **ANSWERS:**
>
> **1** the most expensive   **2** fastest   **3** the most famous
> **4** the most popular   **5** the richest   **6** the highest   **7** the tallest
> **8** the biggest

2a Students work in pairs to answer the questions.

b 🎧 **9.3** Students listen and check.

> **ANSWERS:**
>
> **1** c   **2** a   **3** c   **4** a   **5** b   **6** a   **7** b   **8** c

> **Practice, exercise 2b: Additional activity**
>
> If your students all come from the same country, ask them to prepare
> a similar quiz about their own country instead of the world. Some of
> the topics could be the same, for example *Who was the most popular
> band in (country) in the 20th century?* or *Who is the richest person in
> (country)?*, but students will also need to think of their own ideas.
>
> This quiz could be prepared by a group of students in class or it could
> be done by individuals as homework. Once it has been completed, ask
> other students to try to do the quiz to find out who knows the most
> about their country.

3a Do the example with the class. Students work individually or in pairs
to write five more questions. Circulate and offer help as necessary.
Pay attention to superlative forms, question forms and appropriate
Wh- question words.

> **ANSWERS:**
>
> Who is the oldest person in your family?
> Which is the best restaurant in your town?
> Who is the untidiest / most untidy person you know?
> Which/Where is the most beautiful place in your country?
> Who is the tallest person in your class?
> Who is the most popular singer from your country?
> What is the newest thing in your bag?

b Students work in small groups to ask and answer the questions.
Encourage students to offer extra information whenever possible.

ADDITIONAL PRACTICE

➡ **Resource bank:** Activity 9B *A superlative survey* (Superlative adjectives)
   Study, practice & remember: Practice 2
   Workbook: Grammar focus 2: *Superlative adjectives*, pages 46–47

Vocabulary (PAGE 82)
Shops and services

See *Teaching tips: Working with lexical phrases*, page 21.

1a Focus students' attention on the photos and quickly get a description
of what they can see. Don't worry if students can't give you a
description of everything yet. Students then work either individually
or in pairs to match the words in the box to the photos. Check as a
class. During feedback, drill the pronunciation as necessary.

> **ANSWERS:**
>
> **A** a clothes shop   **B** a bookshop   **C** a baker's   **D** a butcher's
> **E** an optician's   **F** an estate agent's   **G** a post office
> **H** a pharmacy   **I** a shoe shop   **J** a dry-cleaner's
> **K** a hairdresser's   **L** a gift shop

b Ask the whole class the first question and elicit an answer. Students
then work in pairs to answer the questions. Encourage students to
guess the meanings of any unknown words from the context and
deal with any problems during feedback.

> **ANSWERS:**
>
> **1** a post office   **2** a butcher's   **3** a baker's   **4** an estate agent's
> **5** a gift shop   **6** a hairdresser's   **7** a shoe shop   **8** a clothes shop
> **9** a bookshop   **10** an optician's   **11** a pharmacy
> **12** a dry cleaner's

2 As an example, ask a couple of students about the last time they
visited some of the places from exercise 1a. Students then work in
pairs to ask and answer questions.

> **Vocabulary, exercise 2: Additional activity**
>
> For further speaking practice, establish the situation of a tourist
> needing to buy something and see if the students can suggest a
> question. Introduce: *Excuse me. Can you help me? Where can I buy a …
> near here?* and get students to ask and answer in pairs. Circulate and
> help as needed.

ADDITIONAL PRACTICE

➡ **Resource bank:** Activity 9C *Shopping crossword* (Shops and services)
   Workbook: Vocabulary: *Shops and services*, page 47

Reading (PAGE 83)

1a Students work in pairs to discuss the questions.

b Check the meaning of *the coolest place* and *designer clothes*.
Students then read the article to answer the questions. They check in
pairs and then as a class.

> **ANSWERS:**
>
> El Ateneo Grand Splendid in Buenos Aires is the biggest.
> The Old Curiosity Shop is the smallest.
> L'Usine in Ho Chi Minh City, Vietnam is probably the coolest place to
> be.
> Senbikiya in Tokyo has the most perfect products.
> Beacon's Closet in New York has the cheapest designer clothes.

2 Students work individually to decide if the statements are true or
false. They check in pairs and then as a class. During feedback, ask
students to justify their answers with evidence from the text.

ANSWERS:

1 F (You can only buy fruit.)
2 F (They cost $82 a box.)
3 T
4 F (Dickens first wrote about it in 1841.)
5 F (It keeps its old, historical style inside.)
6 T
7 F (It was originally a theatre.)
8 F (It was a factory.)

3 Students work in pairs to discuss the questions.

Reading, exercise 3: Additional activities

a Ask students if they have any famous, strange, beautiful or interesting shops in their home town. As students talk about the shops, elicit/teach any useful vocabulary and write it on the board. Get students to roleplay a situation in a Tourist Information Office, telling a tourist about a shop in their city/country.

b For homework, ask students to write a paragraph about their favourite shop or a strange shop that they know of. When students give you their writing, make sure you provide a comment instead of just marking it. Writing something like *This sounds like a wonderful place to go shopping on a Saturday afternoon.* or *This is one of the strangest shops I have heard of!* can make all the difference to students and encourage them to write more in the future.

Task (PAGES 84–85)

Choose souvenirs from your country

See *Teaching tips: Making tasks work*, page 23.

Preparation (PAGE 84)

Listening

1 Focus students' attention on the photos. They then work in pairs to discuss the questions. Check answers as a class and ask students for ideas for which country the souvenirs come from.

ANSWERS:

A a silk scarf   B a wool scarf   C a bottle of maple syrup
D a toy camel   E Matryoshka dolls

2 Students read the short text quickly to answer the questions. Check as a class.

ANSWERS:

They're from the UK. They like meeting people from different countries and collecting souvenirs from all over the world.

3a 🎧 9.4 Tell students to listen for the souvenirs that the guests will take with them. They check in pairs and then as a class.

ANSWERS:

a silk shirt, jewellery, a toy camel, Matryoshka dolls

b Focus students' attention on the table. Give them a minute to read the table and note the information they need to listen for. Students listen again and complete the information before checking in pairs. Play the recording again if you think students would benefit from it. Check as a class.

ANSWERS:

	Where does he/she live?	What souvenirs does he/she choose?	How does he/she describe the souvenir?
Tina	Thailand	a silk shirt	fantastic, beautiful, colourful
Lee	Thailand	jewellery	better
Karim	Egypt	a toy camel	interesting, not expensive
Oksana	Ukraine	Matryoshka dolls	typical, good, fun, pretty

c Focus students' attention on the Useful language box and give them a minute to read the phrases. Students listen to the recording again and tick the phrases they hear.

ANSWERS:

What do you think? ✓
Why don't we buy a (silk shirt)? ✓
Have you got any ideas for (the children)? ✓
What did you choose for (the little girl / her)? ✓
(Thailand) is famous for (silk products) ... so ... ✓
I think a good souvenir from (Thailand) is (a silk shirt). ✓
(A silk shirt) is a fantastic souvenir. ✓
What's a good souvenir from your country? ✓
That's very typical of (Thailand). ✓
I think jewellery is better, because ... ✓
(Matryoshka dolls) are very typical of (Ukraine). ✓
I think it's a very nice souvenir for (a child). ✓

Task (PAGE 85)

Speaking

1 Give students a few minutes to think of souvenirs to give to the different people from the Taylor family. Circulate and offer help and advice as necessary.

2 Students work in pairs. If you have a monolingual class, students work together to compare their ideas and decide on the best souvenirs. If you have a multilingual class, try to make sure the pairs are made up of people from different countries. Students work together and compare their souvenirs. In feedback you could find out which souvenirs each person would like to receive from their partner.

Task: Speaking: Additional activity

In a multi-nationality class, group students in regions or continents and explain that the people in the photo are on a tour, but they only want to bring back one thing from each region/continent. Students can then try to persuade each other that their ideas are the best.

---

3 Students work in small groups to report what they and their partners talked about.

Share your task

The idea here is to give students a chance to 'perfect' their speaking in this context and provide them with a recording of a 'polished' version. This will provide extra motivation for students, as well as extra practice. Students can either make an audio or video recording, depending on how comfortable they feel and what equipment is available. Students could even use their mobile phones to do this. If possible, they'll need a quiet place to make their recording. Students can either record themselves during the lesson, or as homework and bring the recordings to the next class.

World culture, Find out first:

To help your students prepare for the next class, go through the questions in exercise 1b on page 86. If necessary, discuss ideas for searching for this information on the internet, pointing out the search terms, and suggest other sources of information students could use. Encourage students to use English language websites as much as possible.

World culture (PAGES 86–87)

Famous markets

Culture notes

eBay is an online auction site. If you have something you would like to sell, you can put it on the website and other people can bid for it. It has been hugely successful with many different types of people, especially small businesspeople as it allows them to reach a large audience.

While eBay has become popular in Europe, much of Asia and North America, it doesn't have a presence in every country. In Latin America Mercado Libre is the most common website and in Japan it is Yahoo Japan Auctions.

Galeries Lafayette was founded in 1895 and ten years later moved to its present location on Boulevard Haussman in Paris. The flagship store is an architectural beauty with an amazing glass and steel dome and Art Nouveau staircases. It is now part of an international upmarket department store chain with branches in Berlin, Casablanca, Dubai and Jakarta. In 2009 the company had a turnover in excess of $1 billion.

Walmart started life in 1962 and was founded by Sam Walton. Since then it has grown to be the biggest supermarket retailer in the world, the third largest public operation in the world and, with over two million employees, the biggest private employer in the world. It has operations in numerous countries around the world, including wholly owning the supermarket Asda in the UK.

The company has been heavily criticised over the years, especially for its strong anti-union stance and accusations that it pays poorly. It has a staff turnover rate of about 70% per year and there have also been accusations of sexual discrimination.

Amazon is the world's largest online retailer with a gross income in the region of $60 billion in 2012. The company started by selling books in 1994, but soon diversified to offer CDs, DVDs and practically anything else you can think of. Recently they have also started to produce and sell their own electronic goods in the form of their Kindle line of e-readers and tablets.

In recent years they have come in for criticism due to their legal, but some would say slightly dubious, tax avoidance schemes. Many traditional companies have complained that it is difficult to compete against them if they have to pay local taxes but Amazon doesn't.

Outdoor markets have, despite the stereotypes of rain and fog, always been an important part of London life, and continue to be so. The four markets mentioned on the DVD are just some of the many markets that can be found all over the city. Some of the markets are many hundreds of years old, and this is part of the attraction. They are also popular because of the bargains that can often be found, the products that are sold and the unusual characters that can be found in them.

See the Culture notes on page 77 of this unit for information about **Harrods** and **Macy's**.

Find out first (PAGE 86)

1a Check students understand the concepts of *eBay*, *department stores*, and *second-hand shops*. Students then work in pairs to discuss the question.

b Students work in pairs to answer the questions in the quiz. If some students have not done the research, try to put them with a student who has done it.

c If you have access to the internet and students haven't been able to find the answer to some of the questions, ask students to go online and do some further research. Highlight the search terms. Circulate and offer help with vocabulary and try to encourage people to use only English language websites. Otherwise, tell your students the answers.

ANSWERS:

1 France
2 Galeries Lafayette is in Paris, Harrods is in London and Macy's is in New York.
3 It partially comes from the name of its founder Sam Walton.
4 Amazon
5 markets in the Arab world

View (PAGE 86)

See *Teaching tips: Using the video material in the classroom*, page 24.

2 Go through the words in the glossary to make sure students understand the key vocabulary.

3 ▶ Tell students that the four markets are all famous markets in London. While it is not vital, check the pronunciation of *Borough* /ˈbʌrə/, Camden /ˈkæmdən/ and Portobello /pɔːtəˈbeləʊ/. Make sure students read all of the sentences before they watch the DVD. Students match the sentences to the markets then check in pairs before checking as a class.

ANSWERS:

1 Portobello Market	2 Borough Market	3 Borough Market
4 Camden Market	5 Brick Lane Market	6 Brick Lane Market
7 Camden Market	8 Portobello Market	9 Brick Lane Market

4a Play the DVD again and ask students to answer the questions. They check in pairs and then as a class.

ANSWERS:

Portobello Market: from Monday to Friday, sells fruit and vegetables; on Saturdays, sells clothes
Borough Market: from Thursday to Saturday, sells the best of British food
Brick Lane Market: on Sundays, sells clothes, arts and crafts
Camden Market: every day, sells clothes

b Students work in pairs or small groups to discuss the questions. In feedback, find out which market would be the most popular.

World view (PAGE 87)

5a Give students a minute or two to read through the statements and tick the ones that are true for them.

b Students work in pairs to compare their answers.

World view, exercise 5b: Additional activity

If your students live in the same town or city, elicit some of the places to shop, including a market or two if appropriate. Ask students to work in groups and describe the places, using the DVD as an example. You might like to provide some prompt questions, e.g. *What types of things can you buy there? Who goes there? When is it open? Is there anything special or unique?* Students then work on describing the shopping places in their area.

Once the groups have finished preparing their descriptions, ask each group to describe one shopping area without naming it and ask the other groups to guess which one they are talking about.

Find out more (PAGE 87)

6a Students work individually or in pairs to note any information they might know about the markets that are mentioned in the box.

b Students work in the same pairs to research either all of the markets in exercise 6a or one or two that they have chosen. Focus students' attention on the search terms that they should use. Circulate and help with new vocabulary as necessary.

ANSWERS:

Tsukiji Market: in Tokyo, Japan; sells seafood and fish; biggest market in the world

Mercado del Puerto: in Montevideo, Uruguay; gastronomy

Fes Souk: in Fes, Morocco; sells everything

Bloemenmarkt: in Amsterdam, Netherlands; sells flowers; is a floating market

Write up your research

7 Show students the paragraph prompts and give an example of how they could be filled in by using information from the DVD about one of the markets in London. Students then write about one of the markets they researched in exercise 6a.

Write up your research: Alternative suggestion

Allow your students to write about a market from their home town. Encourage them to do some research, in English if possible, but remember that the most important thing is that they are motivated to write something.

Study, practice & remember

(PAGES 154–155)

See *Teaching tips: Using the Study, practice & remember sections*, page 25.

Practice 1

ANSWERS:

1

1 taller **2** younger **3** better **4** easier **5** more important
6 hotter **7** worse **8** more expensive

2

Sentences 2 & 7 are correct. The others all contain *more* which should be deleted.

Practice 2

ANSWERS:

1

1 The highest **2** The shortest **3** The most popular
4 The oldest **5** the tallest **6** The biggest

2

Students' own answers using:
1 busiest **2** best **3** worst **4** most violent **5** saddest
6 most exciting **7** most boring **8** most difficult

Remember these words

ANSWERS:

1

1 uncomfortable **2** economical **3** cheap **4** easy to use
5 unusual **6** powerful **7** old **8** expensive

2

1 post office **2** hairdresser's **3** butcher's **4** pharmacy
5 estate agent's **6** optician's **7** dry-cleaner's **8** gift shop
9 baker's **10** shoe shop

OVERVIEW

PAGES 88–89

Vocabulary: Clothes

Grammar: Present continuous

Common European Framework: Students have sufficient vocabulary to conduct routine, everyday transactions involving familiar situations and topics.

PAGES 90–91

Listening: Clothes at work

Grammar: Present simple or continuous?

Vocabulary: Describing personality

Common European Framework: Students can understand phrases and expressions related to areas of most immediate priority, for example shopping and employment.

PAGES 92–93

Task: Analyse your personality

Common European Framework: Students can make themselves understood in short conversations that demand descriptions or explanations.

PAGES 94–95

Speaking: Asking for goods and services

Writing: Describing people

Common European Framework: Students can ask about things and make simple transactions in shops, post offices or banks.

Vocabulary (PAGE 88)

Clothes

See *Teaching tips: Working with lexical phrases*, page 21.

WARM UP

Find similar-looking photos of people, for example you could have three photos of women with brown hair and brown eyes, four photos of men with blond hair, etc. Put them up around the classroom so that all the women with brown hair and brown eyes are near each other and all the men with blond hair are near each other in a different part of the room. Each photo should have a number on it to make it easy to identify.

Ask students to go around the classroom and look at the photos. They should choose one of the photos and prepare to talk about it. Circulate and offer vocabulary as necessary. The students can either tell the rest of the class or work in a small group, depending on the class size. The rest of the class or group should guess which photo they are talking about.

The advantage of this activity is that students will subconsciously notice the language they are lacking and so be more receptive to it in the following material. You could use the same pictures and repeat the activity for revision in a later class.

1a Focus students' attention on the pictures and the words for the items of clothing in the box. Students match the items to the pictures. They check in pairs and then as a class.

ANSWERS:

A trousers   B a baseball cap   C a shirt   D a suit   E jeans
F a dress   G shorts   H a jumper   I a skirt   J trainers
K a tie   L sunglasses   M a jacket

b Elicit one or two more items of clothing as examples. Students work in pairs to think of more items. Write their suggestions on the board or invite the students to write their own suggestions on the board.

POSSIBLE ANSWERS:

boxer shorts, a bow tie, a blouse, high-heeled shoes, a T-shirt, a coat

---

Vocabulary, exercise 1b: Additional activities

a Highlight the following words: *trousers, trainers, jumper*. Tell your students that these are all British English words and that American English uses different words. Ask them to use a dictionary or the internet to find the American versions (*pants, sneakers / tennis shoes, sweater*).

This exercise will help to expose students to the fact that British and American English have some differences. It will also encourage them to be more independent learners.

b Ask students, for homework, to look in their wardrobes and find examples of clothes with English written on them. There are a number of different possibilities, including T-shirts with phrases or band names on them, corporate names or slogans on clothing and labels with care instructions.

Ask students to make a note of some of the English they find and include: a) the type of clothing; b) the English word or phrase; c) its meaning. You could also suggest that students take a photo of the clothing if this is possible and maybe even wear some of it to the next class. Once they have done this, put students into groups to share what they found.

This activity will help to reinforce the vocabulary you have introduced in this class as well as making students more independent as they pay attention to the English around them and use this as a learning opportunity.

---

c Students work individually to decide who usually wears the items of clothing in the box in exercise 1a. They check in pairs and then as a class.

ANSWERS:

Usually worn by men: a tie, a baseball cap
Usually worn by women: a skirt, a dress
Usually worn by men and women: a suit, sunglasses, a jacket, shorts, trousers, trainers, a shirt, jeans, a jumper

PRONUNCIATION

See *Teaching tips: Helping students with pronunciation*, page 22.

1 🎧 10.1 Play the recording or model the pronunciation yourself. Pay particular attention to the pronunciation of *suit* /suːt/, *tie* /taɪ/, *trousers* /ˈtraʊzəz/, *skirt* /skɜːt/, *shirt* /ʃɜːt/ and the word stress in *baseball cap* /ˈbeɪsˌbɔːl kæp/ and *sunglasses* /ˈsʌnˌɡlɑːsɪz/.

2 Drill the vocabulary chorally and individually. You might like to drill the vocabulary as part of the sentence *She/He's wearing … .*

ADDITIONAL PRACTICE

➡ **Workbook:** Vocabulary: *Clothes*, page 49; Pronunciation: *Clothes*, page 49

Grammar focus 1 (PAGE 89)

Present continuous

See *Teaching tips: Working with grammar*, page 20.

Read the first two or three sentences with the class and check students understand they need to use the information in the sentences to label the seven people in the picture. Students work individually to name the people. Check as a class.

ANSWERS:

from left to right: Denzil, Frank, Kim, Mel, Pippa, Tom, Val

GRAMMAR

Present continuous

1 Students complete the gaps, using exercise 1 for guidance if necessary.

ANSWERS:

+ is
− isn't
? What is

Highlight:

- that we use the Present continuous for speaking about an action happening now or around now. A timeline will help to show this:

I'm waiting for a bus.

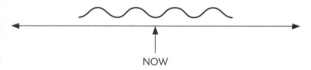

NOW

- the form of the tense: *be + -ing*.
- the different forms of the verb *to be*.
- the contracted forms.
- the inverted word order in questions.

You may want to ask students to read Study 1 on page 156 for a more detailed explanation of the Present continuous.

PRACTICE

1a Tell students they have two minutes to look at the picture and remember as many details as possible.

b Direct students to the questions on page 136. Students work individually or in pairs to answer the questions without looking back at the picture or at the answers on page 133. Conduct feedback as a competition to find out who could remember the most.

2a Go through the example with the class. Students then work individually to write true sentences about themselves. Circulate and monitor.

b Students work in pairs to compare their sentences.

ANSWERS:

1 I'm (not) wearing jeans today.
2 We're / We aren't listening to music at the moment.
3 I'm (not) working alone on this exercise.
4 The sun is/isn't shining today.
5 The teacher is/isn't writing on the board.
6 I'm (not) holding my pen in my left hand.

3a Write a couple of sentences on the board about what people are wearing or doing as an example. Give students a few minutes to write their own sentences.

b Students work in pairs or small groups to compare their sentences.

Practice, exercise 3: Alternative suggestion

Write two questions on the board, for example *Who is wearing blue jeans? Who is sitting near the board?* Elicit the answers and then put students into pairs to write their own questions. Students then work in different pairs to ask and answer their questions.

Practice, exercise 3: Additional activity

Before the class, prepare a number of slips of paper with activities on them, for example *playing the guitar, eating a sandwich, making a pizza, doing homework, having a shower, playing a computer game, watching a comedy*, etc.

Put students into groups and demonstrate the activity by taking a piece of paper and miming the action. The first group to guess the action gets a point. If they can guess the mime by asking a question in the Present continuous they get two points, for example *Are you playing the guitar?* The group with the most points at the end is the winner.

ADDITIONAL PRACTICE

➡ **Resource bank:** Activity 10A *Identity parades* (Clothes; Present continuous); Activity 10B *What's Sam doing?* (Present continuous)

Study, practice & remember: Practice 1

Workbook: Grammar focus 1: *Present continuous*, pages 49–50

Listening (PAGE 90)

Clothes at work

WARM UP

Before the class, arrange for a colleague to come into your class a moment or two after it starts. They could come in on any pretext, ostensibly to give you a message or give you a pencil, for example. When they have gone out, ask students to work in pairs to complete this sentence with as many appropriate clothes words as possible: *He/She is wearing ... .* After a moment or two elicit all of the suggestions and write a description on the board.

If you would like to repeat the activity, and if you can trust your students, walk out of the class yourself for a moment. As you are closing the door, tell them to write a description of what you are wearing. If you think it is better not to go out of the class, ask a student to go out for a minute, but don't tell the class they are going to write a description until he or she has left.

1 Check the meaning of the word *uniform* and the pronunciation, especially of the first syllable /ˈjuːnɪˌfɔːm/. Students work in pairs to discuss the questions.

Listening, exercise 1: Additional activity

You might like to bring in photos of people who wear uniforms, e.g. *police officers, flight attendants, school children* and *receptionists*. Ask students to describe them and say why they are worn. Students could also put them into an order according to whether they like the specific uniforms or not.

2a Talk about the shop assistant with the class as an example. Write the suggestions that your students make on the board. Then they work in pairs to make suggestions about what the other people might wear. Get ideas and put them on the board.

b 🎧 **10.2** Give students a moment to read through the items in the box and deal with any problems. Students listen and write the appropriate letter next to each word then check in pairs. Play the recording again if you think students would benefit from it. Check as a class.

c Give students time to read through the statements. Play the recording again for students to decide if the statements are true or false. They check in pairs and then as a class.

3 Students work in pairs to discuss the questions.

Listening, exercise 3: Additional activity

Write on the board a number of activities, for example *playing football*, *decorating the house*, *going for a run*, *going skiing*, *going to the beach*. Try to choose activities that you know your students would be interested in.

Choose one of the activities and elicit what clothing you would need to do it. Students then complete the rest of the options with appropriate clothing. This activity could be done in class or as homework.

Grammar focus 2 (PAGES 90–91)

Present simple or continuous?

See *Teaching tips: Working with grammar*, page 20.

1a Write on the board *fancy-dress party* and, with the help of the photos, elicit the meaning. Ask students questions, e.g. *Do you like going to fancy-dress parties? When was the last time you went to a fancy-dress party? What did you go to the party as?*

Tell students that the people in the photos are the same people that they have just listened to in exercise 2b. Elicit a description of one of the people. Students then work in pairs to answer the questions. Check ideas for the theme of the fancy-dress party as a class.

b Students quickly read the text to check their ideas.

2 Students work in pairs to discuss the questions.

GRAMMAR

Present simple

1 Write the example sentence on the board. Use timelines to demonstrate the difference between *generally true* and *happening now*, for example:

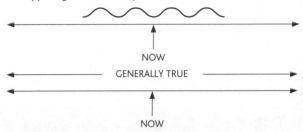

Students then decide which of the alternatives is correct.

2 Read through the words and phrases that we often use with the Present simple. Show how they can be inserted into the example sentence; they can all replace *usually* except *every day*, which goes at the end of the sentence.

Present continuous

3 Write the example sentence on the board. Students choose the correct alternative. Refer them to the previous timelines if necessary.

4 Read through the words and phrases that we often use with the Present continuous. Show how they can be positioned either at the beginning or the end of the example sentence.

You may want to ask students to read Study 2 on page 156 for a more detailed explanation of the Present simple and continuous.

PRACTICE

1a Do the first one with the class as an example. Students work individually to choose the correct alternatives for the rest of the sentences. They check in pairs and then as a class. During feedback, regularly refer back to the timelines and example sentences to reinforce the reasons.

b Students work in pairs to ask and answer the questions.

2a Do the first couple of gaps with the class as examples. Students then work individually to complete the text. Circulate and monitor for common problems to work on during feedback.

b 🎧 **10.3** Students listen and check.

3 Students work in small groups to talk about what they normally wear and what they are wearing at the moment.

ADDITIONAL PRACTICE

Resource bank: Activity 10C *An email home* (Present simple or continuous?)

Study, practice & remember: Practice 2

Workbook: Grammar focus 2: *Present simple or continuous?*, pages 51–52

Vocabulary (PAGE 91)
Describing personality

See *Teaching tips: Working with lexical phrases*, page 21.

1 Check the pronunciation of the words in the box, especially *determined* /dɪˈtɜːmɪnd/, *organised* /ˈɔːgəˌnaɪzd/ and *sociable* /ˈsəʊʃəbəl/. Students then decide if the words are positive or negative. If students don't know a word, allow them to either guess or leave it until later. Students check their ideas in pairs. In feedback, draw two columns on the board marked + and – and ask students to put the words in the appropriate column. Deal with any problems by asking other students to provide examples and definitions before confirming or correcting.

ANSWERS:
Positive: reliable, cheerful, organised, confident, easy-going, friendly, hard-working, sociable, determined, kind
Negative: moody, bossy, shy

2a Give students a few minutes to select three adjectives for each category.

POSSIBLE ANSWERS:
Your personality: students' own answers
A teacher: confident, organised, reliable
A businessperson: determined, hard-working, organised
A nurse: cheerful, hard-working, kind
A shop assistant: cheerful, friendly, hard-working

b Give a couple of sentence heads to help people introduce opinions, e.g. *I think our teacher is … . I'd say that a businessperson normally … .* Students then work in pairs to compare their ideas.

3 Do an example with the class. To make it clear that you are talking about yourself from another person's point of view, draw a stick person on the board and write your name next to it. Then draw another stick person with the name of a friend, relative, colleague or neighbour. Point to the other person and say *He/She thinks I am … .* Students then work in pairs to describe themselves from another person's point of view.

Vocabulary, exercise 3: Alternative suggestion
Before the class, prepare photos of famous people and fictional characters that your students will know. These will vary depending on your students, but might include politicians, actors, characters from films or soap operas, businesspeople or sportspeople. Ask students to write four or five adjectives for some of the photos. Students work in small groups and take it in turns to read out their adjectives and challenge the other members of their group to guess who they are talking about.

Vocabulary, exercise 3: Additional activity
Encourage students to write about the personality of somebody they know well to give them extra practice.

ADDITIONAL PRACTICE
Workbook: Vocabulary: *Describing personality*, page 52

Task (PAGES 92–93)
Analyse your personality

See *Teaching tips: Making tasks work*, page 23.

Preparation (PAGE 92)
Reading and listening

WARM UP
Say a colour and elicit everything in the classroom of that colour, including the colour of the clothes different people are wearing. Put students into small groups and say another colour. In their groups students write down everything they can see of that colour. Elicit the items and award a point to the group with the most items. Repeat the procedure until you run out of colours or the vocabulary becomes repetitive. The winning group is the one with the most points.

1a Elicit two or three colours as a class. Give students one minute to write a list of as many other colours as they can think of.

b Students compare their lists in pairs or small groups and try to add another two colours. Check as a class.

POSSIBLE ANSWERS:
blue, red, yellow, green, orange, purple, brown, pink, black, beige, cream, crimson, violet, amber, emerald, aquamarine, burgundy, royal blue

c Students work in pairs to answer the questions. In feedback, find out which colours are the most and least popular in the class.

2 Make sure your students read the questions before they read the article. Reassure them that they don't have to understand everything, just enough to answer the questions.

ANSWERS:
1 b   2 b

3a 🎧 10.4 Students listen to the recording and answer the two questions. They check in pairs and then as a class.

ANSWERS:
1 red, black, brown, white   2 Yes

b Focus students' attention on the Useful language box and give them a minute to read through it. Students then listen to the recording again and tick the phrases they hear.

ANSWERS:
What's your (least) favourite colour? ✓
What colours are you wearing now? ✓
What does that say about me? ✓
(Red) clothes mean you are a confident person. ✓
You like wearing (black), so you're (reliable). ✓
I think that's absolutely right! ✓
Yes, I'm a very (reliable) person. ✓

Task (PAGE 93)

Speaking

1 Start a conversation with a student by asking them what their favourite colour is. Then make a show of looking for information about them in the text and start to describe them. Stop in the middle of a sentence and ask your students to do the same thing in pairs. Remind them to use the phrases from the Useful language box. Circulate and offer help and encouragement as necessary.

2a Students work in groups to tell each other about either their own personality or that of their partner from the previous exercise.

b Students work in the same groups to discuss the questions.

Share your task

The idea here is to give students a chance to 'perfect' their speaking in this context and provide them with a recording of a 'polished' version. This will provide extra motivation for students, as well as extra practice. Students can either make an audio or video recording, depending on how comfortable they feel and what equipment is available. Students could even use their mobile phones to do this. If possible, they'll need a quiet place to make their recording. Students can either record themselves during the lesson, or as homework and bring the recordings to the next class.

Some additional ideas could include:

- Students record their reaction to the colour analysis.
- Students act as fortune tellers and attempt to 'read' their partner according to their favourite colour.

Language live (PAGES 94–95)

Speaking (PAGE 94)

Asking for goods and services

See *Teaching tips: Using the video material in the classroom*, page 24.

1 Remind students that they looked at shops on page 82 in Unit 9 and so this is a review exercise. Give them a minute to write down as many shops as possible. During feedback check pronunciation.

Speaking, exercise 1: Alternative suggestion

Set the activity up as a competitive group game. Put students into small groups and give them a minute to write down every type of shop they can think of. Elicit a shop from each group and write it on the board. Give one point for each shop a group can provide that hasn't been suggested by a different group. The group with the most points is the winner.

---

2 Students work individually to put the words and phrases into the correct category. Deal with unknown vocabulary during feedback by asking other students to give examples or definitions before you give an answer.

ANSWERS:

at a hairdresser's: an appointment, it suits you, not too short, a haircut, How would you like, hairspray, wash, gel
in a clothes shop: it suits you, too small, a larger size, try it on, too big

3a ⊙ Play the DVD for students to number the phrases they hear from exercise 2 in the correct order. They check in pairs. Play the DVD again if necessary before checking as a class.

ANSWERS:

The words and phrases appear in the following order:
a haircut, an appointment, How would you like, not too short, wash, hairspray, gel, too small, a larger size, try it on, too big, it suits you

b Give students time to read the questions, then play the DVD again for students to answer them. Students check in pairs and then as a class.

ANSWERS:

At a hairdresser's

1 No
2 not too short but not too long
3 £60
4 Because the hairdresser hasn't cut his hair at all.

In a clothes shop

5 4
6 No
7 The second jacket is too small, the third jacket is too big.
8 the fourth jacket

4a Tell your students that all of the phrases were used in the DVD. Complete the first one or two sentences with the class as examples. Students work individually to complete the rest of the sentences then check in pairs.

b ⊙ Students watch the DVD and check their answers.

ANSWERS:

At a hairdresser's

| 1 like | 2 appointment | 3 hair | 4 too, too | 5 wash |
| 6 cut | 7 How's | 8 How much | | |

In a clothes shop

| 1 think | 2 too | 3 size | 4 on | 5 too | 6 suits |
| 7 take | 8 to pay | | | | |

PRONUNCIATION

See *Teaching tips: Helping students with pronunciation*, page 22.

1 Students watch the key phrases and pay attention to the pronunciation. You could ask students to focus on the intonation patterns used, as these are important when asking questions in a shop.

2 Drill the key phrases chorally and individually.

5a Students work in pairs to prepare a conversation in either a hairdresser's or a clothes shop. Circulate and offer help as necessary.

b Students roleplay their conversation. In feedback, invite one or two pairs to perform their conversation for the rest of the class.

Speaking, exercise 5b: Additional activity

Split the class into two, with one half being hairdressers and one half being shop assistants in a clothes shop. Tell the hairdressers they are going to buy some clothes and they need to think about what they want to buy. Tell the shop assistants they are going to get their hair cut and they need to think about what style they want. Give students a couple of minutes to prepare. During this time, circulate and offer help as necessary.

When your students are ready, tell the hairdressers to find a shop assistant and try to find what they want. The shop assistants should stay seated and wait for their customers to come to them. The students then improvise a roleplay to try to buy what they want. If some pairs finish quickly, encourage them to talk to another shop assistant and buy something else.

After a couple of minutes, ask the hairdressers to sit down. It is now the turn of the shop assistants to find a hairdresser to get the haircut they want. During the two sets of roleplays, circulate and make a note of good language use for praise and errors to be corrected later on.

Writing (PAGE 95)

Describing people

1 Focus students' attention on the photos. They then work individually or with a partner to answer the questions. Check as a class and deal with any problem vocabulary, especially *curly hair*, *pony tail* and *slim*. Also, point out the preposition in the phrase *in his forties*.

ANSWERS:
1 Pedro   2 Martha   3 Martha, Kamilla and Paolo   4 Paolo
5 Pedro   6 Martha   7 Pedro   8 Martha, Kamilla and Paolo
9 Pedro   10 Kamilla and Paolo   11 Paolo   12 Kamilla

2 Students complete the table with the words and phrases in the box. Remind students that they can use some of the examples from exercise 1 to help them if they are not sure. Students check in pairs and then as a class.

ANSWERS:
He/She is: in his early twenties, reading a newspaper, carrying a bag, in her teens, holding a book, a nice person in her late thirties, standing up, good-looking, sitting down, wearing lipstick
He/She has got: medium-length hair, short hair, blonde hair

3 Students quickly read the text and match it to one of the photos.

ANSWER:
Martha

4 Students use the description in exercise 3 as a model to write their own description. If you don't have time to do this in class, it can be done as homework.

Writing, exercise 4: Additional activity

Put the descriptions up around the room with a number on them and make sure students can't see the names of the people being described. Students walk around the room and decide which text is talking about which member of the class.

ADDITIONAL PRACTICE

Workbook: Language live: *Asking for goods and services*, page 53; Writing: *Describing people*, page 53

Students can now do Progress test 5 on the Teacher's Resource Disc.

Study, practice & remember
(PAGES 156–157)

See *Teaching tips: Using the Study, practice & remember sections*, page 25

Practice 1

ANSWERS:
1
1 'm watching   2 's playing   3 're waiting   4 're working
5 isn't watching   6 're playing   7 's working
8 'm not waiting
2
1 'm eating   2 isn't buying   3 's sitting   4 'm driving
5 Are you getting   6 's riding   7 Are they playing
8 are you doing

Practice 2

ANSWERS:
1
1 am writing   2 come   3 am sitting   4 are you staying
5 is working   6 play   7 am studying   8 am living
2
1 d   2 f   3 c   4 e   5 a   6 b

Remember these words

ANSWERS:
1
1 dress   2 sunglasses   3 suit, tie   4 trainers
5 jumper   6 jeans   7 jacket   8 shorts
2
Things you wear on your head and neck: sunglasses, a baseball cap, a tie
Things you wear on your feet: trainers
Things you wear on your body: trousers, skirt, shirt, tracksuit
3
1 sociable   2 cheerful   3 bossy   4 shy
5 hard-working   6 determined   7 reliable   8 organised

OVERVIEW

PAGES 96–97

Vocabulary: Animals and natural features

Reading: Working animals

Common European Framework: Students can find and understand relevant information in everyday material, such as letters and brochures.

PAGES 98–99

Listening: Intelligent animals

Vocabulary: Big numbers

Grammar: Question words

Common European Framework: Students can understand and extract the essential information from short recorded passages dealing with predictable everyday matters.

PAGES 100–101

Listening: South Africa

Grammar: Quantifiers: *a lot of, a little, a few, not any, not much, not many*

Common European Framework: Students can give and receive information about quantities, numbers and prices.

PAGES 102–103

Task: Devise a general knowledge quiz

Common European Framework: Students can recall and rehearse an appropriate set of phrases from their repertoire.

PAGES 104–105

World culture: Animals in danger

Common European Framework: Students can generally understand clear, standard speech on familiar matters.

Vocabulary (PAGE 96)

Animals and natural features

See *Teaching tips: Working with lexical phrases*, page 21.

WARM UP

Students work in small groups to make a list of animals. Set the activity up as a contest with the first group to write ten being the winner. If no group has managed to think of ten after two minutes, stop the activity and ask for suggestions. If students show an interest in the names of specific animals, try not to translate, instead encourage them to offer descriptions, e.g. *It's big and lives in the sea.* or mime or imitate the sound of the animal.

1a Focus students' attention on the photos and the words in the box. Elicit which of the words can be seen in the first photo. Students then work in pairs to do the same for the remaining photos. Check as a class and deal with any unused vocabulary that students are unsure of.

ANSWERS:
top left: donkeys, a lake, a mountain
top right: an elephant, a forest
bottom left: a dog
bottom centre: a dolphin, the sea/ocean
bottom right: camels, a desert

b Students work in their pairs to put the words from exercise 1a into the correct category. Check as a class by putting the words on the board in two columns.

ANSWERS:
animals: dog, llama, chimpanzee, dolphin, camel, snake, horse, elephant, rat, whale, donkey, fish
natural features: beach, sea, mountain, ocean, forest, river, volcano, lake, desert, valley

c Students add as many words as possible to the two categories. Check as a class and extend the columns on the board.

POSSIBLE ANSWERS:
animals: cat, lion, tiger, mouse, lizard, cow, goat, sheep
natural features: bay, plain, coast, hill, canyon

2 Students work in pairs to discuss the questions.

Vocabulary, exercise 2: Additional activity

Draw a picture on the board of one of the vocabulary items from exercise 1a. It doesn't matter if the picture is great or not, in fact it helps if it is not immediately obvious. Encourage students to guess what you are drawing by calling out *Is it a ... ?* Students then work in pairs or small groups to do the same to test each other's vocabulary.

ADDITIONAL PRACTICE

➡ **Workbook:** Vocabulary: *Animals and natural features*, page 54

Reading (PAGE 97)

1a Focus students' attention on the photos again. Discuss the work one of the animals does as a class as an example. Accept all possible suggestions and help with any unknown vocabulary. Students then work in pairs to discuss the other jobs the animals might do.

POSSIBLE ANSWERS:
Donkeys, elephants and camels can carry people or objects.
Dogs can help find people or objects that are lost.

b Students quickly read the article to identify which animals are mentioned. If your students need help to read more quickly, give them a time limit of two minutes.

ANSWERS:
horses, donkeys, camels, llamas, elephants, dogs, fish, rats, dolphins

2 Give students enough time to read the questions and deal with any unknown language, for example *improve* (to make something better), *illegal* (not permitted or against the law), *loads* (something that is being carried). Encourage students to read in more detail to find the answers and underline the parts of the text that provide the answers. They check in pairs and then as a class.

ANSWERS:
1 dog **2** fish **3** dog **4** llama **5** dog **6** dog **7** dolphin
8 elephant

3 Students work in pairs to discuss the questions. In feedback, try to encourage as many people as possible to give their opinions.

Listening (PAGE 98)

Intelligent animals

1 Focus students' attention on the photos and elicit the names of the animals pictured. Check the pronunciation. Pay particular attention to the pronunciation of the word *sheep* /ʃiːp/. Students work in pairs to discuss the questions.

> **Listening, exercise 1: Additional activity**
>
> If students seem to be enjoying talking about the questions, ask some more, for example *Which animals make the best pets? Are there any animals that shouldn't be pets? What are the most common pets in your country? What's the strangest pet you have heard of?*

2a 🎧 **11.1** Students listen and number the animals in the order they hear them. They check in pairs and then as a class.

ANSWERS:

whales, dolphins, parrots, dogs, chimpanzees

b Give students a moment to read through the abilities so they know what information they have to listen for. They check in pairs and then as a class.

ANSWERS:

speak to each other: whales, dolphins
speak like humans: parrots
paint pictures: none
use computers: chimpanzees
remember names: dogs
remember numbers: chimpanzees

3 Students work in pairs to answer the questions. During feedback, ask students if they think they are better than the animals at remembering things.

Vocabulary (PAGES 98–99)

Big numbers

See *Teaching tips: Working with lexical phrases*, page 21.

1 Match the first one with the class as an example. Students then work individually to match the rest. They check in pairs before checking as a class. Pay particular attention to the changing vowel sound in the words *five* /faɪv/, *fifteen* /fɪfˈtiːn/, and *fifty* /ˈfɪfti/.

ANSWERS:

1 h   2 c   3 i   4 a   5 g   6 f   7 d   8 b   9 e

2 🎧 **11.2** Play the recording, pausing after each number to give students time to write it down. Students check in pairs. Play the recording again if you think students would benefit from it. Check as a class. During feedback, write both the numeral and the number in words on the board. This will help you to deal with word stress in the next activity.

ANSWERS:

50, 100, 120, 240, 1,500, 8,500, 10,000, 20,000, 32,000,000

PRONUNCIATION

See *Teaching tips: Helping students with pronunciation*, page 22.

1 Students listen again to the numbers and pay attention to the pronunciation. Point out the stressed words and the weak form of *and* /ən/.

2 Drill the numbers chorally and individually.

3a Students work individually or in pairs to guess which number from exercise 2 completes each gap.

b 🎧 **11.3** Students listen and check.

ANSWERS:

1 1,500   2 120   3 50   4 20,000   5 100   6 240   7 8,500
8 32,000,000   9 10,000

ADDITIONAL PRACTICE

Resource bank: Activity 11A *The numbers game* (Big numbers)

Workbook: Vocabulary: *Big numbers*, pages 55–56; Pronunciation: *Big numbers*, page 56

Grammar focus 1 (PAGE 99)

Question words

See *Teaching tips: Working with grammar*, page 20.

1 Students work individually to choose the correct question words. They check in pairs and then as a class. Write the correct questions on the board.

ANSWERS:

1 How many   2 Which   3 How tall   4 How fast   5 How far
6 How long   7 How much   8 What   9 How old

GRAMMAR

Question words with two words (*how* + another word)

1 Students match the question words with the answers. Ask students to remind you of the difference between *How much?* and *How many?* During feedback, highlight:

• the use of *How long?* NOT *How long time?* as this is a common student mistake.

• a range of adjectives we can use after *How* (*big, expensive, cold, hot, near*, etc.)

ANSWERS:

1 f   2 c   3 g   4 a   5 b   6 e   7 d

what* and *which

2 & 3 Read through the examples with your students. Write on the board: ___ *people are wearing red today?* and ___ *did you do before class?* Elicit which word is used to complete each gap. During feedback, highlight:

• that we say *What kind of? NOT Which kind of?*

You may want to ask students to read Study 1 on page 158 for a more detailed explanation of question words.

2 Students work in pairs to ask and answer the questions. Encourage them not to look at the answers and to use their memory. This will be easier if you wrote the questions on the board in Grammar, exercise 1 because students will not need to use their books to remember the questions.

3a Go through the examples and elicit one or two other questions using the table. Students then work individually to write as many questions as possible. Circulate and offer help as necessary.

b Students work in pairs to ask and answer their questions.

ADDITIONAL PRACTICE

➡ **Resource bank:** Activity 11B *The dinner party* (Question words)

Study, practice & remember: Practice 1

Workbook: Grammar focus 1: *Question words*, pages 56–57

Listening (PAGE 100)

South Africa

WARM UP

As a way of recycling the question forms and numbers from the last class, read out the questions from the Grammar focus, exercise 1 as a dictation leaving the question word blank. For example ___ *active volcanoes are there in the world?* Students, working in pairs, need to complete the questions and then remember the answers.

Culture notes

South Africa is a multi-ethnic country with many diverse cultures and languages. In 1934 the country gained independence from Great Britain and in 1961 became a Republic. It was infamous for its apartheid policy of segregating white people of European descent from native Africans and other immigrants. The most famous protester against apartheid was Nelson Mandela, who spent over 28 years as a political prisoner.

Today South Africa has the biggest economy in Africa and is seen as an upper middle income country by the World Bank. This, however, does not take into account the massive disparity between the 'haves' and 'have nots' with about 25% of the country unemployed and living on less than $1.25 a day.

---

1 Focus students' attention on the photos and elicit a quick description of some of the things they can see. Students then work in pairs to discuss the topics.

Listening, exercise 1: Alternative suggestion

If your students are unlikely to know much about South Africa, write this list of words on the board: *Football World Cup 2010, Nelson Mandela, Table Mountain, safari, apartheid*. Elicit what the words have in common and then focus on the photos and follow the procedure for exercise 1.

2a 🎧 **11.4** Make sure the students understand the context before they start to listen. Explain that the *South African Tourist Board* is responsible for encouraging tourists to visit South Africa. Students then listen to the recording and tick the topics from exercise 1 they hear.

ANSWERS:

famous places ✓
wildlife (animals and plants) ✓
natural features (mountains, volcanoes, etc.) ✓

---

b Give students a moment to read through the questions so they know what they have to listen for. Students listen and answer the questions then check in pairs. Play the recording again if necessary. Check as a class. During feedback, if students had problems with any of the questions, play the parts of the recording that give the answers again.

ANSWERS:

1 c   2 b   3 b   4 c   5 a

3 Students work in pairs to discuss the questions.

Grammar focus 2 (PAGES 100–101)

Quantifiers: *a lot of, a little, a few, not any, not much, not many*

See *Teaching tips: Working with grammar*, page 20.

1a Do the first one with the class as an example. Students work individually to choose the correct answers then check in pairs.

b Direct students to audio script 11.4 on page 173 to check their answers.

ANSWERS:

1 aren't   2 have   3 has   4 isn't   5 aren't   6 are

GRAMMAR

Quantifiers: *a lot of, a little, a few, not any, not much, not many*

1 Ask students to quickly remind you of the differences between countable and uncountable nouns (see Unit 6, pages 52–53 of the Students' Book and Study, Practice & Remember, pages 148–149). Go through the example and do number 2 with the class. Students then work individually to complete the rest of the table. They check in pairs before checking as a class. During feedback highlight:

- the weak pronunciation of *a* /ə/ and *of* /əv/.
- the contracted forms: *isn't/aren't any/much/many*.

ANSWERS:

2 a lot of   3 a few   4 not many   5 a little   6 not much
7 not any

You may want to ask students to read Study 2 on page 158 for a more detailed explanation of quantifiers: *a lot of, a little, a few, not any, not much, not many*.

PRACTICE

1 Do the first one with the class as an example. Students read through the text individually and choose the correct answers. They check in pairs and then as a class. During feedback, ask students to justify their answers with reasons from the Grammar box.

ANSWERS:

1 any   2 a little   3 much   4 a lot of   5 a lot of
6 many   7 a few   8 a little

Practice, exercise 1: Alternative suggestion

It is a good idea to get students used to reading a text for basic meaning before they try to focus on the individual words. This is a useful reading skill and will prepare students for reading more difficult texts. In order to promote this skill, ask students to read the text and answer these questions: *Where is the Kalahari Desert? What does 'Kalahari' mean? How long have the Bushmen lived in the Kalahari Desert?* Students should answer these questions first without trying to choose the correct answers. Once you have checked your students have understood the text, continue with the normal procedure for the activity.

2a Create a couple of sentences that are true about your country as an example. Students then work individually to write their own sentences.

b Students work in pairs to compare their sentences. During feedback, ask students to tell you what is similar about their countries.

ADDITIONAL PRACTICE

➔ **Study, practice & remember:** Practice 2

Workbook: Grammar focus 2: *Quantifiers: a lot of, a few, not any, not much, not many,* page 58

Task (PAGES 102–103)
Devise a general knowledge quiz
See *Teaching tips: Making tasks work,* page 23.

Preparation (PAGE 102)
Reading and listening

WARM UP
Introduce the topic of quizzes by asking questions like: *Do you watch quiz shows on TV? Do you have any favourite quiz shows? Would you like to be on a quiz show? Do you do quizzes in magazines to find out your personality / ideal partner? Do/Did you do quizzes at school?*

1a Students work in pairs to discuss the questions. In feedback, find out if there is anything the class has in common.

Culture notes

In the UK quiz shows are very popular and often run on prime time TV. It is also common to have quizzes in pubs with teams of friends competing against each other.

---

b Focus students' attention on the different categories. Check the pronunciation, especially the initial /h/ in *history.* Ask if students think they would be particularly good at answering questions in any of the categories. Students then read the questions and divide them into the five categories. Try to discourage students from shouting out the answers to the questions at this point as this will spoil the next activity.

ANSWERS:
Arts: 7, 10 History: 2, 8 Sport: 5, 9 Science: 3, 4
Countries: 1, 6

2 Focus students' attention on the answers in the box. Elicit the answer to the first question in the quiz. Students then work in pairs to find the answers to the rest of the questions.

ANSWERS:

1 India 2 Vladimir Putin 3 1.6 km 4 150 million km 5 2010
6 Lima 7 Beyoncé 8 Vesuvius 9 tennis 10 Homer

Preparation, exercise 2: Alternative suggestion

You might like to include a level of competition in this exercise. You can either tell students that they will get one point for each correct answer or impose a time limit of three minutes to answer as many questions as possible.

3a 🎧 **11.5** Stress to students that they are going to listen to two other people doing the quiz and that their answers might or might not be correct. Students listen to see if they have the same answers.

b Focus students' attention on the Useful language box. Give them a minute to read through the phrases and deal with any questions. Students then listen to the recording again and tick the phrases they hear.

ANSWERS:

Where is (the River Ganges)? ✓
Who (became President ...)? ✓
How many (kilometres are there ...)? ✓
How (far is it from ...)? ✓
When (did Spain win ...)? ✓
What (is the capital of ...)? ✓
I think it's (in India). ✓
I'm not sure, but I think it's (India). ✓
I've got no idea! ✓
I don't know (either). ✓
I know this one ... it's definitely (2010). ✓

4 Direct students to the answers on page 136. Find out which pair got the most correct answers.

Preparation, exercise 4: Alternative suggestion

If you feel your students need extra help in creating questions, write prompts on the board, e.g. *Where / River Ganges; Who / President of Russia / 26th March 2000,* etc. Elicit each question from the class, drill it and then give the correct answer. Keep a score of who has got the most correct answers if you are running the exercise as a competition.

Task (PAGES 102–103)
Speaking

1a Explain to students that they are going to write their own questions for a general knowledge quiz. Put your students into three teams and ask them to pick a name for themselves. The groups can decide on their own questions, use the information on pages 133, 134 and 136, or use a mix of their own questions and the ideas presented in the Students' Book. If students would like to use their own ideas, it will be easier if they have access to the internet either in class or in a computer lab. Give plenty of time for the teams to decide on and write two questions for each category. Circulate and offer help and support as required, especially checking if the questions are correct, and also reminding students to use the phrases from section a of the Useful Language box.

b Once students have their questions, ask them to write the correct and incorrect answers in a box. Groups may need to be encouraged to mix up the answers so they are not in the same order as the questions.

2a Encourage each team to divide the questions equally between all members to make sure that the activity isn't dominated by stronger students. The members of the team should practise by asking each other the questions and making sure they are comfortable reading them aloud. Try to move between the teams and listen to everyone saying their questions and give advice and feedback. You might want to focus on some of the following:

- weak forms of *do* and *did* in questions.
- sentence stress.
- intonation patterns.

b Invite one team to ask all of their questions while the other two teams confer on the correct answers. To make sure everyone can see the box with the possible answers you might want to copy it onto the board. Allow teams to ask for questions to be repeated if necessary. After the first team has finished asking, check the answers before repeating the procedure with the second and finally the third team. Keep a score of all the points the teams receive.

c Reveal the final score and declare one of the teams the winner. If there is a draw, you might like to have a question ready to ask as a tiebreaker.

3 Students work in pairs to discuss the question. Conduct class feedback to find out the most interesting thing they learnt.

Share your task

The idea here is to give students a chance to 'perfect' their speaking in this context and provide them with a recording of a 'polished' version. This will provide extra motivation for students, as well as extra practice. Students can either make an audio or video recording, depending on how comfortable they feel and what equipment is available. Students could even use their mobile phones to do this. If possible, they'll need a quiet place to make their recording. Students can either record themselves during the lesson, or as homework and bring the recordings to the next class.

Additional idea:

- Students film themselves asking the questions and then post them on a social networking site for other people to answer.

World culture, Find out first:

To help your students prepare for the next class, go through the questions in exercise 1b on page 104. If necessary, discuss ideas for searching for this information on the internet, pointing out the search terms, and suggest other sources of information students could use. Encourage students to use English language websites as much as possible.

World culture (PAGES 104–105)

Animals in danger

Culture notes

The World Wide Fund for Nature (WWF) is an international non-governmental organisation (NGO) whose mission is 'to halt and reverse the destruction of our environment'. It was created in 1961 and has become one of the leading organisations campaigning on behalf of endangered animals around the globe.

In 2013 the organisation had over five million supporters, making it the biggest conservation organisation in the world. It is probably best known for its panda logo, which appears on all of its literature and at its campaign sites. It is currently running thirteen projects to promote and protect the Amazon, the Arctic, sustainable fishing and tigers, among others.

Find out first (PAGE 104)

1a Students work in pairs to talk about their experiences with animals.

b Students work in pairs to answer the questions. If some students have not done the research, try to put them with a student who has done it

c If you have access to the internet and students haven't been able to find the answer to some of the questions, ask students to go online and do some further research. Highlight the search terms. Circulate and offer help with vocabulary and try to encourage people to use only English language websites. Otherwise, tell your students the answers.

POSSIBLE ANSWERS:

Crocodiles live in Africa, Asia, the Americas and Australia. They are a grey-green colour and eat fish, birds, mammals and sometimes other crocodiles. The larger species of crocodiles are very dangerous to humans as they will attack them very quickly.

Giraffes live in Africa and are herbivores. They are an orangey-brown colour with patches of brown. They can be dangerous to humans if they kick.

Monkeys are found all over the world. There are a lot in Africa, South America, Asia and Australia and they can be a wide range of colours. Most species of monkeys are principally herbivores, but their diet ranges from fruits, leaves, flowers, insects and eggs to small reptiles. They can bite and also carry diseases which can be dangerous to humans.

Horses are found all over the world and can be black, brown, grey or white. They are herbivores. They can be dangerous to humans as they can bite or kick.

Elephants live in Africa and Asia. They are grey. They are herbivores and eat grass, tree leaves, flowers, wild fruits, twigs, shrubs, bamboo, and bananas. Elephants can be dangerous to humans if they are mistreated and because of their size.

Zebras live only in Africa and have a distinctive black and white striped coat. They feed mainly on grass and they can be dangerous to humans as they have very sharp teeth and hooves.

Gazelles live in Africa and Asia and are beige in colour. They are herbivores and are not a danger to humans.

Lions live in Africa and Asia and are carnivores – they hunt large mammals like buffalo and wildebeest. They are beigey-brown in colour. They are very dangerous to humans.

View (PAGE 104)

See *Teaching tips: Using the video material in the classroom*, page 24.

2a Go through the words in the glossary to make sure students understand the key vocabulary. Use the photos on the page to help with *ivory* and *savannah*.

b ▶ Students watch the DVD and make a note of the animals they see. During feedback, play the DVD again and pause it every time you see an animal. Elicit the name of the animal and check the pronunciation.

ANSWERS:

gazelles, a monkey, crowned cranes, buffalo, vultures, giraffes, zebras, African elephants, crocodiles, lions

---

View, exercise 2b: Alternative suggestion

Give the remote control to one of the students and ask the other students to tell him or her when to pause. This can give students more feeling of control over the activity and, eventually, over their learning.

---

3 Tell students that this is the audio script for the DVD. Focus students' attention on the words in the box and the text. Elicit the answer for the first gap and then students work individually to complete the rest of the gaps. They check in pairs. Play the recording again to check the answers.

ANSWERS:

1 Twenty   **2** six metres   **3** animal   **4** male   **5** hot
6 crocodiles   **7** lions   **8** man   **9** five

World view (PAGE 105)

4a Check the meaning of *vegetarian* and *give money*. Read through the sentences and tick one or two that you agree with as an example. Give students a minute to decide which statements they agree and disagree with.

b Students work in pairs to compare their ideas. Circulate and make a note of good language to be praised later and language that will need to be corrected.

Find out more ⓢ (PAGE 105)

5a Focus students' attention on the animals in the box. Students work in pairs to brainstorm everything they can think of about them.

b Students work in the same pairs to research either all of the animals in the table or one or two that they have chosen. Focus students' attention on the search terms that they should use. Circulate and help with new vocabulary as necessary and encourage students to use English language websites.

ANSWERS:

Siberian tiger: Lives in Asia / the Russian Far East. There are just under 400. Russian civil war almost wiped them out. There has been heavy poaching of them.

Iberian imperial eagle: Lives in central and south-west Spain. There are just under 300. Loss of habitat, human encroachment and illegal poisoning are killing them.

mountain gorilla: Lives in Africa. There are just under 900. Poaching, habitat loss and disease are killing them.

giant panda: Lives in China. There are 2,000–3,000. Habitat loss and low birthrate are killing them.

hammerhead shark: Lives in warm tropical waters. Exact number unknown. Fishing is killing them.

Write up your research

6 Show students the text about Siberian tigers. Ask the following questions: *Which paragraph gives information about where they live?* (First), *Which paragraph gives information about how many there are?* (Second), *Which paragraph gives information about why they are in danger?* (Second), *Which paragraph gives some extra information?* (Third). Tell students that they should use this as a model for writing up their own research.

Study, practice & remember
(PAGES 158–159)

See *Teaching tips: Using the Study, practice & remember sections*, page 25.

Practice 1

ANSWERS:

1
1 How tall   **2** How much   **3** When   **4** How long   **5** Which
6 What

2
1 Where   **2** Which   **3** How many   **4** How fast   **5** How far
6 How long   **7** When   **8** How much   **9** How far
10 How old

Practice 2

ANSWERS:

1
1 olives   **2** time   **3** biscuits   **4** coins   **5** minutes   **6** food
7 cups   **8** space

2
1 There aren't many potatoes in the cupboard.
2 She hasn't got any potatoes on her plate.
3 There are a lot of potatoes left in the bowl.

3
1 There isn't any rice on the shelf.
2 He's got a little rice in his bag.
3 I haven't got much rice on my plate.
4 There's a lot of rice in the cupboard.

Remember these words

ANSWERS:

1
1 dolphins, fish, whales
2 camels, dogs, donkeys, elephants, horses, llamas, rats
3 dolphins, fish, snakes, whales
4 dogs, fish
5 camels, donkeys, elephants, horses, llamas
6 chimpanzees, elephants, snakes
7 dogs, rats
8 camels, chimpanzees, dogs, donkeys, horses, llamas, rats

2
1 river, lake   **2** mountain, volcano   **3** valley, forest
4 oceans, seas   **5** river, valley   **6** beach, desert

3
1 five point four   **2** six thousand   **3** seventy   **4** eight hundred
5 twenty thousand   **6** three hundred and two   **7** four million
8 two hundred thousand

OVERVIEW

PAGES 106–107

Vocabulary: Celebrations and parties

Grammar: *going to* for future intentions

Pronunciation: Weak form of *to* /tə/

Common European Framework: Students can describe plans and arrangements.

PAGES 108–109

Vocabulary: Weather and seasons

Reading: Celebrating the seasons

Grammar: *would like to* and *want to* for future wishes

Common European Framework: Students can talk about and describe simple desires and wishes.

PAGES 110–111

Task: Plan a festival

Common European Framework: Students can exchange simple or everyday information to organise future events.

PAGES 112–113

Writing: Information to promote a festival

Speaking: Suggestions and offers

Common European Framework: Students can perform and respond to basic language functions, such as information exchange, and express opinions and attitudes in a simple but appropriate way.

Vocabulary (PAGE 106)

Celebrations and parties

See *Teaching tips: Working with lexical phrases*, page 21.

WARM UP

If possible, you might like to start the class off with a mini-party. Prepare the room with soft drinks and some finger food (nothing too extravagant, just some cake and sandwiches will be great). Play some music when your students enter and invite them to have something to eat and drink. Encourage your students to talk about their day, football, television, anything they are interested in, so long as it is in English. This activity will be a surprise for students and serve to change the routine of their classes. It will also help you to set a very strong context for the class.

1a Focus students' attention on the photos. Elicit a quick description of what they can see and check if students can guess what each celebration is. Students then match the celebrations in the box with the photos. Check the word stress of the phrases <u>birth</u>day party, gradu<u>a</u>tion party, <u>wed</u>ding party, coming-of-<u>age</u> party, <u>leav</u>ing party, <u>na</u>tional <u>hol</u>iday, re<u>li</u>gious <u>hol</u>iday.

POSSIBLE ANSWERS:

from left to right: a wedding party or religious holiday, a national holiday, a birthday party, a national holiday

Culture notes

Birthday parties come in many different shapes and sizes in the UK. For children they are usually accompanied by ice cream, cakes and soft drinks. There is usually a birthday cake with the same number of candles as the birthday, for example, if the child is eight years old, he or she will have to blow out eight candles for good luck. The birthday boy or girl will probably receive presents and birthday cards. For adults, there might be a mini-celebration at work or at home, and maybe a social evening with friends in a restaurant or pub.

Graduation parties in the UK are usually only for people graduating from university. There is a formal ceremony where the student invites friends and family and wears a traditional gown and mortarboard. After the ceremony there is usually a dinner and maybe a celebration with friends in a pub. Recently, there has been a growth in proms, which are popular in the USA for students leaving school. Students dress up in formal suits and ball gowns to celebrate the end of their studies.

Wedding parties are also known as receptions. A wedding in the UK might take many forms and take place at any one of a wide variety of locations, for example a church, a mosque, a hotel or a registry office. Afterwards, the reception is usually held in a hotel with dinner, speeches and dancing.

Coming-of-age parties are usually held at the age of 18 in the UK and the USA. There aren't any particularly strong traditions, except for the birthday boy or girl to go out with his or her friends at night.

Leaving parties take place either when a colleague is leaving work or a friend is leaving home for another city or country. In the first case, there is usually a small celebration at work, which may then continue in a nearby restaurant or pub, depending on how long the person has worked at the company. In the second case, there is usually a tearful goodbye in a pub or club.

National holidays in the UK are usually called *bank holidays* to differentiate them from holidays you take off from work or school. They are usually on a Monday and provide the opportunity to get away for the weekend to visit family or get out into the country. The only exceptions in the UK are for special occasions such as the Queen's Jubilee or a royal wedding, when some people have street parties (see the second photo). In the USA, the biggest national holiday is Thanksgiving, which always falls on the fourth Thursday of November. The main tradition for Thanksgiving involves getting together with your family and eating turkey.

Religious holidays are celebrated quite differently depending on the religion involved. In the UK, the only religious holidays which are also national holidays are Christmas and Easter. It is not unusual to see other religious holidays celebrated in different cities, including Jewish, Muslim and Sikh holidays.

b Ask the class the question and elicit responses.

2 Go through the examples with your students. Make sure they understand the verbs in the box and then ask students to work individually or in pairs to match the verbs in box A with the phrases in box B. Check answers as a class by writing them on the board. Encourage your students to make a note of the complete phrases.

ANSWERS:

decorate the house / the table

make traditional food / a cake

hire an entertainer / a band

dress up in party clothes / traditional costumes

take part in a parade / a competition

3a Go through the questions with your students. Give them plenty of time to think of their answers and to make notes. Circulate and offer help as necessary.

Vocabulary, exercise 3a: Alternative suggestion

Prepare a mini-talk before the class to give to your students about a recent celebration or a party you have been to. Make sure you include some of the phrases from exercise 2. Tell your students they should listen to you and tick the phrases they hear. Your students then use your mini-talk as a model to follow.

b Students work in pairs to tell each other about their celebration or party. In feedback, ask students to report back on what their partner said.

Vocabulary, exercise 3b: Additional activity

Prepare strips of paper with the individual phrases from exercise 2 on them. Distribute one to each student. Tell students that they are going to talk for a minute about anything they like, but they must include their phrase. Give them a few minutes to prepare what they want to say. In small groups, each student talks about their chosen topic while the other members of the group listen. At the end, the rest of the group has to identify the phrase that was on the speaker's piece of paper.

ADDITIONAL PRACTICE

Workbook: Vocabulary: *Celebrations and parties*, page 59

Grammar focus 1 (PAGE 107)

going to for future intentions

See *Teaching tips: Working with grammar*, page 20.

1a 🎧 **12.1** Remind students of the celebrations from Vocabulary, exercise 1a. Students listen to the recording and identify which celebration each person is talking about. They check in pairs and then as a class.

ANSWERS:

1 a wedding   **2** a national holiday   **3** a coming-of-age party

b Make sure your students read the items in the box before they listen again. Check students have understood they have to match the speakers to the items. Play the recording. Students then check in pairs. Play the recording again if you think students would benefit from it. Check as a class.

ANSWERS:

Speaker 1: the hairdresser's, drive   **Speaker 2:** the beach, relax
Speaker 3: food, dance

2 🎧 **12.2** Give your students time to read through all of the sentences. Play the recording and pause after each one to give students time to write the word. Students check in pairs and then as a class.

Although there is a pronunciation section later on this page, set the groundwork for it now by drilling the sentences and encouraging students to use the weak form of *to* /tə/.

ANSWERS:

1 meet   **2** drive   **3** work   **4** relax   **5** have   **6** dance

GRAMMAR

going to for future intentions

1 With a weaker elementary class, you might like to remind students of the conjugation for the verb *to be* in the present tense, and remind them of the positive and negative short forms.

Work through the Grammar box with the class, getting students to read the rules. Alternatively, ask students to close their books and remember some of the sentences from exercise 2. Elicit examples of both positive and negative sentences, e.g. *I'm going to meet my friend Monica. I'm not going to work on Monday.* Finally ask students if they can make a question with the prompt *drive to the wedding*.

Highlight:

- the meaning of *going to* for future intentions.
- the form: *be* + *to* + verb.
- the short forms of the verb *to be*.
- the inversion of the auxiliary verb *to be* and the subject to form the question.
- the short answers to the question.

2 Either read the rule in the book or write on the board: *I'm going to a friend's wedding.* Ask students if they can see a difference between this sentence and the other examples. Either elicit or show the absence of a verb after *going to*. Highlight that we usually use this and NOT *going to go*.

You may want to ask students to read Study 1 on page 160 for a more detailed explanation of *going to* for future intentions.

PRACTICE

1a Do the first sentence with the class as an example. Students then work individually to complete the rest of the sentences then check in pairs.

b 🎧 **12.3** Students listen to the recording and check their answers. They then rewrite each sentence to make it true for them.

ANSWERS:

1 I'm going **to** have a party this weekend.
2 My parents **are** going to decorate the house next week.
3 I **am** going to have a holiday abroad this summer.
4 I'm going **to** buy some new clothes this weekend.
5 My friends and I **are** going to have a picnic tomorrow.
6 I'm going **to** make a cake tomorrow afternoon.
7 My best friend is **going** to leave her job next month.

PRONUNCIATION

See *Teaching tips: Helping students with pronunciation*, page 22.

1 Write the first sentence from exercise 1a on the board and model it. Ask students if the pronunciation of *to* is strong like /tuː/ or weak like /tə/. Play the recording of all of the sentences again and ask students to identify if they use the strong or weak pronunciation.

2 Drill the sentences chorally and individually, making sure students use the weak form /tə/.

2a Give students some time to think about their plans and write sentences about them. Circulate and offer ideas if students are having difficulties.

b Elicit some model questions that students could ask and put them on the board. Students then work in pairs to ask and answer questions about their plans. In feedback, ask for the most interesting or exciting plans.

ADDITIONAL PRACTICE

➡ **Study, practice & remember:** Practice 1

Workbook: Grammar focus 1: *going to* for future intentions, pages 59–60; Pronunciation: *Weak forms of* to, page 60

Vocabulary (PAGE 108)
Weather and seasons

See *Teaching tips: Working with lexical phrases*, page 21.

Culture notes

In many cultures, and especially in the UK, the weather can act as a good topic of conversation for small talk when you don't really know somebody that well and you want to fill the silence. You can easily practise this with students by bringing up the topic of the weather in short conversations at the beginning of class or outside the classroom. Talk to them about the weather on your way to work, over the weekend, on your holiday, etc.

There are not many examples of extreme weather in the UK. It gets much colder and there is more snow in other places on the same latitude, and they usually also have more sun and higher temperatures in the summer. However, it is the changeable nature of the weather in the UK that probably leads to it being such a popular topic of discussion.

In recent years it has looked as if the weather patterns might be changing, with wetter summers and colder winters. This has added yet another element to the conversation; is this all because of global warming or is it just a natural variation?

---

1 Students work in pairs to discuss the questions. Check the answers as a class. If your students come from different countries, encourage them to compare their different weather patterns and seasons. If they come from the same country, ask them if they have a favourite or least favourite season.

2 Students work individually to match the phrases in the box with the pictures. They check in pairs and then as a class. During feedback, make sure your students are pronouncing the final -*y* /i/ sound correctly as it is commonly dropped.

ANSWERS:

A It's foggy.   **B** It's cloudy.   **C** It's warm.   **D** It's windy.
E It's icy.   **F** It's cool.   **G** It's sunny.   **H** It's snowing.
I It's cold.   **J** It's raining.   **K** It's hot.   **L** It's wet

---

3 Students work in pairs to answer the questions. Compare ideas with the class for a final feedback session.

Vocabulary, exercise 3: Additional activity

Write on the board: *my last birthday, New Year's Eve, my last holiday, yesterday, last weekend* and add any important national holidays like, for example, Independence Day. Tell students what the weather was like for your last birthday and show the past of the expression introduced in the book, e.g. *It was cold and raining*. Put students into pairs to talk about the weather on the other days. In feedback, see if everybody can agree on what the weather was like.

ADDITIONAL PRACTICE

➡ **Workbook:** Vocabulary: *Weather and seasons*, page 60

Reading (PAGES 108–109)

1a Focus students' attention on the photos and the questions. Students work in pairs to discuss the questions. Elicit ideas and put them on the board.

b Students quickly read the article to see if their ideas were correct. You might like to give a time limit of three minutes to encourage students to read quickly and to find just the answers to the two questions.

ANSWERS:

from left to right: winter in Japan, summer in Sweden and autumn in the USA

---

2 Give your students more time and encourage them to read the text in more detail to check if the statements are true or false. Ask them to underline the part of the text that shows them the answer. This will help with feedback later. Students check in pairs and then as a class.

ANSWERS:

1 T
2 F (Two million people come to see the sculptures.)
3 F (It's when day and night are of equal length.)
4 F (They watch theatre performances in the streets.)
5 F (They celebrate it on the Friday and Saturday nearest to June 24th.)
6 T
7 F (They are most popular in the north-east of the USA.)
8 T

Reading, exercise 2: Additional activities

This is one of the longest texts that students have read so far and there may be quite a lot of vocabulary that students are not sure about. Don't encourage students to ask you about all of the vocabulary they don't understand as this might take a long time, will force people to focus on what they don't know rather than what they do know, and will demand a lot of thinking on your feet. Instead, adopt one or more of the following ideas:

- Ask students to find words associated with a theme. In this text, you might ask students to underline all the words associated with celebrations. This will help students to start developing a basic understanding of words even if they don't fully understand them.

- Put students into pairs and allow them to ask you about a maximum number of words, for example two per pair. They should identify which two words they want to ask you about and write them down before you start answering questions. This will force students to focus on the most important words that they are not sure about.

- Bring in dictionaries for students to use to find definitions of words they are not sure about.

- Show students how to find help with unknown words on the internet.

- Ask students, in pairs, to identify some words they are not sure about. They should then pass these words on to another pair for them to find a definition.

---

3 Students work in pairs to discuss the questions. Check ideas as a class.

Grammar focus 2 (PAGE 109)

would like to and *want to* for future wishes

See *Teaching tips: Working with grammar*, page 20.

1a 🎧 **12.4** Tell students they are going to listen to four sentences, one about each of the festivals. Students listen and decide which festival is being talked about by each speaker. Students check in pairs and then as a class.

> **ANSWERS:**
> **1** Novruz Bayram   **2** Midsummer's Day   **3** Sapporo Snow Festival
> **4** Harvest festival

b Give students time to read the sentences and, if possible, complete them. If students can't remember the words to fill the gaps, tell them not to worry and then play the recording again. Students check in pairs and then as a class. During class feedback, you might like to play each sentence again after you have given the correct answer so students can hear the words in the context of the sentence.

> **ANSWERS:**
> **1** 'd like to   **2** want to   **3** 'd like to   **4** want to

GRAMMAR

***would like to* and *want to* for future wishes**

1 Read through the rules with your students. Try to elicit the difference in meaning between the two forms, but don't push this too much as it is quite subtle. Highlight:

- that basically they mean the same.
- that *want to* is stronger and more direct than *would like to*.
- the form: *would like to* + verb; *want to* + verb.
- the weak pronunciation of *to* /tə/ in both forms, the same as that in *going to* on the previous page.
- the two different short answers to the questions: *Yes, I do.* / *No, I don't.* and *Yes, I would.* / *No, I wouldn't.*

2 Check that students understand the time phrases.

You may want to ask students to read Study 2 on page 160 for a more detailed explanation of *would like to* and *want to* for future wishes.

PRACTICE

a Do the first one as an example with the class. Students work individually to complete the questions then check in pairs.

b 🎧 **12.5** Students listen and check.

> **ANSWERS:**
> **1** Do, would   **2** Are, would   **3** Do   **4** would   **5** Are   **6** Do, would

c Students work in pairs to ask and answer the questions.

ADDITIONAL PRACTICE

Resource bank: Activity 12A *Future walkabout* (*going to* for future intentions; *would like to* and *want to* for future wishes)

Study, practice & remember: Practice 2

Workbook: Grammar focus 2: *would like to* and *want to* for future wishes, pages 61–62

Task (PAGES 110–111)

Plan a festival

See *Teaching tips: Making tasks work*, page 23.

Preparation (PAGES 110–111)

Reading

1 Students work in pairs to discuss the questions. In feedback, ask students to share information about festivals and celebrations in their area.

> **Preparation, exercise 1a: Alternative suggestion**
>
> If your students come from the same country, prepare a list of festivals before the class. Write them on the board and ask students to say what type of festival they are, e.g. *a music festival* or *a folk festival*. Elicit the different activities that people can do at the festivals and ask if students have been to or would like to go to any of them.

2 Make sure students read the questions before they read the website so that they know what they have to look for. Students check in pairs and then as a class. Encourage students to justify their answers by identifying the part of the website that supports them.

> **ANSWERS:**
> **1** July 5th–8th in the heart of the Highlands of Scotland
> **2** Barbara McDowell, Salsa Fling, The Protractors
> **3** Scottish haggis, Scotch broth, Scottish shortbread
> **4** drawing classes, face-painting, arts and crafts workshops
> **5** hotels and a campsite
> **6** music and dancing
> **7** Auldhay Station, Aberdeen Airport

3a 🎧 **12.6** Students listen to the conversation and identify which of the things on the website the people talk about. They check in pairs. Play the recording again if you think students would benefit from it.

> **ANSWERS:**
> They talk about the dates, the music, the food, the activities for children and the accommodation.

b Focus students' attention on the Useful language box and make sure students read all of the phrases before they listen again and tick the ones they hear.

> **ANSWERS:**
> When is the festival going to happen? ✓
> What (music) are you going to have? ✓
> How about (food)? ✓
> It's going to be (at the beginning of July / at the end of November). ✓
> (Salsa Fling) are going to play at the festival. ✓
> We're going to have (cookery demonstrations). ✓
> We've got a lot of (activities for children). ✓
> There's going to be (traditional Scottish dancing). ✓

Task (PAGE 110)

Speaking

1 Put students into pairs. Give the context by explaining that your students are going to plan a local festival using the questions from Preparation, exercise 2 as prompts. Remind students to use the language from the Useful language box, as well as *would like to* and *want to*. Circulate and offer help and encouragement as necessary.

2 Split up the pairs and put students into small groups. Students talk about the festival they planned with their original partner. You could end the activity by having the class vote on what they think is the best festival.

Share your task

The idea here is to give students a chance to 'perfect' their speaking in this context and provide them with a recording of a 'polished' version. This will provide extra motivation for students, as well as extra practice. Students can either make an audio or video recording, depending on how comfortable they feel and what equipment is available. Students could even use their mobile phones to do this. If possible, they'll need a quiet place to make their recording. Students can either record themselves during the lesson, or as homework and bring the recordings to the next class.

Some additional ideas could include:

- Students film themselves talking about their proposed festival as if it were a television advertisement.
- Students record a conversation with a classmate with one person asking questions about the festival and the other one answering.

Language live (PAGES 112–113)

Writing (PAGE 112)

Information to promote a festival

Culture notes

Boi Bumbá festivals are held predominantly in the north and north-east of Brazil, in and around the Amazon. The biggest and most famous of these festivals is held in Parintins, about 500 km from Manaus, the capital of the state of Amazonas in Brazil.

There are many different versions of the festival, and as many different stories about the origin. Basically, all the festivals start with a play which tells the story of Francisco, a farmer, and his (usually) ugly, pregnant wife Catirina, who wants to eat beef tongue. Francisco kills a bull for his wife, but it turns out the bull is the farm owner's favourite. A priest and a doctor both fail to revive the bull and Francisco is just about to be sent to jail when a shaman performs a ritual that finally brings the bull back to life and spares Francisco from jail. The end of the story is a huge party that celebrates the bull's life and usually spills out into the streets afterwards.

The festival in Parintins is very popular with the residents of the city and draws tourists from all around the world. There is a 35,000 capacity arena for the play, and the tickets are all free. The main problem with seeing the festival is getting to the city as it is quite remote with access only by the Amazon River or plane.

1a Focus students' attention on the three photos. Students work in pairs to discuss the questions. Elicit ideas and put them on the board. Make sure that students know the word *bull* to describe the third picture.

b Students quickly read the text and check the answers to the questions. Check as a class.

ANSWERS:

1 The photos show the Boi Bumbá festival.
2 It takes place in Brazil.
3 They're celebrating the story of a bull which comes back to life.

2 Make sure students read the statements first and then the text to find out if they are true or false. They check in pairs and then as a class.

ANSWERS:

1 T
2 F (There are many festivals.)
3 T
4 F (There are three nights.)
5 T
6 F (Tickets are free.)

3 Students match the paragraphs with the descriptions. This will help students to structure their own writing later on.

ANSWERS:

a 3   b 2   c 1

4 Give students some time to remember the festival they planned from page 110. Encourage them to make notes before they start writing and to refer to the text about *Boi Bumbá* for inspiration. If students would prefer, allow them to write about a real local festiva

5 Students work individually to write about their festival.

Writing, exercise 5: Alternative suggestion

Instead of asking students to write individually, you might like to ask them to do some collaborative writing. This can have the benefit of encouraging weaker writers, improving group identity and changing the focus of writing to make it more interesting. Some ways you can do this include:

- having students work in groups of three and take responsibility for writing about just one of the points from exercise 3.
- suggesting students use an online program like Google Docs to enable them to write collaboratively and produce one text between them.
- putting students into groups and allowing them to decide how they will produce the text.

Speaking (PAGE 113)

Suggestions and offers

See *Teaching tips: Using the video material in the classroom*, page 24.

1 Focus students' attention on the photo. Set a context by saying the three women are organising a birthday party. Students then work in pairs to discuss the question.

2a ▶ Students watch the DVD and answer the question. Make sure students understand they only have to say how many ideas are mentioned, not what the ideas are. Students check in pairs and then as a class.

ANSWER:

4

b Make sure students read the phrases for giving suggestions before they watch the DVD again to put them in order. They check in pairs and then as a class.

ANSWERS:

b, f, e, d, a, c

c If students don't remember the answer, play the end of the recordin again for them to check.

ANSWER:

They decide to go to an open-air concert in the park.

3a Do the first one as an example. Students work individually to put the rest of the sentences in the correct order, then check in pairs.

b ⏵ Students watch the recording to check their answers. Quickly check with the class and put the correct sentences on the board.

ANSWERS:

1 Why don't we go out for a meal?
2 Where shall we go?
3 How about Thai Kitchen?
4 Let's go bowling!
5 That sounds like a good idea.
6 I'll phone and book some tickets.
7 Shall I ask Ben if he wants to come?
8 Yes, OK then.

PRONUNCIATION

See *Teaching tips: Helping students with pronunciation*, page 22.

1 Students watch the recording of the key phrases again and pay attention to the pronunciation. If you wrote the sentences on the board for the previous question then you can use this to focus on specific areas that might cause problems, for example intonation, sentence stress or weak forms.

> **Pronunciation, exercise 1: Alternative suggestion**
>
> Draw these two intonation patterns on the board:
>
>
>
> Write the following sentence on the board: *Let's go to the cinema.* and provide a model of the intonation similar to the second diagram. Try to make sure you go down after the first syllable of *cinema*. Ask students which intonation pattern on the board best resembles your model and elicit the second one.
>
> Then write on the board the question: *Do you want to go out?* and model it with an intonation pattern similar to the first diagram. Try to make sure you go up on *out*. Ask students which intonation pattern on the board best resembles your model this time and elicit the first one.
>
> Tell students to watch the key phrases and pay attention to the intonation patterns. Tell students that only one of the phrases follows the first pattern and ask them to identify which one it is (sentence 7).
>
> Ask students: *How is sentence 7 different to the others?* Elicit that it is the only *yes/no* question. Tell your students that when we ask a question of this type we usually use the same rising intonation pattern.

2 Drill the key phrases chorally and individually.

4a Read through the three situations with students and elicit one or two ideas for each one. This will help less imaginative students to start their conversations. Students work in pairs to select one of the situations and write a conversation based on it. Circulate and offer help and encouragement as necessary.

b Students practise their conversation in pairs. Finish off the class by inviting one or two pairs to perform their conversations for the class.

ADDITIONAL PRACTICE

🔁 **Resource bank:** Activity 12B *The school party* (Suggestions and offers)

Workbook: Writing: *Information to promote a festival*, page 62; Language live: *Suggestions and offers*, page 63

Students can now do Progress test 6 on the Teacher's Resource Disc.

Study, practice & remember
(PAGES 160–161)

See *Teaching tips: Using the Study, practice & remember sections*, page 25.

Practice 1

ANSWERS:

1
    1 I am going to see a film this evening.
    2 He is not going to play tennis this weekend.
    3 Are you going to visit us next week?
    4 I am going to book the tickets today.
    5 She is going to have a haircut tomorrow.
    6 I am not going to get up early tomorrow.
    7 Are they going to arrive tonight?
    8 Is he going to do his homework this evening?

2
    1 're going to have   2 'm not going to drive
    3 are you going to start   4 's going to meet
    5 'm going to clean   6 aren't going to study

Practice 2

ANSWERS:

1
    1 Do you want to have a sandwich?
    2 I'd like to buy two tickets please.
    3 I don't want to get up early tomorrow.
    4 Would you like to share a taxi with me?
    5 She doesn't want to cook dinner.
    6 Do you want to use my pen?
    7 Would you like to have some cake?
    8 They want to play football this weekend.

2
    1 Do   2 would   3 like   4 doesn't   5 Would   6 like
    7 don't   8 Do

3
    1 Do   2 would   3 want   4 like   5 wants   6 'd
    7 don't   8 speak

Remember these words

ANSWERS:

1
    1 make   2 decorate   3 hire   4 take part   5 dress up
    6 hire   7 decorate   8 take part

2
    1 ✗   2 ✓   3 ✓   4 ✗   5 ✓   6 ✗   7 ✗   8 ✓

OVERVIEW

PAGES 114–115

Vocabulary: School and university subjects

Grammar: *have to* and *don't have to*

Pronunciation: Weak form of *have to*

Common European Framework: Students can talk about and assign responsibilities.

PAGES 116–117

Vocabulary: Education and training

Listening: Two career paths

Common European Framework: Students can express plans and expectations in simple everyday contexts such as education and work.

PAGES 118–119

Reading: From slates to iPads

Grammar: *might* and *will*

Common European Framework: Students can use an idea of the overall meaning of short texts on everyday topics to derive the probable meaning of unknown words from the context.

PAGES 120–121

Task: Complete a careers questionnaire

Common European Framework: Students can respond appropriately to forms and questions about personal habits and routines.

PAGES 122–123

World culture: A dream come true

Common European Framework: Students can write short, basic descriptions of events, past activities and personal experiences.

Vocabulary (PAGE 114)

School and university subjects

See *Teaching tips: Working with lexical phrases*, page 21.

Culture notes

Compulsory education in the UK is from the ages of 5–16. From the ages of 5–7 most children go to infant schools, and then from 8–11, most children go to junior schools. These two types of school are usually the same institution and are called primary schools. From 11–16 most students go to secondary or senior schools. From 16–18 students can either stay at their secondary school or go to a sixth form college.

Education from 5–18 is free, although there is also a small private sector. Universities are no longer free, with many universities charging up to £9,000 a year. Most degrees take three years to complete.

The names of the different types of schools can cause problems. The vast majority of students go to *state schools*, which are the free ones. There are also *public schools*, which charge fees but are called *public* because they have to show their accounts to the public every year, and *private schools*, which are run as private businesses.

At the age of 16 most students take their GCSE exams (GCSE standing for General Certificate of Secondary Education). These are national exams and enable students to leave with qualifications in the individual subjects they studied. At the age of 18 students then take their A-Levels (the A standing for Advanced). They can use these to enter university.

WARM UP

Write on the board: *I love(d) school because … .* and *I hate(d) school because … .* Ask students to raise their hands if they love or loved school. Put all of these students into one group. Put all of the students who hate or hated school into another group. Give the two groups five minutes to complete the sentences in any way they like. Then pair students up with somebody from the other group and ask them to compare their ideas.

1a Focus students' attention on the photos and the subjects in the box. Students work in pairs to match the subjects to the photos. Check as a class. During feedback check the pronunciation and meaning of any unknown vocabulary. Note that *information technology* is often referred to as *I.T.*

ANSWERS:

from left to right: performing arts, science/maths, engineering, geography

---

b Students work in their pairs again to add three more subjects to the list. Elicit ideas and put them on the board.

POSSIBLE ANSWERS:

food technology, chemistry, physics, biology

Vocabulary, exercise 1b: Additional activity

Draw a table on the board with three columns. Label the columns: *school*, *university* and *both*. Ask students to complete the table with the subjects from exercises 1a and b, according to what is available at school or university where they live.

In the UK, the possible answers would be:

School: science (at university you usually study a specific area of science, e.g. physics), design and technology

University: performing arts, medicine, law, leisure and tourism, engineering

Both: geography, languages, business studies, history, information technology, literature, media studies, economics, maths

---

2 Do the first one as a class as an example. Students then work in pairs to answer the rest of the questions. During feedback, if there is any disagreement, encourage students to try to justify their answers before saying what you think.

POSSIBLE ANSWERS:

good with numbers: business studies, science, economics, maths
good with people: medicine, leisure and tourism
good at art: design and technology
good at remembering facts: law, history
good with your hands: design and technology
good with machines: engineering
good at writing: literature, media studies
good at speaking: languages, performing arts

---

3 Students work in pairs to discuss the questions.

ADDITIONAL PRACTICE

➡ **Workbook:** Vocabulary: *School and university subjects*, page 64

Grammar focus 1 (PAGE 115)

have to and don't have to

See *Teaching tips: Working with grammar*, page 20.

1 Focus students' attention on the email. Students read the questions first and then the email to find the answers. They check in pairs and then as a class.

> **ANSWERS:**
> **1** a teacher training course   **2** next month

2 Check the meaning of *part-time* and *full-time*. Students read the email again to find the correct answers. They check in pairs before checking as a class.

> **ANSWERS:**
> **1** doesn't like   **2** children   **3** hasn't   **4** part-time
> **5** doesn't live

GRAMMAR

have to and *don't have to*

1 Check students understand *necessary*. They then read through the sentences and match them to the meanings. Students check in pairs and then as a class. During feedback, highlight that:

- the third person positive form is *has to*.
- the third person negative form is *doesn't have to*.
- *don't have to* (not necessary) is not the opposite of *have to* (necessary). If students are interested in how to express negative obligation, you could remind them of *can't* (meaning *not OK or not allowed*) from Unit 5.

> **ANSWERS:**
> **1** a   **2** a   **3** b   **4** b

You may want to ask students to read Study 1 on page 162 for a more detailed explanation of *have to* and *don't have to*.

PRONUNCIATION

See *Teaching tips: Helping students with pronunciation*, page 22.

1 🎧 **13.1** Remind students of the weak forms that they have looked at in previous units. Elicit, if possible, the strong and weak forms of *to* /tuː/ and /tə/. Write *have* on the board and ask them how they think it's pronounced. Students will probably suggest /hæv/ but the more common pronunciation is /hæf/. Play the recording and ask students to pay attention to the pronunciation of both *have* and *to*.

2 Drill the sentences chorally and individually.

PRACTICE

1a Elicit answers for the first couple of sentences as examples. Students then work individually to complete the rest of the sentences. Circulate and monitor.

b Students work in pairs to compare their ideas.

> **POSSIBLE ANSWERS:**
> **1** **a** have to, **b** have to, **c** don't have to
> **2** **a** have to, **b** have to, **c** don't have to
> **3** **a** don't have to, **b** have to, **c** don't have to

ADDITIONAL PRACTICE

➡ **Study, practice & remember:** Practice 1

> **Workbook:** Grammar focus 1: *have to* and *don't have to*, page 65; Pronunciation: *have to*, page 66

Vocabulary (PAGE 116)

Education and training

See *Teaching tips: Working with lexical phrases*, page 21.

1a Check students understand *degree*, *earn*, *unemployed* and *career*. Also, check the pronunciation of *course* /kɔːs/. Do the first one as an example with the class, but don't confirm the answer yet. Students work individually to choose the correct answer for the rest of the sentences. They then check in pairs.

b Students read the college advert to check their answers. Encourage them to underline the collocations to make it easier to refer to them in the future. Check as a class.

> **ANSWERS:**
> **1** fail   **2** get   **3** get   **4** do   **5** choose   **6** for   **7** have   **8** to
> **9** be   **10** earn

2 Do the first one or two as an example. Students then work in pairs to categorise the phrases. Check as a class.

> **ANSWERS:**
> **college/university:** fail an exam, get into university, get a degree, do a course, apply for a course, have an interview, train to be
> **work:** choose a career, apply for a job, have an interview, train to be, be unemployed, earn money

3a Point out to students that they also need to think about the form of the verbs. Do the first one as an example and ask them questions to guide them, e.g. *Is it first, second or third person? Is it past or present?* Students then work individually to complete the sentences. They check in pairs before checking as a class.

> **ANSWERS:**
> **1** train   **2** degree   **3** failed   **4** are   **5** have   **6** earning
> **7** for   **8** do   **9** get   **10** career

b Give students a minute or so to think about which sentences they agree with or are true for them.

c Students work in pairs to compare their ideas.

> **Vocabulary: Additional activities**
>
> If you have the time, it is a good idea to get students to investigate other related verb phrases. Some ideas include:
>
> - asking students to find more collocations with the verbs from exercise 1a. You could ask students to find two more collocations for each verb or allocate one verb per student and ask them to find five more collocations that they think are interesting. Students then present their findings to their classmates.
>
> - asking students to find other verbs that collocate with the nouns, for example *take an exam, pass an exam, cheat in an exam*. Just as with the verbs, you could ask students to focus on one noun phrase or look at all of them.
>
> - encouraging students to keep a notebook for any new verb/noun phrases that they come across.
>
> - keeping a record of new verb/noun phrases in class by putting them on a wall or creating a digital file so that students can easily refer to them and even add to them.

ADDITIONAL PRACTICE

→ **Resource bank:** Activity 13A *Education crossword* (School and university subjects; Education and training)

Workbook: Vocabulary: *Education and training*, page 66

Listening (PAGE 117)

Two career paths

1   Students work in pairs to discuss the questions. If some or all of your students are not in work, change the last question to *What is your ideal job?*

2   🎧 **13.2** Make sure students read the topics before they listen so that they know what to listen for. Students then listen to the recording and mark each topic: L for Lorraine (the woman) and M for Martin (the man).

> **ANSWERS:**
> 1 L   2 M   3 M   4 L   5 M   6 M

> **Listening, exercise 2: Alternative suggestion**
> If you have a weaker elementary class, or students who need to increase their confidence in their listening skills, you might like to ask students to look at the pictures and guess which sentence applies to which person before listening to check their ideas.

3   Ask students to read the questions and deal with any unknown language, e.g. *worth* in question 6. Students then listen to the recording and answer the questions. They check in pairs. Play the recording again before checking answers as a class.

> **ANSWERS:**
> 1 No, she didn't.   2 No, they weren't.   3 at 16   4 Yes, she did.
> 5 60   6 over £30 million   7 engineering and maths   8 maths
> 9 No, he didn't.   10 No, he didn't.   11 No, it's stress free.
> 12 No, he wouldn't.

4   Students work in pairs to discuss the questions.

Reading (PAGE 118)

WARM UP

Write on the board: *school now* and *school 50 years ago*. Elicit ideas for differences between the two from the class.

1   Students work in pairs to discuss the questions. During feedback, be careful not to overload your students with your own ideas about the education system. Also, if your school doesn't have a lot of technology, make sure you stress that technology is only a tool and cannot do your learning for you.

2   Check students understand *slate* by using the picture of the old classroom. Make sure students read the questions before reading the article so they know what to look for. Ask students to read the article quickly to find which things are mentioned. To help with feedback, it is a good idea to get students to underline the part of the text that mentions each thing. Students check in pairs and then as a class.

> **ANSWERS:**
> studying grammar, using the internet, learning Chinese

3   Check that students know what they have to do by pretending to join two sentence halves. Give students time to read the text again to find the answers. They check in pairs before checking as a class.

> **ANSWERS:**
> 1 e   2 a   3 b   4 c   5 f   6 d

4   Students work in pairs to discuss the questions.

Grammar focus 2 (PAGE 119)

might and *will*

See *Teaching tips: Working with grammar*, page 20.

1a   To give students a context, tell them that all of these sentences come from the reading text but discourage them from looking at the text again until they have tried to complete the sentences from memory. Students complete the sentences with one of the words then check in pairs.

b   Students read the last paragraph of the reading text again to check their answers.

> **ANSWERS:**
> 1 might   2 won't   3 might not   4 will

GRAMMAR

might and *will*

1   Students look at the four sentences from exercise 1a again and match the modal verbs to the definitions. Give your students a few minutes to think about this and then have them check with a partner. During feedback, highlight:
   - the meaning of the verbs, i.e. the idea of *prediction*. As a contrast, refer back to the language of *going to* in Unit 12 about *intentions*. Ask students to organise the words *will*, *won't*, *might* and *might not* on a line:

   ←————————————————————————→
   WILL   MIGHT   MIGHT NOT   WON'T

   - the short forms: *'ll* and *won't*.
   - the pronunciation of the short forms *I'll, he'll, we'll*, etc.

> **ANSWERS:**
> 1 Sentence 4   2 Sentence 2   3 Sentence 1   4 Sentence 3

2   Elicit the use of the infinitive without *to* after these modal verbs, e.g. *I will play.* NOT *I will to play.*

> **ANSWER:**
> the infinitive without *to*

3   Students work individually to change the sentences into the negative form. They check in pairs and then as a class. During feedback, highlight:
   - the fact that we don't use a short form for *might not*.
   - the pronunciation of *won't* /wəʊnt/.

> **ANSWERS:**
> 1 Students won't do all their homework on computers.
> 2 English might not be the most important language.

You may want to ask students to read Study 2 on page 162 for a more detailed explanation of *might* and *will*.

PRACTICE

1   Do the first one as an example with the class. Students work individually to choose the correct answers then check in pairs before checking as a class.

ANSWERS:
1 will disappear   2 won't go, might study   3 might go, might travel
4 will study   5 might need   6 will take

2a Focus students' attention on the photos and quickly elicit some of the things that they can see in them. Complete the first one or two sentences so that they are true for you. Students then work individually to complete the sentences about themselves. Circulate and offer help and advice whenever necessary.

b Students work in pairs or small groups to compare their sentences.

Practice, exercise 2b: Additional activity

When students are listening to each other in exercise 2b, encourage them to keep a note of what is said. Next, put students into pairs or small groups with different people. They should then tell their new partner or group what their original partner said, but include one false sentence. The other students have to guess what the false sentence is.

ADDITIONAL PRACTICE

Resource bank: Activity 13B *Looking into the future* (*might* and *will*)

Study, practice & remember: Practice 2

Workbook: Grammar focus 2: *might* and *will*, page 68

Task (PAGES 120–121)

Complete a careers questionnaire

See *Teaching tips: Making tasks work*, page 23.

Preparation (PAGES 120–121)

Reading

WARM UP

Prepare a number of definitions for jobs on strips of paper. If you have ten students, you will need five definitions, if you have sixteen students, you will need eight definitions, and so on. Write the definition on one piece of paper and the job on a different piece. For example, *This person works in a restaurant and brings you your food.* and *Waiter*. Use some of the jobs from Unit 1 to help recycle vocabulary. Before your students enter the classroom put out the strips of paper on the chairs.

When students come in, ask them to read the strip of paper on their chair and then walk around and find the person with the corresponding definition or job. Encourage them to read the definitions and not just show them to each other. When they have found their partner, they should sit down together and write more definitions for other jobs. To finish off the activity, have students read some of their definitions aloud and invite other students to guess what the job they are describing is.

1 Focus students' attention on the photos and elicit what the jobs are or might be. Students work in pairs to discuss the questions. During feedback, you might also want to ask students if there are any jobs they would hate to do.

2 Focus students' attention on the careers questionnaire on the opposite page. Check the meaning of *mainly indoors, mainly outdoors, sympathetic, working hours, regular hours* and *smart*. Be especially careful with *sympathetic* as it is a false friend for *nice* or *friendly* in various languages. Give students a few minutes to complete the questionnaire.

3a 13.3 Tell students they are going to listen to two people talking about the questionnaire. Make sure they read the two questions first, then play the recording. Students check in pairs and then as a class.

ANSWERS:
1 a's   2 some but not all of them

---

b Focus students' attention on the phrases in the Useful language box. Give them a couple of minutes to read through the phrases and deal with any problems that may arise. Students then listen to the recording and tick the phrases they hear. They check in pairs and then as a class. You may need to play the recording again for students to check as a lot of the phrases are used. If you do this, pause after each sentence to give students time to find and tick it.

ANSWERS:
What does that mean? ✓
What does it say? ✓
What else? ✓
Yes, that's true. ✓
I think that's partly true. ✓
That's not right. ✓
That's rubbish! ✓
I like doing things and being active. ✓
I'll work as hard as I can. ✓
I might be a bit bossy sometimes. ✓
I won't be horrible to people. ✓
I'm not good at maths or business. ✓
I'm a journalist at the moment ... ✓
I'd like to be a designer. ✓

Task (PAGE 120)

Speaking

1a Students work in pairs to compare their answers to the questionnaire. In feedback, you could find out if the class had anything in common in their answers.

b Direct students to page 133 to find out what their answers mean.

Speaking, exercise 1b: Alternative suggestion

Direct students to page 133, but instead of reading to find out what their own answers mean, ask them to find out what their partners' answers mean. They should then tell their partner what the results are.

---

2 Working in the same pairs, students discuss their findings. Circulate and offer help and encouragement and remind them to use the language from the Useful language box. You might like to make a note of good language use to praise at the end of the class and other language that needs to be corrected.

3 Students work in small groups to talk about their own or their partner's results and their reactions.

Share your task

The idea here is to give students a chance to 'perfect' their speaking in this context and provide them with a recording of a 'polished' version. This will provide extra motivation for students, as well as extra practice. Students can either make an audio or video recording, depending on how comfortable they feel and what equipment is available. Students could even use their mobile phones to do this. If possible, they'll need a quiet place to make their recording. Students can either record themselves during the lesson, or as homework and bring the recordings to the next class.

Some additional ideas could include:

- Set up and record an interview with one student asking the questions from the questionnaire and another student answering.
- Students put their answers on a piece of paper. Shuffle and redistribute the answers anonymously and ask students to record themselves interpreting the results. In a later class, play the recordings and ask students to guess who gave the original answers.

World culture (PAGES 122–123)

A dream come true

Culture notes

The British Isles have always been a destination for immigrants, from the Romans of the 1st century, the Anglo-Saxons of the 4th to 8th centuries, the Vikings of the 8th to 10th centuries to the Normans from the 11th century and countless other groups after that.

In the second half of the 20th century Britain saw increasing levels of immigration from former colonies, especially the Caribbean and the sub-continent of India, Pakistan and Bangladesh. These more recent waves of immigration have often been accompanied by worries expressed by various groups that this is changing the nature and the culture of the UK. It is worth noting, however, that these worries are normally more widespread during times of economic difficulties when people are struggling to find work and find it easiest to blame somebody else.

The Royal Ballet began life in 1931 as the Sadler's Wells Ballet. In 1956 it gained a royal charter and changed to its current name. It is based in the Royal Opera House in Covent Garden in London, although it often tours around the UK and the world. It is seen as one of the premier ballet companies in the world.

Find out first (PAGE 122)

1a Students work in pairs to try to guess the answers to the quiz. If some students have not done the research, try to put them with a student who has done it.

b If you have access to the internet and students haven't been able to find the answer to some of the questions, ask students to go online and do some further research. Highlight the search terms. Circulate and offer help with vocabulary and try to encourage people to use only English language websites. Otherwise, tell your students the answers.

ANSWERS:

1 b   **2** a   **3** b   **4 a** Dominica, **b** Brazil, **c** Argentina   **5** Cuba

View (PAGE 122)

See *Teaching tips*: *Using the video material in the classroom*, page 24.

Culture notes

Santiago de Cali is the official name for the Colombian city where Fernando Montaño was born, and which is more commonly known simply as Cali. It is on the west coast of Colombia on the Pacific Ocean. It is Colombia's third biggest city and is famous for its cheap plastic surgery and excellent sporting infrastructure.

2a Set the scene and make sure students understand the meaning of the key vocabulary by reading through the glossary with them. Ask questions about each of the words to make sure they have understood, for example *Do you have an audition for a play in a theatre? Might you receive a scholarship if you're very clever but very poor? Can you give me some examples of training a footballer might do?*

b ⊙ Make sure students read through the topics before they watch the DVD so they know what they have to pay attention for.

ANSWERS:

1 his early life in Cali   **2** his dreams when he was a child   **3** his time in Cuba   **4** coming to London and starting to learn English   **5** how he keeps fit   **6** his other interests

3 Give your students the chance to read through the questions and clear up any doubts before they watch the DVD again. Students check in pairs. Play the DVD again if you think students would benefit from it. Check as a class.

ANSWERS:

1 3 or 4   **2** 12   **3** Cuba   **4** She saw him dance and invited him to an audition.   **5** No, he didn't.   **6** every day   **7** to be a principal dancer with the Royal Ballet   **8** drawing, acting, modelling clothes

World view (PAGE 123)

4a Check the meaning of *I can't stand ...* . Give students a minute or two to read through the statements and tick the ones they agree with and put a cross next to the ones they disagree with.

b Students work in pairs to compare their ideas and see if they can agree on their favourites. In feedback, find out who is the class's favourite artist, dancer, etc. You might choose not to have a group discussion on who is their favourite politician if you don't think it is appropriate.

Find out more ⓢ (PAGE 123)

5a Students work in pairs to make notes of any information they already know about the people in the box.

b Students work in the same pairs to research either all of the people in the box or one or two that they have chosen. Focus students' attention on the search terms that they should use. Circulate and help with new vocabulary as necessary and encourage students to use English language websites.

> **ANSWERS:**
>
> **Carlos Acosta:** Born in 1973 in Colombia. Principal guest artist with the Royal Ballet. He's won many awards and tours around the world.
>
> **Antônio Carlos Jobim:** Born in 1927 in Brazil, died in 1994. Songwriter and composer. Wrote *The Girl from Ipanema*, one of the most recorded songs of all time.
>
> **Eva Perón:** Born in 1919 in Argentina, died in 1952. Married to Juan Perón, she was the first lady of Argentina. A strong supporter of labour rights who also ran several charitable organisations.
>
> **Frida Kahlo:** Born in 1907 in Mexico, died in 1954. Painter. Her work is considered as emblematic of national and indigenous tradition.
>
> **Mario Vargas Llosa:** Born in 1936 in Peru. Writer, journalist and essayist. Won the 2010 Nobel Prize for literature.

Write up your research

6 Show students the paragraph on Carlos Acosta. Ask students to locate the information about where he is from, why he is famous and his main achievements. Tell students they should use this paragraph as a model to write up their own findings about one of the people they researched.

Study, practice & remember

(PAGES 162–163)

See *Teaching tips: Using the Study, practice & remember sections*, page 25.

Practice 1

> **ANSWERS:**
>
> **1**
> **1** don't have to **2** doesn't have to **3** have to **4** has to **5** don't have to **6** have to **7** have to **8** has to
>
> **2**
> **1** don't has – don't have
> **2** don't – can't
> **3** Does we have – Do we have
> **4** doesn't has – doesn't have
> **5** paying – pay
> **6** has to – have to
> **7** Does they have – Do they have
> **8** don't – can't
>
> **3**
> **1** You have to wear a seatbelt when you drive in Britain.
> **2** Do you have to do military service in your country?
> **3** My brother doesn't have to wear a uniform at his school.
> **4** I don't have to have a visa to visit Italy.
> **5** Does your friend have to take an exam this week?
> **6** My parents don't have to work anymore.
> **7** You have to go outside if you want to smoke.
> **8** Do they have to book tickets for the film?

Practice 2

> **ANSWERS:**
>
> **1** (Possible answers)
> **1** won't **2** might **3** will **4** won't **5** will **6** will **7** will **8** might
>
> **2**
> **1** c **2** h **3** g **4** a **5** d **6** f **7** e **8** b

Remember these words

> **ANSWERS:**
>
> **1**
> **1** performing arts **2** medicine **3** leisure and tourism **4** media studies **5** engineering **6** geography **7** information technology **8** history **9** maths **10** business studies
>
> **2**
> **1** in **2** for **3** got **4** into **5** was **6** in **7** take **8** to **9** failed **10** earn

OVERVIEW

PAGES 124–125

Vocabulary: Ways of communicating

Grammar: Present perfect (unfinished time)

Common European Framework: Students can simply describe basic past events and relate them to the present.

PAGES 126–127

Reading and vocabulary: Technology

Grammar: Present perfect (with *ever*)

Pronunciation: *have*

Common European Framework: Students can locate and identify specific information in shorter texts on matters of familiarity.

PAGES 128–129

Task: Take part in a game

Common European Framework: Students can tell a basic story or simply describe something.

PAGES 130–131

Speaking: Telephoning

Writing: A text message

Common European Framework: Students can identify and follow the main points in simple TV programmes or short films.

Vocabulary (PAGE 124)

Ways of communicating

See *Teaching tips: Working with lexical phrases*, page 21.

WARM UP

Elicit from the group as many different ways of communicating as possible, even if they aren't used today. Some of these could include *art*, *sign language*, *television*, *email*, *phones*, *body language*, *writing*, etc. Put students into small groups and ask them to try to put the items into chronological order from the oldest to the newest. The order that students come up with isn't important, and there is probably no agreed answer in any case, but the opportunity to talk about different ways of communicating will set a good context for this unit.

Vocabulary, exercise 1: Additional activity

Before looking at the exercises, focus students' attention on the photo. Ask: *Is there anything unusual or strange in this photo?* Students might suggest something about how the person looks very traditional, but is using a modern mobile phone.

---

1 Check the meaning of *landline* and *up-to-date*. Students work in pairs to discuss the questions. In feedback, elicit ideas from different students and see how many people agree.

2 Check the meaning of *smartphone* and the meaning and pronunciation of *Wi-Fi* /ˈwaɪˌfaɪ/ and *attachment* /əˈtætʃmənt/. Complete the first sentence with the class as an example. Students work individually to complete the rest of the sentences, then check in pairs before checking as a class.

ANSWERS:

1 a smartphone   **2** a smartphone, a laptop, a tablet computer, an internet connection, a Wi-Fi connection   **3** a smartphone, a laptop, a tablet computer   **4** a smartphone, a laptop, a tablet computer   **5** a smartphone, a landline   **6** a smartphone, a landline   **7** a smartphone, a laptop, a tablet computer   **8** a smartphone, a laptop, a tablet computer

3 Talk about the first verb phrase in exercise 2 with the class as an example. Students then work in pairs to discuss the questions. In feedback, find out if there is anything that none of the students ever do.

ADDITIONAL PRACTICE

➡ **Workbook:** Vocabulary: *Ways of communicating*, page 69

Grammar focus 1 (PAGE 125)

Present perfect (unfinished time)

See *Teaching tips: Working with grammar*, page 20.

1 Make sure that your students read the questions before they read the text. Check the meaning of *so far* (up until now), *on hold* (when you are on the phone and asked to wait for a moment) and *assignment* (a piece of homework or a project). You might like to encourage your students to read the text quickly by giving them a time limit of two minutes.

ANSWERS:

1 one   **2** one

2a Students work individually to complete the sentences. Encourage them not to look at the text yet. Students check in pairs.

b Students check their answers with the text. Ask them to underline the corresponding sentences in the text so that they can refer back to them later if they need to.

ANSWERS:

1 have   **2** has   **3** hasn't   **4** have, haven't   **5** have

GRAMMAR

Present perfect (unfinished time)

1 Look again at the completed sentences from exercise 2a. Give students a couple of minutes to analyse the sentences and decide which is the correct rule. Tell the class this is the Present perfect, and highlight that:

- the action or state is in the past but connected to the present.
- the time period in each case is not finished. Note that this use of the Present perfect usually shows that the period of time is not finished but that the activity/action/state is.
- we do not know, or it is not important, exactly when these things happened.

ANSWERS:

1 not finished   **2** don't say

2 Read through the words and phrases that we often use with the Present perfect. Ask students to read the text again and find examples.

3 Use sentence 5 from exercise 2a to show the form for the Present perfect (using sentence 1 might be confusing because of the use of *have* as the main verb). Students then look at the example sentences to find the regular and irregular past participles. Also, highlight:

- the use of *have/has*.
- the negative forms in sentences 3 and 4.
- the question forms.

ANSWERS:

Regular past participles: watched, downloaded
Irregular past participles: had, done, read, been

After checking the answers, you might like to direct students to the Verb list on page 175.

4 Give students a few minutes to find more examples of the Present perfect in the comments in exercise 1. During feedback, ask students what the time period is to reinforce the idea that it is unfinished.

Potential problem with the Present perfect

The difference between the Present perfect and the Past simple can cause problems for many learners. This might be because their first language has an equivalent of the Present perfect, but this is used slightly differently. Alternatively, it might be because their first language doesn't use anything similar to the Present perfect in English.

The key to the difference between the two tenses is to remember that the Past simple always refers to a specific time in the past. The time might be explicit or implicit, but there always is one. It is not true to say that the action is always finished, it might be either the time or the action that has finished.

The Present perfect, on the other hand, refers to an indefinite time. It could be, for example 'some time in history', 'some time in my life' or 'some time in the last two weeks'. It is also important to remember that we are looking at this indefinite time from the present, which is why it is a present tense and not a past one.

Many students will take time to both understand and produce the Present perfect appropriately. Expose your students to the tense as often as possible and offer patient assistance and correction whenever it is needed.

You may want to ask students to read Study 1 on page 164 for a more detailed explanation of the Present perfect (unfinished time).

PRACTICE

1a As an example complete the first sentence with the class so that it is true for you. Students then work individually to complete the rest of the sentences about themselves. Circulate and monitor.

ANSWERS:

Students' own answers using:
1 've made   **2** 've sent   **3** 've spent   **4** 've written   **5** 've watched   **6** 've read   **7** 've received   **8** 've taken

b Students work in pairs to compare their sentences. In feedback, find out if there is anything the whole class has in common.

Practice, exercise 1b: Alternative suggestion

After students complete their sentences, ask them to walk around the class and read their sentences to as many people as possible with the objective of trying to find somebody who wrote the same as them. Do an example with some of the students by saying your sentences and them saying theirs. When you have something the same, act out writing down the student's name and then move on to another student. Make sure students talk to lots of different people by encouraging them to move around.

Practice, exercise 1b: Additional activity

If you have a strong elementary class, you could ask students to find out some extra information about each of the points. To ask for this extra information students will often need to use a Past simple question, so provide a model on the board, for example:

A: I've made two phone calls so far today.

B: Who did you call?

A: I called my boss and my sister.

However, do not insist too much on them producing the correct forms all the time, instead treat it as an opportunity to expose them to a language point that they will cover in more detail in the future.

ADDITIONAL PRACTICE

Study, practice & remember: Practice 1

Workbook: Grammar focus 1: *Present perfect (unfinished time)*, pages 69–70

Reading and vocabulary (PAGES 126–127)

Technology

See *Teaching tips: Working with lexical phrases*, page 21.

WARM UP

As a way of revising the grammar point of the last class, and of setting a context for this one, prepare a number of questions about communicating on strips of paper using the Present perfect tense. For example, *How many text messages have you sent today? How many hours have you spent on your computer this week?* Cut up the questions and place one on each desk. When your students come into the room, they should read the question on their desk and then ask the people sitting around them. In feedback, students report back to the class what their neighbours said.

1a Check the meaning and pronunciation of *viruses* /ˈvaɪərəsəz/. Students work in pairs and try to guess the answers. Elicit some of the ideas that students have, but don't confirm any answers yet.

b Students quickly read the article to check their answers. Ask students to underline the part of the text that shows the answers to help with feedback later. Check as a class.

ANSWERS:

1 c   **2** c   **3** c

2 Show students they have to match the beginnings of the sentences in A to the endings of the sentences in B. Give students time to read the text in more detail. They match the sentence halves and check in pairs before checking as a class. Encourage students to justify their answers if there is any disagreement.

ANSWERS:

1 d   2 g   3 e   4 f   5 b   6 a   7 c

3a Give students time to read through the questions. Ask them if they have any doubts about the meaning of the words and phrases in bold. If students do have doubts, find the phrase in the text and ask questions about the context to make the meaning clearer.

b Students work in pairs to ask and answer the questions. Circulate and monitor for any interesting answers.

c Students work in pairs or small groups to talk about the article. During feedback, find out what the class thought was the most interesting or surprising fact.

ADDITIONAL PRACTICE

➡ **Workbook:** Vocabulary: *Technology*, page 70

Grammar focus 2 (PAGE 127)

Present perfect (with *ever*)

See *Teaching tips: Working with grammar*, page 20.

1 🎧 **14.1** Make sure students read the questions before they listen to the recording so they know what to listen for. They check in pairs. Play the recording again if you think students would benefit from it. Check as a class.

ANSWERS:

Conversation 1
1 10 or 12
2 Yes, she does.
Conversation 2
3 last summer when she was on holiday
4 at an open-air concert in a park
Conversation 3
5 It's slow and keeps stopping.
6 homework assignments and photos

Grammar focus 2, exercise 1: Alternative suggestion

Before listening, ask students to look at the questions and predict what the answers might be. Give your students some examples, e.g. *a number, a yes or no answer, a time or day, a place*. After students have listened and checked their answers, go back and see if their predictions were correct.

This type of activity will help students develop their listening skills as they will be more able to find information if they know what they are listening for. It is also an authentic listening strategy as we usually make predictions about what we are going to hear in our first language, even if these predictions are not explicit or if we are unaware of them.

---

2 Students listen to the recording again and complete the gaps. They check in pairs and then as a class.

ANSWERS:

Conversation 1
1 forgotten   2 have
Conversation 2
3 Have   4 haven't
Conversation 3
5 ever   6 had

Grammar focus 2, exercise 2: Alternative suggestion

If you have a class of stronger elementary students, ask them to try to complete the gaps before listening to check their answers. This will provide more of a challenge and encourage them to think more about the possible answers.

GRAMMAR

Present perfect (with *ever*)

1 Remind students of the Present perfect used with unfinished time from page 125 and the form. Write on the board: *Have you ever forgotten your password?* Elicit that the word that refers to time in this sentence is *ever*. Ask students what *ever* refers to and elicit that it is *your life*. Ask students if we know, or are interested in, *when* you forgot your password. Elicit that we are not, that what we are interested in is *whether* you forgot your password at some time in your life, not *when*. Read through the rules with your students. They then decide which alternative is correct. During feedback, highlight:

• that *ever* is usually only used in questions.

• the short answer only uses the auxiliary verb *have* or *has*.

ANSWERS:

1 b   2 a   3 a

You may want to ask students to read Study 2 on page 164 for a more detailed explanation of the Present perfect (with *ever*).

PRONUNCIATION

See *Teaching tips: Helping students with pronunciation*, page 22.

1 🎧 **14.2** Remind students of the strong and weak forms that they have looked at before, for example those in Units 4, 5 and 12. Write the word *have* on the board and elicit the pronunciation /hæv/ and /həv/. Play the recording and ask students to notice which one is used. Read through the examples.

Potential problem with the pronunciation of *have*

In questions *have* is usually unstressed because it is not the main word, and so not important compared to the content word, in this case the main verb. In short answers, however, it is important as it is the only verb we have, so it is stressed. If you have stronger students, you might like to talk about this as it can be good to give a reason for the seeming idiosyncrasies of a language.

2 Drill the sentences chorally and individually.

PRACTICE

1a Go through the example and do the first question with the class. Students then work individually to write questions using the prompts. Circulate and monitor. Students check in pairs.

ANSWERS:

1 Have you ever bought anything online?
2 Have you ever lost your mobile phone?
3 Have you ever made a phone call in English?
4 Have you ever spent more than a week without a phone or computer?
5 Have you ever done a dangerous sport?
6 Have you ever stayed awake for the whole night?
7 Have you ever studied in a foreign country?

b Students write three more questions. Circulate and offer help as necessary.

2 Students work in pairs to ask and answer their questions. You might like to ask students to make a note of the answers to help with feedback. During feedback, ask students to report on what their partners said.

ADDITIONAL PRACTICE

Resource bank: Activity 14A *The Traveller's Club* (Present perfect (with *ever*)); Activity 14B *Revision board game* (Revision of all language in the Students' Book)

Study, practice & remember: Practice 2

Workbook: Grammar focus 2: *Present perfect (with* ever*)*, pages 71–72; Pronunciation: *Strong and weak forms of* have, page 73

Task (PAGES 128–129)

Take part in a game

See *Teaching tips: Making tasks work*, page 23.

Preparation (PAGES 128–129)

Reading and listening

Culture notes

The game in this task is based on a popular quiz show on BBC Radio 4 called *Just A Minute*. If you would like to get an idea of what the programme is like, you can find videos and audio recordings online by doing a search for *Just a Minute*, or going directly to the BBC Radio 4 website.

1 Focus students' attention on the game and the rules at the top of the page. Make sure students read the questions first so they know what they are looking for. Students then read the rules to find the answers and check in pairs before checking as a class. Reassure any students who seem confused that you are going to give them lots of examples.

ANSWERS:

1 two or more
2 the game board, topics and questions, a watch or timer
3 by taking as many squares on the board as possible by talking for one minute about the topic or question related to that letter

2a 🎧 **14.3** Give students time to read the questions before they listen to the recording to find the answers. Students check in pairs. Play the recording again if you think students would benefit from it. Check as a class.

ANSWERS:

1 M ('Mobile phones')   2 Yes

b Focus students' attention on the Useful language box. Play the recording again and ask students to tick the phrases they hear.

ANSWERS:

So, let me think. ✓
I'm going to talk about ... ✓
What I mean is, ... ✓
What else? ✓
... and things like that. ✓

Task (PAGES 128–129)

Speaking

1a Put students into small groups and make sure they have everything they need to play the game. Set the groups up so that they have students who are roughly of the same level. This will mean that stronger students don't win easily and leave the weaker ones with no squares. Set a time limit before the games start, so that you can stop the groups if they are very slow to finish.

Speaking, exercise 1a: Alternative suggestion

If you think some of your students are still not sure about how to play the game then set up an example with three or four of the strongest students in the class. Sit around a table and invite the rest of the class to stand around and watch. Play the game for a few turns so that everyone can see a successful turn and a failed turn. Students then split up into groups to play the game themselves.

b Students play the game. If some groups finish before the others, ask them to play again or change the members of the group with another group of fast finishers. Circulate and offer help, advice and act as referee as required. Remind students to use the Useful language box.

2 Talk about these questions as a class. If students found it difficult, ask why and talk about ways to overcome this problem in the future.

Share your task

The idea here is to give students a chance to 'perfect' their speaking in this context and provide them with a recording of a 'polished' version. This will provide extra motivation for students, as well as extra practice. Students can either make an audio or video recording, depending on how comfortable they feel and what equipment is available. Students could even use their mobile phones to do this. If possible, they'll need a quiet place to make their recording. Students can either record themselves during the lesson, or as homework and bring the recordings to the next class.

Language live (PAGES 130–131)

Speaking (PAGES 130–131)

Telephoning

See *Teaching tips: Using the video material in the classroom*, page 24.

Culture notes

When mobile phones were first introduced to the market it came as something of a surprise that texting would be popular, as it was just assumed that people would want to talk on their mobiles. Today, however, people send more text messages than they make phone calls and the numbers are increasing as sending texts gets cheaper and cheaper.

1 Focus students' attention on the photo, but ignore the message for now. Students work in pairs to discuss the questions. In feedback, find out who chats the most, who sends the most text messages, etc.

2a ▶ Check the meaning of *dropping*. Make sure students read the sentences before they watch the first part of the DVD and tick the things they see or hear. They check in pairs and then as a class.

ANSWERS:

a woman putting her coat on ✓
a man giving his name and phone number ✓

b Give students time to read the form before they watch again and complete it. They check in pairs and then as a class.

ANSWERS:

Taxi for Mr / Ms: Richard Goodley
From (address): 29 Market Street
To: train station
Pick-up time: 9.45
Number of passengers: 2

3a ⊙ Check the meaning of *ringing*, *looking for* and *apologising*. Ask students to watch the second part of the DVD and tick the things they see or hear. They check in pairs and then as a class.

ANSWERS:

a mobile phone ringing ✓
a woman looking for her mobile phone ✓
a woman apologising ✓

b Play the second part of the DVD again and pause for students to write appropriate responses. Students check their ideas in pairs. Elicit suggestions and put them on the board and deal with any errors.

POSSIBLE ANSWERS:

1 Hello, it's (name) speaking.
2 I'm fine thanks. You?
3 I'm just leaving work.
4 Yes, how about we meet for a coffee?
5 Who are you with?
6 Yes, sure.

4 ⊙ Check the meaning of *angry* and *wrong number*. Students watch the third part of the DVD and tick the things they see or hear. They check in pairs and then as a class.

ANSWERS:

a man getting angry ✓
a man dialling a wrong number ✓

5a Tell students that all the phrases come from the DVD they have just seen. Complete the first sentence with the class as an example. Students work individually to complete the rest and then check in pairs.

b ⊙ Students watch the DVD to check their answers.

ANSWERS:

1 here   2 Who's   3 talk   4 call   5 soon   6 speaking
7 about   8 that   9 number

PRONUNCIATION

See *Teaching tips: Helping students with pronunciation*, page 22.

1 Play the DVD again and ask students to focus on the pronunciation of the key phrases.

2 Drill the key phrases chorally and individually.

6a Focus students' attention on the conversation in exercise 3b. Demonstrate how some of the details can be changed, for example names and alternative expressions. Students work in pairs to write their own conversation. Circulate and monitor.

b Students practise their conversations. In feedback, invite one or two of the pairs to perform their conversations for the class.

Writing (PAGE 131)

A text message

Culture notes

Although 'text speak' is commonly used, especially by young people, it isn't as widespread as some people seem to think. One of the reasons for this is the advent of predictive text, which means people only have to start texting a word and the phone can predict what it is going to be. This has had the effect of speeding up normal texting.

It is, however, possible to see examples of 'text speak' on the internet, in online forums and comments on blogs and other websites. It is good for students to be able to recognise 'text speak', but they shouldn't be too concerned about producing it.

'Text speak' has caused a lot of debate about whether the standards of written English are declining. Every year there will be something in the papers about how exams are full of text talk that is indecipherable to the general population. Although there is a lot of talk about declining standards, there is no actual evidence to back this up. On the contrary, it seems that people today are writing far more than they used to.

1 Focus students' attention on the photo on page 130 again. Ask them what the message is in the photo. Elicit *See you tomorrow.* and show how it is created with the letter *c* sounding like *see* /siː/, the letter *u* sounding like *you* /juː/, the number *2* replacing *to* and the changed spelling of *morrow* to *moro*. Ask students why they think some people like to do this and if they think it really is quicker than writing out the words in full. Students then work in pairs to discuss the questions.

2 Do one or two examples with the class. Show how the vowels are often missed out and the sounds of the letters are important. Students then work individually or in pairs to match the words to the 'text speak'.

ANSWERS:

1 abt   2 n   3 r   4 @   5 btw   6 4   7 gr8
8 xx   9 luv   10 u   11 c u   12 thx   13 2
14 2moro   15 wd   16 ur

3 Tell your students that all of the messages in this exercise make up one conversation. Translate the first sentence into English with the class as an example. Students then work to decipher the other messages and put them in order. Check as a class.

ANSWERS:

d, a, c, b, e

4   Do the first sentence on the board with the class as an example. Students then work individually or in pairs to rewrite the rest. Invite students to come to the board to write their sentences and ask for alternatives from the class.

POSSIBLE ANSWERS:
1 Hi, Alex. r u free 2moro? Wd u like 2 go 2 c a movie? Luv Ed
2 OK What wd u like 2 c?
3 How abt The Queen n I? It's @ Odeon @ 7.30.
4 Gr8 what time?
5 Abt 7.15?
6 C u there. Btw, I haven't got any money – can u pay 4 my ticket?
7 I'll lend u the money.
8 Thx 4 that! C u 2moro. Luv xx Alex

5   Remind students of the conversation in 'text speak' in exercise 3. Students work in pairs to prepare their own conversation. Students can either do this on paper or by using their mobile phones. Be aware, though, that, depending on what type of price plan they have, some people will have to pay for their text messages and so may not wish to send real texts.

Looking ahead: Additional activity

If this is the end of your term, then it might be useful to talk to students about their future plans for their English studies. There are a number of ways of doing this and a number of things you might want to talk about. Some of them include:

• asking students to set objectives for themselves over the next six months.

• if students have a holiday after the term, discussing what they can do to improve their English during that time.

• pointing out parts of the material that you might not have covered, for example some parts of the Workbook, that they could use once the term has finished.

• reviewing language that students have covered and that they might need to work on in the future.

• motivating your students by showing them how much they have learnt and improved over the course of the last term.

ADDITIONAL PRACTICE

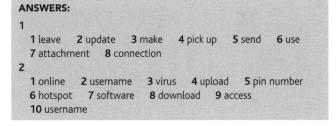 **Workbook:** Language live: *Telephoning*, page 73; Writing: *A text message*, page 73

Students can now do Progress test 7 and the End of course test on the Teacher's Resource Disc.

Study, practice & remember
(PAGES 164–165)

See *Teaching tips: Using the Study, practice & remember sections*, page 25.

Practice 1

ANSWERS:
1
　1 forgotten　2 sent　3 bought　4 walked　5 left
　6 checked　7 watched　8 read
2
　1 's broken　2 've eaten　3 haven't done　4 's phoned
　5 Have you checked　6 haven't seen　7 Has he fixed
　8 've taken
3
　1 have　2 has　3 haven't　4 hasn't　5 haven't　6 hasn't
　7 has　8 haven't

Practice 2

ANSWERS:
1
　1 met　2 failed　3 sung　4 told　5 stayed　6 owned
　7 eaten　8 left
2
　1 Have you ever played basketball? Yes, I have.
　2 Have you ever been to New Zealand? No, I haven't.
　3 Has he ever had a job interview? No, he hasn't.
　4 Has she ever eaten Chinese food? Yes, she has.
　5 Have you ever tried horse-riding? No, I haven't.
　6 Have they ever seen a camel? Yes, they have.
　7 Has she ever written a letter in English? No, she hasn't.
　8 Have you ever taken a driving test? Yes, I have.

Remember these words

ANSWERS:
1
　1 leave　2 update　3 make　4 pick up　5 send　6 use
　7 attachment　8 connection
2
　1 online　2 username　3 virus　4 upload　5 pin number
　6 hotspot　7 software　8 download　9 access
　10 username

Pearson Education Limited
Edinburgh Gate
Harlow
Essex CM20 2JE
England
and Associated Companies throughout the world.

www.pearsonelt.com

First published 2013
Third impression 2015

ISBN: 978-1-4479-3686-2

Set in Bliss Light 8.5pt/10.5pt
Printed in Malaysia, CTP-PJB

Cover images: *Front:* **Fotolia.com:** Kushnirov Avraham

Illustrated by: Pavely Arts, Kathy Baxendale, Graham Humphreys/The
Art Market, Ed McLachlan